C000241296

"You'll never be able to say that you 'just didn't know'.]
brand. Knowing the international aid sector from the inside
it hurts. This book is a must-read for every professional an
alike."

Bill Easterly, *Author of* The White Man's Burden ʌʌʌ ɪ ʜᴇ ɪʏʀᴀɴɴʏ ᴏʀ Experts

"The programme evaluation literature often focusses on measuring the direct effects of
programmes. This book shows convincingly that we should pay more attention to unintended consequences, and provides the tools to do so. Highly recommended!"

A. Mushfiq Mobarak, *Kasoff '54 Professor of Economics, Yale University*

"It's not often that a book on aid is this original and this important. Dirk Jan Koch
turns a forensic eye on an issue that normally merely provokes handwringing: the unintended consequences of aid. In a text full of case studies, precise typologies and practical
suggestions for practitioners, he provides a wonderful guide to what they are, and what
to do about them."

Duncan Green, *Oxfam & London School of Economics,*
Author of How Change Happens

"*Foreign Aid and Its Unintended Consequences* will leave many readers shaking their
heads in disbelief at how foreign assistance can get things so wrong. Koch's book offers
a compelling and honest analysis of the pathologies of aid's unanticipated and unwanted
consequences. His original typology of these effects will stimulate much debate and discussion by students, practitioners, and scholars alike, while also pointing to real opportunities for aid's transformation. This book offers a ray of hope for anyone desperate for
ideas on how to radically reform the global development sector."

Nilima Gulrajani, *Senior Research Fellow, ODI*

"This book holds the golden message for the young professionals we train to set foot in
the field of international development to always change perspective and to keep a continuous eye for the unexpected. It encourages them in their role as change agents by providing evidence-based guidance on how to best play their part."

Sara Kinsbergen, *Programme Director AMID Young Professional Programme,*
Radboud University

"***** (5 stars)! No taboos, no blind spots. This book investigates all potential claims
about side effects of development assistance and tells us which ones we should be more
vigilant about. A great read!"

Axel Dreher, *Chair of International and Development Politics, Heidelberg University,*
and Editor, Review of International Organizations

"This book is an admirably thorough and evidence-based exploration of – negative and
positive – unintended consequences of international development cooperation. The book
is compelling as it is written by an insider academic who has engaged in and observed
development for decades. Dirk Jan Koch provides us with a razor-sharp analysis without
ever losing his commitment or his belief that development policy and practice can indeed
be improved."

Thea Hilhorst, *Professor of Humanitarian Studies,*
Institute of Social Studies, The Hague

"This is an important book for anyone with an interest in accelerating development – advocates and champions of development can gloss over its unintended consequences, but to ensure the best chance of really helping people, policymakers must pay them more attention. The concepts and tools laid out should be essential reading in every development agency, charity or research institution."

Ian Mitchell, *Director of Development Cooperation in Europe,*
Center for Global Development

"In this erudite and highly readable book, Dirk-Jan Koch examines a comprehensive range of aid-related problems and their possible solutions. The book's focus on getting to grips with 'unintended consequences' is both original and productive, and opens up important new perspectives on development policy and humanitarian action. This book will be hugely useful to both researchers and reflective practitioners involved in trying to make aid work better."

David Lewis, *Professor of Anthropology and Development,*
London School of Economics

"This book will be extremely useful for students on Development Studies courses and anybody interested in development because the author provides a very balanced discussion of the effects, intended and unanticipated, of international development interventions. The author develops a coherent typology, but also shows how better design and planning can help to mitigate potential adverse effects. Dirk-Jan Koch presents a nuanced assessment that counters the excessively negative view of development so widespread in public perceptions."

Oliver Morrissey, *Professor of Development Economics, Nottingham University*

"The international development community has become increasingly adept at answering ever narrower questions about design and performance, while continuing to neglect the less manageable–but no less impactful–realm of the unanticipated, unintended, and unexpected. Koch's particular mix of practical experience and analytical introspection reminds us of how important it is to focus on the unintended effects of aid (both negative and positive!), and encourages us to become better observers, smarter planners, and more honest partners for change."

Pablo Yanguas, *Author of* Why We Lie about Aid

"This fascinating book explores the unintended effects of international development cooperation. Koch draws insights from complexity theory and uses empirical evidence in developing a robust typology for understanding unintended effects in international development cooperation. This intellectually rich book provides an opportunity for development workers to be self-critical and reflexive. This is a must-read book for development practitioners, policymakers, and academics interested in international development cooperation."

Emmanuel Kumi, *University of Ghana*

"An excellent book that is constructively critical of aid as we know it. Based on lived experience, this book adds to our understanding of the good, the bad and the ugly of international aid–and how to do international cooperation better."

Stefan Dercon, *Oxford University, Author of* Gambling on Development

"Accessible, well-researched, original, at times provocative, *Foreign Aid and Its Unintended Consequences* shatters myths about development aid. Koch argues that donors and aid agencies should be more aware of the outcomes they don't always intend. While not shying away from criticism and even controversy, the book is ultimately hopeful and constructive, outlining actionable steps to harmonize goals and impacts."

Mark Schuller, *Author of* Killing with Kindness

"In the development world, the ostrich syndrome is often the norm, hiding the problems everyone knows about. In this highly original book, Dirk-Jan Koch takes us on a journey around the world, with many examples, showing the myriad of possible effects, both positive and negative, that urgently need to be uncovered. This an urgent read for those who want to move away from hypocrisy and are interested in unintended effects."

Valéry Ridde, *Director of Research, Centre of Population et Développement, CEPED, Université de Paris Cité*

Foreign Aid and Its Unintended Consequences

Foreign aid and international development frequently bring with it a range of unintended consequences, both negative and positive. This book delves into these consequences, providing a fresh and comprehensive guide to understanding and addressing them.

The book starts by laying out a theoretical framework based on complexity thinking, before going on to explore the ten most prevalent kinds of unintended effects of foreign aid: backlash effects, conflict effects, migration and resettlement effects, price effects, marginalization effects, behavioural effects, negative spillover effects, governance effects, environmental effects, and ripple effects. Each chapter revolves around a set of concrete case studies, analysing the mechanisms underpinning the unintended effects and proposing ways in which policymakers, practitioners, and evaluators can tackle negative side effects and maximize positive side effects. The book also includes personal testimonies, a succinct overview of unintended effects, and suggestions for further reading.

Providing a clear overview of what side effects to anticipate when planning, executing, and evaluating aid, this book will be an important resource for students, development practitioners, and policymakers alike.

Dirk-Jan Koch is Chief Science Officer of the Netherlands Ministry of Foreign Affairs, and is Special Professor of International Trade & Development Cooperation at Radboud University, the Netherlands. Views expressed in this book do not represent the official views of these institutions.

Rethinking Development

Rethinking Development offers accessible and thought-provoking overviews of contemporary topics in international development and aid. Providing original empirical and analytical insights, the books in this series push thinking in new directions by challenging current conceptualizations and developing new ones.

This is a dynamic and inspiring series for all those engaged with today's debates surrounding development issues, whether they be students, scholars, policy makers and practitioners internationally. These interdisciplinary books provide an invaluable resource for discussion in advanced undergraduate and postgraduate courses in development studies as well as in anthropology, economics, politics, geography, media studies and sociology.

For more information about this series, please visit: www.routledge.com/Rethinking-Development/book-series/RDVPT

Foreign Aid and Its Unintended Consequences

Dirk-Jan Koch

Routledge
Taylor & Francis Group

LONDON AND NEW YORK

Designed cover image: ©Maarten Wolterink

First published 2024
by Routledge
4 Park Square, Milton Park, Abingdon, Oxon OX14 4RN

and by Routledge
605 Third Avenue, New York, NY 10158

Routledge is an imprint of the Taylor & Francis Group, an informa business

© 2024 Dirk-Jan Koch

The right of Dirk-Jan Koch to be identified as author of this work has been
asserted in accordance with sections 77 and 78 of the Copyright, Designs and
Patents Act 1988.

The Open Access version of this book, available at www.taylorfrancis.com, has been made available
under a Creative Commons Attribution-Non Commercial-No Derivatives (CC-BY-NC-ND) 4.0 license.

Trademark notice: Product or corporate names may be trademarks or registered trademarks,
and are used only for identification and explanation without intent to infringe.

British Library Cataloguing-in-Publication Data
A catalogue record for this book is available from the British Library

ISBN: 9781032412184 (hbk)
ISBN: 9781032412146 (pbk)
ISBN: 9781003356851 (ebk)

DOI: 10.4324/9781003356851

Typeset in Sabon
by Newgen Publishing UK

Funded by Radboud University.

Contents

Figures

Glossary: operational typology of the unintended consequences of international development efforts

Effect	Definition	Subtypes
Backlash effect (Chapter 3)	Unintended backlash effects occur when an external action leads to an opposite reaction that affects the achievement of the intended effect. The backlash effect is by definition a macro-level effect, as reactions that are opposite to the expectation at the individual level fall under the heading of behavioural effects.	Anti-aid backlash Anti-foreign values backlash
Conflict effects (Chapter 4)	Unintended conflict effects occur when the external intervention strengthens rebel groups or increases tensions between individuals, (ethnic) communities, or recipients and non-recipients.	Direct conflict effects Indirect conflict effects
Migration and resettlement effects (Chapter 5)	Unintended migration and resettlement effects occur when an external intervention creates a movement of population, either towards or away from the intervention, which was not the objective of the intervention. These movements can be either voluntary or involuntary.	Aid-induced resettlement Migratory push effects Migratory pull effects
Price effects (Chapter 6)	Unintended price effects occur when an external intervention distorts prices in recipient or adjacent villages, communities, cities, or regions, or affects the exchange rates of local currencies.	Downward price effects Upward price effects The Dutch disease
Marginalization effects (Chapter 7)	Unintended marginalization effects occur when an external intervention contributes to an increase in inequality by weakening or leaving behind already vulnerable groups, in either a relative or an absolute sense.	Elite capture effects Regressive targeting effects Charitable consumerism effects

(Continued)

Effect	Definition	Subtypes
Behavioural effects (Chapter 8)	Unintended behavioural effects occur when recipients or affected persons respond to an external intervention in unintended ways due to psychological factors that were insufficiently taken into consideration when the intervention was designed.	Rebound effects Backfire effects Motivational crowding-out effects
Negative spillover effects (Chapter 9)	Unintended negative spillover effects materialize when an external intervention negatively affects thematic or geographic areas or institutions outside of the intervention area.	Negative institutional spillover effects Negative thematic spillover effects Negative geographic spillover effects Fungibility
Governance effects (Chapter 10)	Unintended governance effects occur when external interventions unintentionally influence the quality and reach of institutions at any level in the recipient country.	Corruption effects Democracy effects Tax effects
Environmental effects (Chapter 11)	Environmental trade-off effects occur when social and economic progress unintentionally contributes to environmental degradation.	Carbon surge effects Biodiversity decline effects Animal welfare reduction effects
Ripple effects (Chapter 12)	Ripple effects occur when there are positive spillover effects beyond the beneficiary, intervention, area, or thematic focus. They can be considered unintended if the donor or implementing agency did not take into account that these spillovers could happen in its formal evaluation parameters.	Thematically synergetic effects Catalytic effects Human interaction effects

1 Introduction

Understanding the unintended consequences of international development

---

The questions guiding this introduction:

- Why do I think all of us in the field of international development ought to understand unintended effects better?
- Which myths about unintended effects need to be unlearned before reading this book?
- What do I want to achieve with this book?
- How will I go about doing that?

1.1 Why study unintended consequences in international development?

While a diplomat at the Netherlands embassy in the DRC, I was also teaching a master's course in International Cooperation and Development at the Catholic University of Kinshasa. The course dealt with issues such as the impact of development aid. The DRC had received over USD 10 billion in aid over the previous decade, the largest peacekeeping mission on earth and the largest debt write-off in history. After 15 two-hour lectures, I asked the students: 'Having read all the literature and listened to the lectures, do you think that development aid helps or hinders your country?' After a while, the first student, Irène, raised her hand.

Well, I think it helps the country. Take me, for instance. My cousin has been working for an international NGO, Caritas, for ten years and has earned a good salary. He has paid for my high school and university tuition fees, and now I am interning at a bank. When I finish university, they will hire me! So development aid is definitely working.

This was clearly different from the effects that all that aid was intended for. I was perplexed: I had been teaching them about all the different effects of aid that I had learnt from textbooks, from fungibility to the Dutch disease. But these unintended side effects were definitely not part of that curriculum.

Unintended effects are often less innocent than Irène's story. When the United Nations sent a peacekeeping mission to Haiti to protect civilians, the cholera that the blue helmets brought with them from Nepal killed at least 10,000 Haitians in 2010. Being aware of the risk of unintended effects is key: if the United Nations had had a more open attitude

DOI: 10.4324/9781003356851-1

This Chapter has been made available under a CC-BY-NC-ND license.

combined with better monitoring and evaluation, they would have detected the threat and installed a sewage system earlier, preventing many unnecessary deaths.[1]

I wrote this book intending to prevent situations like the one in Haiti. And not just similar side effects of poor implementation, but especially negative side effects of poor design and planning. It is meant as a call to action for all of us as students, evaluators, researchers, policymakers, practitioners, and communicators of international development. Let's break out of our tunnel vision and end our myopic focus on desired outcomes and predetermined indicators. And let's look at *all* the consequences of our actions, whether positive (like Irène's experiences in the DRC) or negative (like the cholera outbreak in Haiti).

I tried searching for 'unintended effects' in official policy evaluations, but found very few. This surprised me, because when I was working in the DRC, I had witnessed so many of these unintended effects with my own eyes. I had seen how sexual violence had hit the headlines, but the action taken to prevent it had also contributed to an explosion in the number of fictitious reports of rape, with innocent men being put in jail as a result.[2] I had seen how rents in certain Goma neighbourhoods had skyrocketed because of a peacekeeping mission. The result? The citizens of Goma had been forced out of that part of the city, and had to move to unsafe areas with no electricity or streetlights.[3] So although international development and cooperation do inevitably cause a whole range of unintended effects – both positive and negative – these are constantly glossed over in official policy evaluations. I had seen these unintended effects at first hand and academics were also writing about them. But in the official evaluation reports they were pretty much nowhere to be found.

I wrote this book since I feel that my master's studies in international development, and even my training as a PhD candidate, have left me woefully unprepared to become an effective policymaker in the international development sector. Why? Even though I was trained to design, implement, and assess the stated objectives of foreign assistance programmes, there was scarcely any room for unintended effects at all. I learned in great detail how to measure the efficiency and effectiveness of programmes in terms of the objectives formulated in advance, yet I was blind to the unintended effects. Of course, I had to read some authors who were critical of aid in general terms, but that did not equip us to categorize unintended effects or enable us to think about how to mitigate the negative ones. In short, this is the book I wish my professors had told me to read back when I was a student. If I had read this book 20 years ago, quite a few of my own 'aid accidents' as a policymaker and practitioner could have been avoided.

1.2 Five myths about unintended effects that you need to discard before reading the book

Luckily, this book does not start from zero. Over the last seven years or so, a loose group of committed academics and professionals mapped different characteristics of side effects of international cooperation, such as Olga Burlyuk, Gergana Netcheva, Jonny Morell, and Zumera Jabeen. I had the opportunity to work with all of them, and together we have busted five myths regarding unintended effects: that they can't be anticipated; that they're unavoidable; that they're always downplayed; that they're always negative; and that they're an objective phenomenon.[4]

1.2.1 Myth 1: unintended effects can't be anticipated

One of the most common misconceptions about unintended effects is that they are completely unforeseen and unanticipated. Yet this is often not the case: effects that are not intended might very well be anticipated. However, the action is executed regardless when those effects are deemed less important or less likely (or both). Zwart argues that these unintended effects are not a consequence of what Merton calls 'ignorance, error, or ideological blindness,' but the result of protracted deliberations on intervention dilemmas.[5]

The humanitarian intervention for Rwandese refugees in and around Goma in the DRC in 1994 is a good example. After the genocide and the winning of the war by the Tutsi, both the genocidaires and moderate Hutu were fleeing Rwanda. Most of them (about 1 million) sought refuge in Goma, North Kivu. Cholera was killing 600 people per day. Right from the start, the aid agencies knew there were genocidaires among the refugees.[6] Because the aid agencies couldn't target only the non-genocidaires, the unintended but anticipated effect of the relief effort was that those involved in the genocide were receiving aid and could regroup. In the second half of 1994, it became clear that a substantial portion of the aid was being siphoned off by the genocidaires, who were staging military attacks back in Rwanda with the refugee camp as a base.[7] In late 1994, the French section of Médecins Sans Frontières pulled out of the camps, as they estimated that the unintended – but anticipated – negative effects began to outweigh the positive ones. Other aid agencies continued until 1996, when Rwandan government soldiers invaded the refugee camps and sent the aid agencies packing. Hence, it was not that the unintended effects were unanticipated: it was just that the willingness to accept the collateral damage (unintentionally financing genocidaires) differed between the aid agencies. I will discuss this example in more detail in Chapter 4 on conflict effects.

1.2.2 Myth 2: unintended effects are unavoidable

While unintended effects may be anticipated and accepted, this doesn't mean they are unavoidable. Granted, all actions are bound to create some unintended effects, be it big or small. But at the same time, no particular unintended effect is wholly unavoidable. For instance, the large influx of goods, cash, or people that occurs as a result of international cooperation in areas where these were previously scarce is bound to create some distortions, but also these unintended effects can be mitigated or even avoided.

For decades, in-kind food aid from rich high-income to low-income countries was found to reduce the incentives for the local food production, leading to increased food insecurity in the long run.[8] But the practice has continued as the short-term benefits were deemed larger than the 'unavoidable' long-term costs, and because United States (US) and Canadian farmers benefited from it.[9] However, it appeared that the unintended effects of food aid long assumed to be 'unavoidable' actually turned out to be avoidable after all. Avoiding this effect simply involves purchasing food locally rather than shipping it from the United States or Canada. Policy changes by organizations like the World Food Programme from the 2000s onwards have shown that it is possible to support local producers while providing food relief. An initial impact assessment shows that the 'double effect' (suppressing local markets) was largely avoidable, and that it was possible to stimulate local farmers' organizations close to food-deprived areas, without causing prices to skyrocket.[10] I will deal with this case in more detail in Chapter 6 on price effects.

1.2.3 Myth 3: unintended effects are always downplayed

Just because agencies in the field of international development have a stake in downplaying side effects, they are not always downplayed. For example, in Chapter 13, I show how research into the side effects of humanitarian aid to South Sudan was swept under the rug by aid actors. However, what I also found in that research is that exaggerating the unintended effects of public action has become something of a national sport for the detractors of international cooperation.

Exaggerated unintended effects are alleged unintended effects of an intervention that, at closer inspection, are not occurring, or at least not to the degree or with the certainty as suggested. For instance, exaggerated unintended effects popped up in the discussion around deregulation (reducing government rules). One of the arguments advanced by proponents of deregulation is that regulation has unintended effects. I investigated one of these 'unintended effects' claims – one that relates to the negative side effects of regulating the extraction of 'conflict' minerals.[11] It turned out that the unintended effects were inflated by those parties who stood to gain from international deregulation!

The narrative that public action has unintended effects and should therefore be limited is pervasive. The critics of public action have employed this tactic in many areas beyond regulating the extraction of minerals, and the conclusion is always that a rollback of regulation or collective action is required. An interesting example is provided by the 2015 Nobel Prize in Economics Laureate Sir Angus Deaton. He thinks that the unintended effects of international aid on the quality of governance are so great that aid should be reduced as soon as possible: 'Negative unintended consequences are pretty much guaranteed … the pernicious effects are always there.'[12] Geske Dijkstra verified this claim using a detailed meta-analysis, which showed that the unintended effects Sir Deaton referred to were exaggerated.[13] While I believe that paying attention to unintended governance effects is more than warranted (see Chapter 10), it is important to recognize when they are being overstated.

1.2.4 Myth 4: unintended effects are always negative

Unintended effects are all too often reduced to undesirable effects.[14] Yet, many unintended effects in international development are clearly positive.[15] When I assessed the unintended effects in international development with the Dutch government, we found that the largest category was the category with positive spillover effects. One evaluation, called *Work in Progress–Evaluation of the ORET Programme: Investing in Public Infrastructure in Developing Countries*, showed how work on a port (focussed on improving transport) had an impact on a different sector (tourism): 'An unintended consequence of the ORET-financed works is the unexpected increase in tourism due to the extended beach.'[16] This is a catalytic spillover effect, as the unintended effects were found in a different sector (tourism) than the targeted sector (transport). More on these ripple effects can be found in Chapter 12.

Nevertheless, in this book, the majority of unintended effects that I report are negative. This is because unintended positive effects tend to get integrated into the intended effects over time.[17] Let's take the example of de-worming interventions. These started as a health intervention, and the higher education test scores were a positive but unintended side effect. However, nowadays donors and agencies present de-worming campaigns in light of their beneficial effects on health as well as education. Since outcomes are now an integral aspect of de-worming project documents, they have now become intended effects.

1.2.5 *Myth 5: unintended effects are an objective phenomenon*

If there are unintended effects of international development, we should just improve our measurement tools, and ensure that our randomized control trials are more adaptive to spot surprising results. That would do the trick, right? Well, things are a bit more complicated: we confirmed that what might be considered unintended by one group (e.g. the programme developers) might not be unintended by another group (e.g. those implementing, funding, or receiving the programme).[18]

For instance, Kamanzi shows that while aid may fail from the donor's perspective, it can still play a huge role for the livelihoods of the recipients and aid intermediaries, such as district officials.[19] By analysing the 18-year rural development programme of the Dutch embassy in Bukoba, Tanzania, Kamanzi shows that the livelihoods of local aid intermediaries, such as district officials, had improved due to the programme. Interestingly, a harsh international evaluation showed that poverty effects for the target group were insufficient, but their analysis omitted this large group of unintended beneficiaries: aid intermediaries.[20] Kamanzi shows how the local district officers maximized the number of training courses for which they would receive a stipend from the implementing partners. The aid intermediaries invested these stipends in income-generating activities for their retirement: schooling for their children, housing, and plots of land.[21] This had a trickle-down effect on the wider population. So poverty reduction was achieved through a positive effect very much intended by the local intermediaries but not necessarily by the donors. This goes to show that what is 'unintended' really depends on the eyes of the beholder, so despite a hint of objectiveness, an unintended effect is a highly subjective phenomenon.[22]

1.3   What do I want to achieve with this book?

1.3.1 *Avoid the mistakes that I made*

Abandoning these myths enables us to understand unintended effects better. But understanding them leaves much in the way of practically dealing with them. For instance, how the unintended effects of international cooperation efforts are handled in evaluations tends to be haphazard and superficial.[23] Researchers often stumble upon unintended effects accidentally during their research and report on them in a couple of lines towards the end of the report. They had not planned to investigate them systematically or developed any appropriate research methods.[24] What is needed here is a more targeted and systematic approach. That means developing an operational typology and more insight into the underlying mechanisms that cause the unintended effects. That is exactly what this book sets out to do.

The book develops this typology to enable international cooperation workers and researchers to get more serious about unintended effects. This typology provides a scientifically robust framework to determine whether international development interventions 'have generated or can be expected to generate significant positive or negative, intended or unintended, higher-level effects.'[25] Currently, the percentage of evaluations that mentions unintended effects (for Norwegian, Dutch, and US aid) hovers between 10 and 15 per cent. With this book's help, I hope this number will increase.

Through this book I aim to contribute to a change in policies and practices. As you will discover, the most vulnerable, whether women, voiceless citizens, or staff members from aid agencies that work in the countries where they originate from (compared to expatriate staff), are too often disproportionately affected by the mistakes made in international development. We need to make sure that they have a seat at the table. This enables to plan mitigating measures for those who experience any adverse effects.

I find it encouraging that the development sector takes some unintended effects, especially unintended conflict effects, more seriously now than two decades before. Back then, working in a 'conflict-sensitive way' was unheard of, whereas nowadays 'conflict-scans' and 'conflict-monitoring' are part and parcel of development programming, partly because of an impressive push by the peacebuilding field (see Section 4.3). But despite a sector-wide push to 'doing development differently' and 'adaptive management,' implementation has been lacklustre.[26] Suppose we can become more conflict-sensitive in our ways of working. In that case, we surely must be able to also become more environmentally sensitive (Chapter 11) and more sensitive about a potential backlash (Chapter 3), just to mention two of the side effects treated in this book. And if we can capitalize on positive ripple effects (Chapter 12), why not invest in them?

1.3.2 *Protecting international solidarity*

Am I too ambitious or even pretentious to say that I hope the book will achieve more than 'just' unintended consequences being taken more seriously? To me, this professionalization of the international development sector is a stepping stone to something bigger: the protection of international solidarity as such. Let me explain.

The rise in social indicators in low-income countries over the last few decades has been remarkable. Because of the coronavirus disease 2019 (COVID-19) pandemic and the Russian invasion of Ukraine, they have been plateauing. Still, since the end of colonialism, life has gotten much better in nearly all low-income countries. Mothers are less likely to die when giving birth and children are less likely to die before they are five. More children are learning to read and write, and they are less likely to go to bed hungry.[27] Progress has been uneven across countries, sectors, and groups, but it has been undeniable. While we need to credit first and foremost governments, organizations, and individuals in low-income countries for this, progress would have been much slower without, for instance, the donated bed nets and the teacher salaries being paid.

> The nurse, Placide, of the health centre in South-West Rwanda is showing me around in the basic facilities of his centre. It is hygienic, the garden is maintained well and while I don't see any fancy machines, the basics are well arranged. The nurse takes the patient registry and shows how the number of visits has been increasing over the years. I ask him if there is a problem: does the rise in visits indicate a rise in health problems? 'Far from it, ever since there is health insurance, we see that people now come to visit us when they have health problems. The most vulnerable, the *indigènes*, would never come because of the costs. However, the *indigènes* now also have health insurance, free of charge. We can alleviate quite some of their illnesses, such as malaria, as we can also provide basic medication free of charge.'
>
> I visited the health centre in 2005, when Rwanda was still piloting–with international support–its community-based health insurance system. Membership increased from less than 10 per cent in 2003 to 74 per cent in 2013. The government was in the driver's seat in rolling out the program, and over two-thirds of the premiums were

paid for by Rwandans themselves. However, donors covered the premiums of the *indigènes,* paid for the pilot schemes, and provided technical assistance.[28] When I now look at Rwanda's health statistics, the progress has been remarkable: when I was toured around by Placide, the life expectancy was only 55 years, now it is 69. This wouldn't have been possible without international solidarity: in 2019 health expenses were USD 56 per capita in Rwanda, of which USD 21 was provided by international actors.[29] Before we spend a book on unintended effects (also of aid to Rwanda!), it is essential to acknowledge that the intended effects have often been achieved, and have contributed to dramatic improvements in the human condition over the last decades, not just in Rwanda, but across many low-income countries.

There is an enormous body of academic evidence, compiled in rigorous impact evaluations and meta-analysis that foreign aid can effectively achieve intended objectives. Over the last fifteen years, the independent research organization 3ie has been composing 'evidence maps.' These are schematic overviews of aid effectiveness, showing that an increasing number of interventions are evidence-based. For some sectors, such as health and education, we now have bold evidence on what works when and where (and what not). While the evidence of the effectiveness of aid in newer sectors, such as the promotion of information and communication technologies, is still patchy, many interventions can now be considered evidence-based, from specific interventions in the field of Mental Health and Psychosocial Support to Conditional Cash transfers.[30]

With the massive challenges that the world is facing right now, the need for more evidence-based international development interventions is unmistakable. Climate change is getting out of hand, global inequality is reaching alarming levels, and autocracy is rising. Many of the problems are intertwined, and more actors, governments, and people than ever are involved in solving these global challenges. But while we need a forward-looking, comprehensive, and ambitious international development sector to deal with these challenges, the international development sector is increasingly facing headwinds from all sides: financially, ideologically, and politically.

While the OECD heralds 'record' foreign aid levels of over USD 200 billion annually,[31] increasing amounts are being spent within donor countries themselves, especially on the reception of refugees. Many high-income countries – including Denmark, Finland, Italy, Norway, Switzerland, and the UK – reduced support for the world's poorest countries to fund refugee reception closer to home. Out of a survey of thirty rich countries, twelve reduced their development spending in 2022.[32] And while Western leaders solemnly pledge funds for the reconstruction of Ukraine (which is needed), this funding is often taken away from the poorest countries.

Ideologically, the international development sector faces criticism from a new generation of activists and academics, who highlight neo-colonial practices or even racism in the sector. They criticize the top-down priority setting in Western capitals, the lack of follow-up on promises to work more with local actors, and the unequal treatment of international and national staff members. There is a strong call to 'decolonize development,' to which the traditional aid agencies have difficulty responding.[33]

Lastly, the international development sector is facing political headwinds. Parliamentarians in many donor countries are eager to exploit the smallest mistake by development agencies for electoral gains, and often do so successfully. They demand more regular reporting from donor agencies on cases of fraud and sexual exploitative abuse and they use the information they receive to feed the 'management by outrage' cycle. This leads to a reduction in public support for official development assistance, which makes it easier to engage in budget cuts. This way, the crisis entrenches itself.

We as development professionals can respond to these financial, ideological, and political headwinds in two ways. One is to retreat, go on the defence, and hope the crisis in international development will blow over. We can try to brush off criticism from the left as ideologically driven, rather than attempting to learn from it. To appeal to right-wing xenophobia to get allocated at least some of the 'migration management' funding. Or we can take a headlong rush. To learn from the criticism, to adapt to the changed circumstances, and to develop a new and confident narrative and practice. I choose the latter: the book aims to push innovation and collaboration in the sector. It aims to professionalize it, so that it comes stronger out of the storms that it currently faces. Too often professionals in the development sector erroneously think they protect their organization and the sector by concealing side effects. In the short run, this might indeed protect their reputation, but in the end, it only worsens things as lessons aren't learnt, performance lacks, and adaption to new challenges is too slow.

I choose for this flight forward as there are just too many global challenges that require effective international collaboration. Neither runaway climate change nor rising levels of inequality will go away if we look to the other side. Still too many kids go to bed hungry across the globe. There are so many community workers, educators, and nurses across the globe walking the extra mile to fight this hunger and other forms of poverty, so let's not give up on them, but learn how to support them better.

1.4 Reading guide for the remainder of the book

The approach I take in this book is a 'critical-constructive approach.' It is critical because it assesses research reports, evaluations, and practices of international development agencies through a rather critical lens. I understand the ideological and institutional drivers of these organizations (having been part of one myself), so I know when to take their publications with a pinch of salt. At the same time, the approach is constructive, since I aim to see how I can contribute to improving the practices of these same agencies. So if you expect this book to be another 'dead aid' book, I must disappoint you. Over the course of the book, you will find a more fine-grained analysis of what can go wrong with external interventions (and what can go better than expected). Still, the basic premise of this book is that international solidarity is needed, especially in the face of the climate crisis and rising global inequality. Yet, you will be equally disappointed if you expect this book to tell you that the development sector can make do with a few managerial fixes here and there. This book attempts to come towards a 'radical reform' agenda as proposed by Gulrajani: one that fundamentally changes how the international development sector is structured.[34]

For those unfamiliar with development studies, the academic backbone of the development sector: there is no other social science discipline as preposterous as this one. While economists tend to stick to financial woes, political scientists to governance troubles, and sociologists to inequality, development scholars claim to combine them all. They aim to solve low-income countries' economic, political, social, and environmental problems. Not just in one, but in all of them! But this weakness of the discipline is also its strength: by combining insights and research methods across the social sciences, it can connect dots that other disciplines consider separate. It can combine anthropologists' detailed ethnographic fieldwork with economists' sweeping macroeconomic analyses and shed new light on both of them. But while development *academics* adopt this wide-eyed lens, aspiring development *practitioners* – like me at the start of my career – are often trained with a much more 'rigorous' way of thinking, with little space for the unexpected. In this book, I propose to bridge this gap between the practice and the study of international development.

This book is structured along the lines of a research I carried out with Professor Joost de Laat and his team at the Centre for Global Challenges of Utrecht University. Based on the text-mining of about 700 evaluation documents, we made a 'top ten' of unintended effects. This book follows these effects in ascending order. It starts with the category of unintended effects found least in the evaluations assessed as part of this research (the backlash effect) and ends with the category encountered most often (catalytic spillover effects).[35] I claim in no way that the ten categories (and the thirty sub-categories!) are exhaustive: this book is a first attempt to taxonomize unintended effects, the start of a discussion rather than the end of it.

The book aims to be both academically sound and easily accessible to a wide audience. I will start with a theoretical chapter, and then break down the taxonomy of unintended effects chapter by chapter.[36] But the book can also be read without its academic backbone: every chapter includes various concrete examples, including a testimony by somebody unintentionally affected by international development efforts, positively or negatively.[37] Every chapter concludes with recommendations on better dealing with the encountered side effects. I subdivide the recommendations into the three main target audiences of this book: (1) policymakers, (2) practitioners, and (3) evaluators.[38]

This book is not just informative; it is also a call to action. A call to break free from our tunnel vision, let go of our sacred cows, and be self-critical, without being defeatist. That's why this book concludes with a set of discussion questions designed to spark debate with your peers. I hope that reading this book not only makes you more aware of potential side effects, but also motivates you to take a stance in your organization to challenge existing paradigms. To plead for more transparency and willingness to learn, not to bury but to redeem development. Let's redesign the incentives in the aid system to allow for complexity and learning.

While we need effective international development efforts more than ever to deal with the global challenges, it is often rightly being criticized. I hope this book contributes to the professionalization of the sector so that these criticisms can be overcome and international solidarity will thrive.

Notes

1 The unintended cholera outbreak is actually an example of the negative geographic spillover effect, dealt with in Chapter 9.

2 The testimony of Masamba in Chapter 8 on behavioural responses provides more background on this example.

3 This is an example of the upward price effect, which will be discussed in Section 6.2.

4 For a more at-length discussion on these misunderstandings, see Dirk-Jan Koch and Lau Schulpen, 'Introduction to the special issue "unintended effects of international cooperation",' *Evaluation and Program Planning* 68 (2018), 202–209, https://doi.org/10.1016/j.evalprogplan.2017.10.006

5 Frank de Zwart, 'Unintended but not unanticipated consequences,' *Theory and Society* 44, no. 3 (2015): 283–297, www.jstor.org/stable/43694760

6 Jason Stearns, *Dancing in the Glory of Monsters: The Collapse of the Congo and the Great War of Africa* (New York, NY: Public Affairs, 2012).

7   Linda Polman, *War Games: The Story of Aid and War in Modern Times* (London: Penguin UK, 2010).

8   Paul J. Isenman and H. W. Singer, 'Food aid: Disincentive effects and their policy implications,' *Economic Development and Cultural Change* 25, no. 2 (1977): 205–237, https://doi.org/10.1086/450944

9   Ryan Cardwell and Pascal L. Ghazalian, 'The Effects of Untying International Food Assistance: The Case of Canada,' *American Journal of Agricultural Economics* 102, no. 4 (2020): 1056–1078.

10 World Food Programme, *P4P Impact Assessments: Synthesis of Preliminary Findings* (Rome: WFP, 2015). www.wfp.org/publications/p4p-impact-assessment-reports

11 Dirk-Jan Koch and Sara Kinsbergen, 'Exaggerating unintended effects? Competing narratives on the impact of conflict minerals regulation,' *Resources Policy* 57 (2018): 255–263, https://doi.org/10.1016/j.resourpol.2018.03.011

12 Angus Deaton, *The Great Escape* (Princeton, NJ: Princeton University Press, 2013), 312 and 317.

13 Geske Dijkstra, 'Aid and good governance: Examining aggregate unintended effects of aid,' *Evaluation and Programme Planning* 68 (2018): 225–232, https://doi.org/10.1016/j.evalprogplan.2017.09.004

14 Patrick Baert, 'Unintended consequences: A typology and examples,' *International Sociology* 6, no. 2 (1991): 201–210, https://doi.org/10.1177/026858091006002006

15 Robert Klitgaard, ' "Unanticipated consequences" in anti-poverty programmes,' *World Development* 25, no. 12 (1997): 1963–1972, https://doi.org/10.1016/S0305-750X(97)00106-X

16 IOB, *Work in Progress–Evaluation of the ORET Programme: Investing in Public Infrastructure in Developing Countries* (The Hague: Netherlands Ministry of Foreign Affairs, 2015). www.government.nl/documents/reports/2015/07/01/iob-work-in-progress-evaluation-of-the-oret-programme-investing-in-public-infrastructure-in-developing-countries, 2020. Interestingly, the same programme also had negative unintended effects, showing that one programme can have both positive and negative side effects simultaneously.

17 Robert K. Merton, 'The unanticipated consequences of purposive social action,' *American Sociological Review* 1, no. 6 (1936): 897, https://doi.org/10.2307/2084615

18 David Mosse, *Cultivating Development: An Ethnography of Aid Policy and Practice* (London: Pluto Press, 2005), 346.

19 Adalbertus Kamanzi, *Our way: Responding to the Dutch aid in the District Rural development programme of Bukoba Tanzania* (Leiden: African Studies Centre, 2007).

20 IOB, *Poverty, Policies and Perceptions in Tanzania: An Evaluation of Dutch Aid to Two District Rural Development Programmes. Evaluation Report 296* (The Hague: Policy Operations Department IOB, 2004). www.tanzaniagateway.org/docs/poverty_policies_perceptionsinTanzania.pdf

21 Kamanzi, *Our way*, 123.

22 This is confirmed for health interventions: Anne-Marie Turcotte-Tremblay, Idriss Ali Gali Gali, and Valéry Ridde, 'The unintended consequences of COVID-19 mitigation measures matter: Practical guidance for investigating them,' *BMC Medical Research Methodology* 21, no. 1 (2021): 28, https://doi.org/10.1186/s12874-020-01200-x

23 See, for instance, Martin de Alteriis, 'Considering Unintended Consequences: Evidence From Recent Evaluations of U.S. Foreign Assistance Programs,' *American Journal of Evaluation* 41, no. 1 (2020): 54–70, https://doi.org/10.1177/1098214018804081

24 Ibid., 63.; Henrik Wiig and Jørn Holm-Hansen, *Unintended Effects in Evaluations of Norwegian Aid: A Desk Study* (Oslo: Norad, 2014), 16, www.norad.no/en/toolspublications/publications/2014/unintended-effects-in-evaluations-of-norwegian-aid/

25 OECD/DAC Network on Development Evaluation, *Better Criteria for Better Evaluation: Revised Evaluation Criteria, Definitions and Principles for Use* (Paris: OECD, 2019), 11, www.oecd.org/dac/evaluation/revised-evaluation-criteria-dec-2019.pdf

26 Dan Honig and Nilima Gulrajani, 'Making good on donors' desire to do development differently,' *Third World Quarterly* 39, no. 1 (2017): 68–84, https://doi.org/10.1080/01436 597.2017.1369030

27 Hans Rosling, Ola Rosling, and Anna Rosling Rönnlund, *Factfulness: Ten Reasons We're Wrong About the World–and Why Things Are Better Than You Think* (London: Sceptre, 2018).

28 Management Sciences for Health, *The Development of Community-Based Health Insurance in Rwanda: Experiences and Lessons* (Medford, MA: MSH, 2016), https://msh.org/wp-content/uploads/2016/04/the_development_of_cbhi_in_rwanda_experiences_and_lessons_-_technical_brief.pdf

29 Institute for Health Metrics and Evaluation, 'Rwanda,' accessed on 1 February 2023, www.healthdata.org/rwanda

30 International Initiative for Impact Evaluation, 'Africa Evidence Map,' last modified on 17 September 2019, https://gapmaps.3ieimpact.org/evidence-maps/africa-evidence-gap-map

31 OECD, *ODA Levels in 2022–Preliminary Data. Detailed Summary Note* (Paris: OECD, 2023), www.oecd.org/dac/financing-sustainable-development/ODA-2022-summary.pdf

32 Samuel Lovett, 'Rich countries increasingly the recipients of their own aid, new figures show,' *The Telegraph*, 13 April 2023, www.telegraph.co.uk/global-health/climate-and-people/rich-countries-increasingly-the-recipients-of-their-own-aid/

33 Peace Direct, *Time to Decolonise Aid: Insights and Lessons from a Global Consultation* (London: Peace Direct, 2021), www.peacedirect.org/publications/timetodecoloniseaid/

34 Nilima Gulrajani, 'Transcending the great foreign aid debate: Managerialism, radicalism and the search for aid effectiveness,' *Third World Quarterly* 32, no. 2 (2011): 199–216, https://doi.org/10.1080/01436597.2011.560465

35 There are two caveats to note here. First, the proposed typology is not fully consistent with the mutually exclusive, collectively exhaustive (MECE) principle. Some unintended effects could fall into more than one category: e.g. unintended gender effects are now spread across various unintended effects (e.g. behavioural and backlash effects). I could also have chosen to come up with a separate 'unintended gender effect' category, but in the end I decided to stick to a maximum of ten categories, as to keep it digestible. Moreover, I do not capture all possible unintended effects: this indicates that the categories are not exhaustive. Second, personally I take the order of the chapters with a pinch of salt: it is only based on the times it occurs in Dutch evaluations. If an unintended effect is counted less often in evaluations, it might just mean that the blind spot in this regard is larger, not that this unintended effect is less prevalent.

36 If you would like to understand how the taxonomy was developed, see Dirk-Jan Koch, Jolynde Vis, Maria van der Harst, Elric Tendron, and Joost de Laat, 'Assessing international development cooperation: Becoming intentional about unintended effects,' *Sustainability* 13, no. 21 (2021): 11571, https://doi.org/10.3390/su132111571

37 The testimonies are write-ups of the personal experiences of the people involved. The testimonies adhere to journalistic, and not to academic standards. For instance, no triangulation of the testimonies has taken place.

38 The distinction between recommendations for policymakers and practitioners can be slightly blurred, but recommendations for policymakers tend to focus more on the sector as a whole, and for practitioners focus more on the organization and the programme level. Recommendations for policymakers often concern politicians as well, and those for the evaluators often hold for researchers and students.

Further reading

de Alteriis, Martin. 'Considering unintended consequences: Evidence from recent evaluations of U.S. foreign assistance programs.' *American Journal of Evaluation* 41, no. 1 (2020): 54–70. https://doi.org/10.1177/1098214018804081

Baert, Patrick. 'Unintended consequences: a typology and examples.' *International Sociology* 6, no. 2 (1991): 201–210. https://doi.org/10.1177/026858091006002006

Cardwell, Ryan, and Pascal L. Ghazalian. 'The effects of untying international food assistance: The case of Canada.' *American Journal of Agricultural Economics* 102, no. 4 (2020): 1056–1078. https://doi.org/10.1002/ajae.12084

Deaton, Angus. *The Great Escape.* Princeton, NJ: Princeton University Press, 2013.

Dijkstra, Geske. 'Aid and good governance: Examining aggregate unintended effects of aid.' *Evaluation and Programme Planning* 68 (2018): 225–232. https://doi.org/10.1016/j.evalprogplan.2017.09.004

Gardner, Katy, David Lewis, Vered Amit, and Christina Garsten. *Anthropology and Development: Challenges for the Twenty-First Century.* London: Pluto Press, 2015.

Gulrajani, Nilima. 'Transcending the great foreign aid debate: Managerialism, radicalism and the search for aid effectiveness.' *Third World Quarterly* 32, no. 2 (2011): 199–216. https://doi.org/10.1080/01436597.2011.560465

Honig, Dan, and Nilima Gulrajani. 'Making good on donors' desire to do development differently.' *Third World Quarterly* 39, no. 1 (2017): 68–84. https://doi.org/10.1080/01436597.2017.1369030

Institute for Health Metrics and Evaluation. 'Rwanda.' Accessed on 1 February 2023. www.healthdata.org/rwanda

International Initiative for Impact Evaluation. 'Africa Evidence Map.' Last modified on 17 September 2019. https://gapmaps.3ieimpact.org/evidence-maps/africa-evidence-gap-map

IOB. *Poverty, Policies and Perceptions in Tanzania: An Evaluation of Dutch Aid to Two District Rural Development Programmes. Evaluation Report 296.* The Hague: Policy Operations Department IOB, 2004. www.tanzaniagateway.org/docs/poverty_policies_perceptionsinTanzania.pdf

IOB. *Work in Progress–Evaluation of the ORET Programme: Investing in Public Infrastructure in Developing Countries.* The Hague: Netherlands Ministry of Foreign Affairs, 2015. www.government.nl/documents/reports/2015/07/01/iob-work-in-progress-evaluation-of-the-oret-programme-investing-in-public-infrastructure-in-developing-countries

Isenman, Paul J., and H. W. Singer. 'Food aid: Disincentive effects and their policy implications.' *Economic Development and Cultural Change* 25, no. 2 (1977): 205–237. https://doi.org/10.1086/450944

Kamanzi, Adalbertus. *Our Way: Responding to the Dutch Aid in the District Rural Development Programme of Bukoba Tanzania.* Leiden: African Studies Centre, 2007.

Klitgaard, Robert. '"Unanticipated consequences" in anti-poverty programmes.' *World Development* 25, no. 12 (1997): 1963–1972. https://doi.org/10.1016/S0305-750X(97)00106-X

Koch, Dirk-Jan, and Sara Kinsbergen. 'Exaggerating unintended effects? Competing narratives on the impact of conflict minerals regulation.' *Resources Policy* 57 (2018): 255–263. https://doi.org/10.1016/j.resourpol.2018.03.011

Koch, Dirk-Jan, and Lau Schulpen. 'Introduction to the special issue "unintended effects of international cooperation".' *Evaluation and Program Planning* 68 (2018): 202–209. https://doi.org/10.1016/j.evalprogplan.2017.10.006

Koch, Dirk-Jan, Jolynde Vis, Maria van der Harst, Elric Tendron, and Joost de Laat. 'Assessing international development cooperation: Becoming intentional about unintended effects.' *Sustainability* 13, no. 21 (2021): 11571. https://doi.org/10.3390/su132111571

Lovett, Samuel. 'Rich countries increasingly the recipients of their own aid, new figures show.' *The Telegraph,* 13 April 2023. www.telegraph.co.uk/global-health/climate-and-people/rich-countries-increasingly-the-recipients-of-their-own-aid/

Management Sciences for Health. *The Development of Community-Based Health Insurance in Rwanda: Experiences and Lessons.* Medford, MA: MSH, 2016. https://msh.org/wp-content/uploads/2016/04/the_development_of_cbhi_in_rwanda_experiences_and_lessons_-_technical_brief.pdf

Merton, Robert K. 'The unanticipated consequences of purposive social action.' *American Sociological Review* 1, no. 6 (1936): 894–904. https://doi.org/10.2307/2084615

Mosse, David. *Cultivating Development: An Ethnography of Aid Policy and Practice.* London: Pluto Press, 2005.

OECD. *ODA Levels in 2022–Preliminary Data. Detailed Summary Note.* Paris: OECD, 2023. www.oecd.org/dac/financing-sustainable-development/ODA-2022-summary.pdf

OECD/DAC Network on Development Evaluation. *Better Criteria for Better Evaluation: Revised Evaluation Criteria, Definitions and Principles for Use.* Paris: OECD, 2019. www.oecd.org/dac/evaluation/revised-evaluation-criteria-dec-2019.pdf

Peace Direct. *Time to Decolonise Aid: Insights and Lessons from a Global Consultation.* London: Peace Direct, 2021. www.peacedirect.org/publications/timetodecoloniseaid/

Polman, Linda. *War Games: The Story of Aid and War in Modern Times.* London: Penguin UK, 2010.

Rosling, Hans, Ola Rosling, and Anna Rosling Rönnlund. *Factfulness: Ten Reasons We're Wrong about the World–and Why Things Are Better Than You Think.* London: Sceptre, 2018.

Stearns, Jason. *Dancing in the Glory of Monsters: The Collapse of the Congo and the Great War of Africa.* New York, NY: Public Affairs, 2012.

Turcotte-Tremblay, Anne-Marie, Idriss Ali Gali Gali, and Valéry Ridde. 'The unintended consequences of COVID-19 mitigation measures matter: Practical guidance for investigating them.' *BMC Medical Research Methodology* 21, no. 1 (2021): 28. https://doi.org/10.1186/s12874-020-01200-x

Wiig, Henrik, and Jørn Holm-Hansen. *Unintended Effects in Evaluations of Norwegian Aid: A Desk Study.* Oslo: Norad, 2014. www.norad.no/en/toolspublications/publications/2014/unintended-effects-in-evaluations-of-norwegian-aid/

World Food Programme. *P4P Impact Assessments: Synthesis of Preliminary Findings.* Rome: WFP, 2015. www.wfp.org/publications/p4p-impact-assessment-reports

de Zwart, Frank. 'Unintended but not unanticipated consequences.' *Theory and Society* 44, no. 3 (2015): 283–297. www.jstor.org/stable/43694760

2 For those who love theory
Explaining unintended effects with complexity theory and bounded policy learning

From this theoretical chapter you will learn:

- How are the key terms 'international development' and 'unintended effects' defined in this book
- Why we need to use complexity thinking – and not linear thinking – in international development
- How to better understand unintended effects, make use of the positive ones, and mitigate against the negative ones
- The meaning of key relevant concepts in complexity thinking: feedback loops, non-linearities, interconnectivities, alternative impact pathways, and adaptive agents
- That complexity thinking in international development does not mean that we should abandon planning, but move towards adaptive planning
- That there are ideological, institutional, and technical limits to policy learning in the international development sector

When I was doing my master's studies in Development Management at the LSE, I was trained extensively in linear programming: from inputs to outputs, to outcomes, to intended effects. I loved the sense of direction and certainty that this provided, and how it professionalized the development sector by measuring progress at various stages of implementation. I went almost straight from university to working for the Netherlands Ministry of Foreign Affairs, where I imposed this framework on the recipients of funding from our organization. I now apologize to everybody I pushed into this linear straightjacket. It took me twenty years to discover that the international development process is a lot messier than I learned at university. All kinds of unexpected things happen with the funding we provide. This is not something that I ever could have learned from the reports I would receive from the funding recipients, who all echoed the same linear thinking – they had little choice after all. I gradually learned these lessons through living, working, and researching with an open mind (always with local researchers) in low-income countries. This book is a write-up of that two-decade long journey. I hope that learning these lessons will go faster for you than it did for me!

DOI: 10.4324/9781003356851-2

This Chapter has been made available under a CC-BY-NC-ND license.

"Dear Mr. Gandhi, We regret we cannot fund your proposal because the link between spinning cloth and the fall of the British Empire was not clear to us."

Figure 2.1 The challenges of linear planning in a nutshell.

Source: Written by M. M. Rogers and illustrated by Ariv R. Faizal, Wahyu S., Ary W. S. Creative team for Search for Common Ground Indonesia.

2.1 What are we actually talking about?

Before we go any further, a short note on two of the book's key concepts. In the social sciences, we normally use formal terms such as 'unintended effects' or 'unintended consequences.' In this book, these terms are used interchangeably with 'side effects.' I use a simple definition of unintended effects: the consequence of an action that differs from the consequence that was aimed for when starting it.[1] This definition means that many problems I have encountered in the international development sector are excluded. If a programme fails to meet its objectives, this is not necessarily an unintended effect. For instance, I once visited the Niger Delta in Nigeria to evaluate a programme my organization was implementing. We had promised to build 'Information Resource Centres' so that the population would be better informed about their rights. The programme was a failure: the population ended up barely using these centres. But this failure does not constitute an unintended effect: the programme just didn't meet its objectives. One would speak of unintended effects if politicians would have used these Information Resource Centres to start a new political party, or by rebels to start a rebellion.

Unexpected events are also excluded from this definition. For instance, with colleagues from Radboud University, I was researching Private Development Initiatives (small NGOs from the Global North operating in the Global South) and they worked fine. However, when COVID happened, they lost half of their funding because they couldn't engage in regular offline fundraising (e.g. village festivals). This is not an unintended effect either, but an extraneous event.[2]

The second key term used in this book is 'international development.' The title of this book refers to 'aid,' but this is just for marketing purposes: if the term 'development' is used without 'aid,' a potential reader might think that this is a book about the side effects of property development or child development. The term 'international development' stands on its own, referring to the efforts of agencies, governments, and individuals in the Global North to promote sustainable progress in the Global South (often with or via local partners).[3] Elements of what 'sustainable progress' means are very contested, as will become clear in Chapter 3. At any rate, these international development efforts can take various forms, such as long-term development programmes, life-saving humanitarian aid, and peacebuilding activities. While the definition of 'unintended effects' I use is narrow (as explained above), my definition of 'international development' is deliberately broad as I try to get an insight into the broader field of international solidarity. This ranges from individual acts to government programmes and private sector initiatives and from international adoption to tax evasion crackdowns and fair trade schemes.

2.2 Complexity thinking in international development

Since development programmes are affected by a wide range of sociocultural, economic, political, legal, administrative, and often ecological factors – all of which interact in complex and unpredictable ways – international development is a messy business. A useful approach for making sense of this messiness is complexity thinking.[4]

Complexity thinkers use ten key concepts, five of which are of particular importance for this book, and which are shown in the figure below.[5] Complexity thinkers argue that there are multiple (1) *feedback loops*, (2) *interconnections*, (3) *non-linearities*, and (4) *alternative impact pathways*, in a system composed of (5) *adaptive agents* that lead to both intended and unintended effects.[6] Complexity thinking can be a particularly useful approach to understanding the unintended effects of international cooperation efforts by providing an 'understanding of the mechanisms through which unpredictable, unknowable, and emergent change happens.'[7] Outputs, outcomes, and effects are linked in many ways, leading to multiple layers of unintended effects. In every chapter, I will highlight the key concepts of complexity thinking that explain the emergence of the respective unintended effects.

Let's return to the cartoon of Gandhi's funding request being turned down by an external donor (Figure 2.1). Although fictional, it can teach us a great deal about the limits of linear thinking. Gandhi's spinning wheel campaign ended up creating a mass movement that eventually beat the British Empire, but the potential donor from the cartoon fails to see this great potential. This is because linear thinking is inadequate at capturing the complexity of the Indian independence struggle. For instance, it cannot account for how Gandhi's campaign for domestic cloth production did not only lead to more cloth, but also to a revived national consciousness. This is an example of an *alternative impact pathway*. It also cannot account for how the independence movement simmered under the surface for years and suddenly came to fruition, with millions on the streets: the Indian struggle for independence was a process wrought with *non-linearities*.

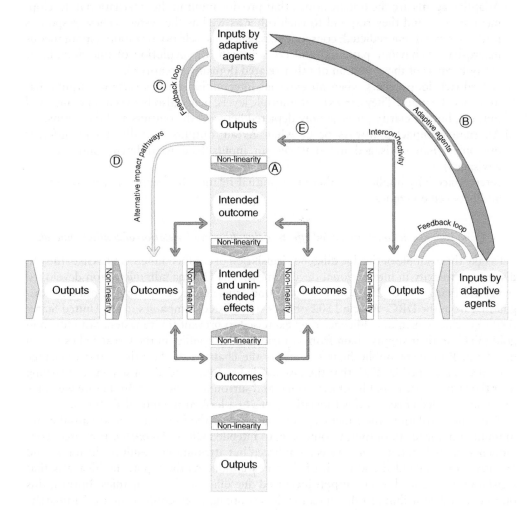

Figure 2.2 Key terms of complexity thinking in international development.

Source: Image designed by Ymke Wieringa.

Imagine putting periodic targets on the size of the Indian independence movement relative to cloth production funding! We can further think of the *interconnections* with other anti-colonial movements, *feedback loops* of colonial violence and increasing anti-colonial fervour, and *adaptive agents* such as the two Cold War superpowers that both had a stake in the decolonization of India.

Let's flesh out these concepts in more detail and apply it to a more current international development example: the conflict minerals legislation.

Let's go through the key terms one by one:

a **Non-linearities** can exist anywhere in the system, and certain thresholds of outputs sometimes need to be achieved before certain outcomes can be attained. These processes are non-linear in the sense that the thresholds serve as tipping points that can exponentially increase the pace of the process.

b **Adaptive agents** are the organizations that provide input in the international development system, and they respond to each other as well as the system. These responses
lead to several unpredicted consequences, such as self-organization (spontaneous
macro-level behaviour patterns) and co-evolution (the evolution of one domain or
entity because of the evolution of other related domains or entities).

c A **feedback loop** occurs when an external intervention creates certain outputs that
influence the input. They can exist at multiple levels, hence also between outcomes and
outputs, but for clarity purpose only depicted between the outputs and the inputs.

d **Alternative impact pathways** occur when certain outputs lead directly to different
outcomes than envisaged (or that certain inputs lead to different outputs than
envisaged).

e **Interconnectivity** implies that there is a mutual relationship between various outputs
and between outcomes.

2.2.1 Complexity in action: unintended effects of due diligence legislation of conflict minerals

Let's take the example of the due diligence legislation of conflict minerals as a case study to
discuss complexity in international development. The Obama administration developed
the Dodd-Frank Act of 2010, and inserted one article concerning conflict minerals originating from the DRC. Article 1502 obliges stock-listed companies in the United States
(US) to declare which due diligence they exercised to prevent tin, tungsten, tantalite, and
gold (3TG) in their supply chain from contributing to conflict in the Great Lakes region
of Africa. Prominent public figures, such as the chair of the Securities and Exchange
Commission, argued in 2017 that the law has led to 'unintended consequences washing
over the Democratic Republic of the Congo and surrounding areas.'[8] But before we move
to the unintended effects of this legislation, let's first look at the intended effects.

With this legislation, the American government had the following linear causal chain
in mind: input leads to output, to outcome, to intended effect. An *output* is a direct consequence of the input, an *outcome* is an indirect, but attributable, result of the input, and
an *effect* is the intended end result of the intervention. As the input, the idea was that
legislation would lead to an output: increased due diligence by companies. In turn, this
output would contribute to the outcome: less sourcing from conflict mines. Ultimately,
this outcome would lead to the intended effect: less funding for rebels and less conflict.

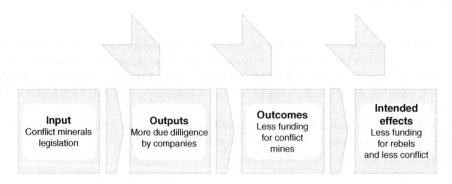

Figure 2.3 The effects of conflict mineral legislation through a linear lens.

Source: Image designed by Ymke Wieringa.

This linear chain played out as intended, at least to a certain degree, for certain minerals. For instance, the number of tin, tungsten, and tantalite (3T) mines controlled by rebels decreased significantly after the Dodd-Frank Act went into effect. IPIS, an independent research group, found in their 2009/2010 survey that 56 per cent of the 3T mines were under the influence of armed actors, whereas the 2013–2015 survey found this remained the case in only 21 per cent of the mines.[9] The intended effect seems to have been achieved, at least to a certain degree for three out of four minerals.

But looking beyond the predetermined parameters, unintended outcomes of the Dodd-Frank Act were also abound. Based on a review of twelve studies, the legislation had (at least) three unintended effects: (1) increased funding for rebels in and around gold mines, with a substantial share of the rebels moving from the T3 to the gold mines[10]; (2) a weakened position for female miners[11]; and (3) reduced bargaining power for artisanal miners.[12]

Since I was living in the eastern DRC in that period and visited some of these conflict mines myself, I came to realize that linear thinking could explain the intended effects but not those unintended effects. Complexity thinking proved a much more useful tool, as Figure 2.4 illustrates. I will go through the five key concepts one by one.

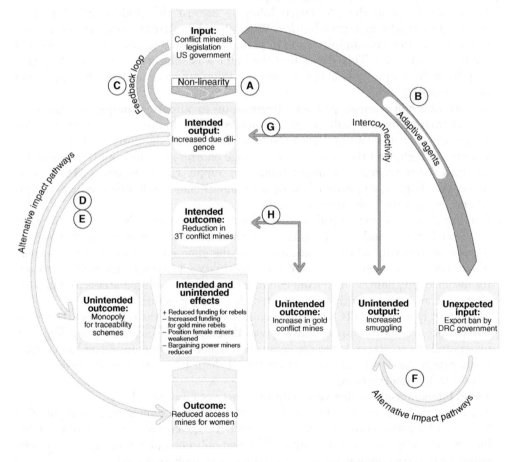

Figure 2.4 Conflict minerals legislation's intended and unintended effects through a complexity lens.

Source: Image designed by Ymke Wieringa.

a Non-linearity (outputs or outcomes only kicking in after a tipping point)
The conflict minerals legislation didn't automatically lead to a steady increase in due diligence by companies, because there was no traceability scheme yet for minerals to certify that minerals are coming from a specific approved mining site. In the first year (2011) there was no increase in due diligence, but rather a disengagement effect: many companies simply stopped sourcing from the DRC and the Great Lakes region altogether. Only when a critical number of companies rallied behind one traceability initiative, the initiative reached a 'tipping point' and many other companies started to use it.

b Adaptive agents (agents providing inputs influencing other agents)
The behaviour of other actors who provide inputs in the system is not fixed, as linear thinking assumes. When the Dodd-Frank Act was adopted, the first reaction of the DRC government was to come to a total export ban of minerals from the eastern DRC for one year as to tidy up the sector to prepare it for the roll-out of the Dodd-Frank Act. This initially undermined the goal of the Dodd-Frank Act, which aimed to initiate extra due diligence by companies, not a total export ban.

c Feedback loop (from outputs back to inputs)
Many companies in the US started lobbying against the Dodd-Frank Act, as it increased their administrative burden. When President Trump came into office, one of the first acts of his administration in January 2016 was to suspend this section of the Dodd-Frank Act. This shows that the input was subject to a negative feedback loop from the output: a backlash to increased due diligence leads to the suspension of Article 1502.

d, e, and f: Alternative impact pathways (from inputs to outputs, or outputs to outcomes)
d One alternative impact pathway of the increased due diligence was the unintended emergence of a monopolized traceability scheme. Since the costs of a traceability scheme are high, and the first-move advantage enormous, a monopoly emerged for one traceability scheme (the International Tin Supply Chain Initiative, iTSCi). This reduced the bargaining power of the miners: they all had to sell their products via this scheme and pay the levies imposed on them.

e Another alternative impact pathway was that it reduced women's access to mines. To be allowed to mine and wash the ores – something often done by women – they needed to get a 'miner card,' which became a way for the mining officials to extract all kinds of services from women. Thus, while the traceability scheme was intended to protect, for instance, pregnant women from entering the mines, it reduced access to mines for all women and subsequently weakened female miners' position.

f The export ban by the DRC government aimed to flush out the rebels from the mines, but another alternative impact pathway was that it actually increased smuggling. The miners and the rebels needed to earn cash and finance their operations, and since legitimate export was no longer possible, many of them (they are also adaptive agents) went (further) underground.

g and h: Interconnectivity (between outputs or between outcomes)
g The increased focus on due diligence by the international community (an output) also had a similar effect as the export ban by the DRC government: there was a notable increase in smuggling (another output). The two outputs (one intended, the other one unintended) were communicating vessels, they were interconnected.

h Contra to linear thinking, due diligence for the 3Ts was interconnected with the due diligence for gold (or the lack thereof). There is a big difference between gold and other conflict minerals worldwide and in the DRC: whereas with the 3Ts you need to transport tons for a reasonable profit, you need only one kilo of gold to make a lot of money. So, when the due diligence requirements for the 3Ts went up and many of the 3T conflict mines could not be exploited anymore, many rebels moved to the gold mining sector. There was a clear interconnection between different outcomes. There was a so-called waterbed effect: the more successful the policy was in one domain (3T), the more dislocation towards the gold sector took place.

By inserting more complexity into a policy assessment, we get a more granular view of causal mechanisms and the intended and unintended effects. By no means do I claim that we now have a complete overview of all the effects of the Dodd-Frank Act, as probably many more processes were set in motion, but at least it gives a more comprehensive overview than a linear model could ever do.

Complexity thinkers can be quite radical when it comes to abandoning planning. One complexity thinker argues that 'development planning should abandon prescriptive, goal-oriented decision making and prediction about future states.'[13] While I understand that planning has downsides, I am not sure we should abandon efforts such as the Sustainable Development Goals. Let us be more open about the trade-offs between them, and their shortcomings. As you can see in Figures 2.2 and 2.4, I still use the classical terms from linear development management thinking (inputs, outputs, outcomes, and effects), but I have abandoned the linear causal chain. Easterly suggests that there should be less planning in development.[14] I disagree: I think that there should be more *adaptive* planning.[15]

2.3 Bounded policy learning explaining the persistence of unintended effects

Did we learn from these side effects? Since the parliament of the European Union tasked the European Commission to develop a conflict minerals legislation in 2012 as well, this presents a perfect case to find out if the Europeans learned from the American mistakes. The Europeans always seem to take longer to make laws, so we can easily compare the European conflict minerals legislation of 2017 with the American one of 2010 to see if lessons were learnt.[16] The good news is that, while not all lessons were learnt, the Europeans designed the law so that the likelihood of some negative side effects had become substantially lower.

The advocacy coalition framework provides some clues for understanding which lessons are being learnt (and which ones not!). Advocacy coalitions comprise individuals who belong to different groups (e.g. civil servants, journalists, academics, and politicians) but share underlying core principles and often interests. These actors share normative and causal beliefs and engage in coordinated activity over time. Regarding the US and EU conflict mineral laws discussed here, two opposing transatlantic advocacy coalitions emerged: pro-regulation and anti-regulation. Both pushed the EU to consider the side effects of the US law, but in very different ways.

The pro-regulation camp proposed as the main takeaway that the EU regulation should have a global scope because of the unintended consequences of stigmatising one region. According to them, the disengagement effect had left legitimate miners unemployed in a stigmatized DRC, which could have been avoided. The EU learned this lesson and gave its conflict minerals law a global coverage. Because the regulation was now active in multiple risky regions, companies could no longer afford to disengage from the traceability scheme.

The anti-regulation camp also stimulated that lessons would be learnt. They argued that the EU regulation should not require that companies declare that they had nothing to do with conflict mines. They proposed that companies declare they had done their utmost to minimize the risks they were sourcing from conflict mines, a subtle but important difference. According to them, this effort-based approach would also reduce the disengagement effect, and the EU took on board this lesson as well.

While the EU did learn, this policy learning was a politicized process bounded by clear limits. Advocacy coalitions socially constructed evidence about the unintended effects to further their respective agendas. While those with stakes against regulation exaggerated the unintended effects,[17] those who had an interest in the legislation downplayed side effects or focussed on different ones. The degree of learning depended on the frames and the strength of advocacy coalitions and was not a neutral, technical process. This is something we will observe throughout this book. The lessons from advocacy coalitions with stronger frames ('blood minerals') were taken up more readily than those with less attractive frames ('let's reduce the administrative burden for our companies'). Similarly, advocacy coalitions with growing and increasingly vocal membership (like Nobel Prize Laureate Denis Mukwege) were more likely to see their proposed lessons learnt.

The two opposing advocacy coalitions did not substantially learn from each other. But when they did, a neutral platform such as the Organisation for Economic Cooperation and Development (OECD) played an important facilitating role. For this, the OECD ensured that its agenda was set in a multi-stakeholder way, with members of opposing advocacy coalitions (non-governmental organizations [NGOs] and businesses) jointly determining the forum's direction. This forum helped overcome technical boundaries to learning: limits related to a lack of information. For instance, in the beginning, little was known about the shift of rebels from 3T to goldmines. When this technical information was provided, lessons were learnt in this regard by both advocacy coalitions. The unanticipated unintended effects of the American initiative hence became anticipated unintended effects in the European case.

Yet, even though some policy learning took place when the Europeans crafted their law, there are clear limits: hence, I will use the 'bounded policy learning' model in this book, with technical, institutional, and ideological limits to learning.[18] In this case, overcoming ideological and institutional boundaries proved especially hard. Ideological boundaries are limits based on deep-held convictions. Concerning the conflict minerals debate, I found that the anti-regulation coalition had a hard time accepting that the DRC government imposed the mining embargo. They wanted to blame the Dodd-Frank Act for the disengagement effect because they wanted to believe that the side effect was the unintended effect of a market intervention, not the intended effect by a national government.

I also encountered institutional boundaries to learning, which are limits that result from organizational interests. For instance, representatives from traceability schemes often displayed a tunnel vision. They were neither willing to learn about the 'smuggling' side effect nor willing to learn about the effects of monopolistic traceability schemes on miners. These institutional boundaries to learning are cemented through a pervasive conflict of interests in the international development sector as many evaluators and researchers are too donor-dependent, according to Ridde and Sardan.[19]

This book aims to overcome these three boundaries to learning. It provides the tools to overcome technical boundaries to learning. It provides a personal insight into my ideological blind spots, in the hope that it invites you to research your own. Lastly, by communicating openly about the mistakes my organizations and I made, I encourage you to share your dilemmas and errors as well: together we can make the international development sector fit to face the global challenges of the 21st century.

Notes

1 Baert, 'Unintended consequences.' I use the terms effects, consequences, impacts, and results interchangeably, as they all refer to a final stage in programme implementation. Of course this final stage can set in motion new processes, so the usage of these terms remains tricky.

2 Sara Kinsbergen, Marieke Pijnenburg, Tom Merlevede, Luca Naus, and Dirk-Jan Koch, 'The differential impact of the COVID-19 crisis on small-scale development initiatives, a cross-country comparison,' *VOLUNTAS: International Journal of Voluntary and Nonprofit Organizations* 33 (2022): 497–523, https://doi.org/10.1007/s11266-021-00385-z

3 I need to make two caveats to this definition. First, I include in my definition of international development all activities that are officially counted as Official Development Assistance (ODA) by the OECD, irrespective of whether I agree that they are counted as ODA. For example, because currently taking care of asylum seekers in donor countries can be counted as ODA (in the year of their arrival), this is also covered in the book. Second, the terms Global North and Global South are fluid categories (e.g. China belongs both to the Global North and to the Global South). At the moment countries and governments start behaving as donors, I consider them to be (also) part of the Global North.

4 Michael Bamberger, Jos Vaessen, and Estelle Raimondo, *Dealing with Complexity in Development Evaluation* (Thousand Oaks, CA: Sage Publications, 2016), 5.

5 The other concepts are 'emergence,' 'sensitivity to initial conditions,' 'phase space,' 'chaos and the edge of chaos,' and 'self-organization and co-evolution.'

6 Emery Brusset, Cedric de Coning, and Bryn Hughes, *Complexity Thinking for Peacebuilding Practice and Evaluation* (London: Springer, 2016).

7 Ben Ramalingam, Harry Jones, and John Young, *Exploring the Science of Complexity: Ideas and Implications for Development and Humanitarian Efforts* (London: Overseas Development Institute, 2008), ix.

8 Michael S. Piwowar, 'Reconsideration of conflict minerals rule implementation,' *United States Securities Exchange Commission*, 31 January 2017, www.sec.gov/news/statement/reconsideration-of-conflict-minerals-rule-implementation

9 OECD, *Mineral supply chains and conflict links in Eastern Democratic Republic (IPIS)* (Paris: OECD, 2015), www.oecd.org/corporate/mne/mineral-supply-chain-eastern-drc.htm

10 Yannick Weyns, Lotte Hoex, and Ken Matthysen, *Analysis of the interactive map of artisanal mining areas in eastern DR Congo: 2015 update* (Antwerp: International Peace Information Service, 2016), https://ipisresearch.be/publication/analysis-interactive-map-artisanal-mining-areas-eastern-dr-congo-2/

11 Marie Rose Bashwira Nyenyezi, *Navigating obstacles, opportunities and reforms: women's lives and livelihoods in artisanal mining communities in eastern DRC*, doctoral thesis (Wageningen: Wageningen University & Research, 2017), https://doi.org/10.18174/413901

12 Christoph Vogel, Josaphat Musamba, and Ben Radley, 'A miner's canary in Eastern Congo: Formalisation of ARtisanal 3T mining and precarious livelihoods in South Kivu,' *The Extractive Industries and Society* 5, no. 1 (2018): 73–80, https://doi.org/10.1016/j.exis.2017.09.003.

13 Nour-Eddine Sellamna, *Relativism in Agricultural Research and Development: Is Participation a Post-Modern Concept? Working Paper 119* (London: Overseas Development Institute, 1999), 13, www.files.ethz.ch/isn/102317/wp119.pdf

14 William R. Easterly, 'Planners vs. searchers in foreign aid,' presented at *Asian Development Bank's Distinguished Speakers Program* at Manila, Philippines, 18 January 2006, http://users.nber.org/~rdehejia/!@$devo/Lecture%2002%20Aid/Easterly_Searchers_vs_Planners.pdf

15 Lena Gutheil and Dirk-Jan Koch, 'Civil society organizations and managerialism: On the depoliticization of the adaptive management agenda,' *Development Policy Review*, 41, no. 1 (2022): e12630, https://doi.org/10.1111/dpr.12630

16 Dirk-Jan Koch and Olga Burlyuk, 'Bounded policy learning? EU efforts to anticipate unintended consequences in conflict minerals legislation,' *Journal of European Public Policy* 27, no. 10 (2020): 1441–1462, https://doi.org/10.1080/13501763.2019.1675744

17 See, for example, this alarmist title on babies 'dying in Congo due to Dodd-Frank law': Jeffry Bartash, 'More babies may be dying in Congo due to Dodd-Frank law on "conflict minerals",' *MarketWatch*, 20 July 2018, www.marketwatch.com/story/more-babies-may-be-dying-in-congo-due-to-dodd-frank-law-on-conflict-minerals-2018-07-20

18 Dirk-Jan Koch and Marloes Verholt, 'Limits to learning: The struggle to adapt to unintended effects of international payment for environmental services programmes,' *International Environmental Agreements: Politics, Law and Economics* 20, no. 3 (2020): 507–539, https://doi.org/10.1007/s10784-020-09496-2

19 Valéry Ridde and Jean-Pierre Olivier de Sardan, 'The development world: Conflicts of interest at all levels,' *Revue internationale des études du développement* 249 (2022): 247–269, https://doi.org/10.4000/ried.1530

Further reading

Baert, Patrick. 'Unintended consequences: A typology and examples.' *International Sociology* 6, no. 2 (1991): 201–210. https://doi.org/10.1177/026858091006002006

Bamberger, Michael, Jos Vaessen, and Estelle Raimondo. *Dealing With Complexity in Development Evaluation*. Thousand Oaks, CA: Sage Publications, 2016.

Bartash, Jeffry. 'More babies may be dying in Congo due to Dodd-Frank law on "conflict minerals".' *MarketWatch*, 20 July 2018. www.marketwatch.com/story/more-babies-may-be-dying-in-congo-due-to-dodd-frank-law-on-conflict-minerals-2018-07-20

Bashwira Nyenyezi, Marie Rose. *Navigating Obstacles, Opportunities and Reforms: Women's Lives and Livelihoods in Artisanal Mining Communities in Eastern DRC*. Doctoral thesis. Wageningen: Wageningen University & Research, 2017. https://doi.org/10.18174/413901

Brusset, Emery, Cedric de Coning, and Bryn Hughes. *Complexity Thinking for Peacebuilding Practice and Evaluation*. London: Springer, 2016.

Easterly, William R. 'Planners vs. searchers in foreign aid.' Presented at *Asian Development Bank's Distinguished Speakers Program* at Manila, Philippines, 18 January 2006. http://users.nber.org/~rdehejia/!@$devo/Lecture%2002%20Aid/Easterly_Searchers_vs_Planners.pdf

Gutheil, Lena, and Dirk-Jan Koch. 'Civil society organizations and managerialism: On the depoliticization of the adaptive management agenda.' *Development Policy Review* 41, no. 1 (2022): e12630. https://doi.org/10.1111/dpr.12630

Kinsbergen, Sara, Marieke Pijnenburg, Tom Merlevede, Luca Naus, and Dirk-Jan Koch. 'The differential impact of the COVID-19 crisis on small-scale development initiatives, a cross-country comparison.' *VOLUNTAS: International Journal of Voluntary and Nonprofit Organizations* 33 (2022): 497–523. https://doi.org/10.1007/s11266-021-00385-z

Koch, Dirk-Jan, and Olga Burlyuk. 'Bounded policy learning? EU efforts to anticipate unintended consequences in conflict minerals legislation.' *Journal of European Public Policy* 27, no. 10 (2020): 1441–1462. https://doi.org/10.1080/13501763.2019.1675744

Koch, Dirk-Jan, and Marloes Verholt. 'Limits to learning: The struggle to adapt to unintended effects of international payment for environmental services programmes.' *International Environmental Agreements: Politics, Law and Economics* 20, no. 3 (2020): 507–539. https://doi.org/10.1007/s10784-020-09496-2

OECD. *Mineral supply Chains and Conflict Links in Eastern Democratic Republic (IPIS)*. Paris: OECD, 2015. www.oecd.org/corporate/mne/mineral-supply-chain-eastern-drc.htm

Piwowar, Michael S. 'Reconsideration of conflict minerals rule implementation.' *United States Securities Exchange Commission*, 31 January 2017. www.sec.gov/news/statement/reconsiderat ion-of-conflict-minerals-rule-implementation

Ramalingam, Ben, Harry Jones, and John Young. *Exploring the Science of Complexity: Ideas and Implications for Development and Humanitarian Efforts*. London: Overseas Development Institute, 2008.

Ridde, Valéry, and Jean-Pierre Olivier de Sardan. 'The development world: Conflicts of interest at all levels.' *Revue internationale des études du développem*ent 249 (2022): 247–269. https://doi. org/10.4000/ried.1530

Sellamna, Nour-Eddine. *Relativism in Agricultural Research and Development: Is Participation a Post-Modern Concept? Working Paper 119*. London: Overseas Development Institute, 1999. www.files.ethz.ch/isn/102317/wp119.pdf

Vogel, Christoph, Josaphat Musamba, and Ben Radley. 'A miner's canary in Eastern Congo: Formalisation of artisanal 3T mining and precarious livelihoods in South Kivu.' *The Extractive Industries and Society* 5, no. 1 (2018): 73–80. https://doi.org/10.1016/ j.exis.2017.09.003

Weyns, Yannick, Lotte Hoex, and Ken Matthysen. *Analysis of the Interactive Map of Artisanal Mining Areas in Eastern DR Congo: 2015 Update* (Antwerp: International Peace Information Service, 2016). https://ipisresearch.be/publication/analysis-interactive-map-artisanal-mining-areas-eastern-dr-congo-2/

3 Backlash effects

For every action, there is an equal and opposite reaction

Unintended backlash effects occur when an external action leads to an opposite reaction that affects achieving the intended effect. The backlash effect is by definition a macro-level effect, as reactions that are opposite to the expectation at the individual level fall under the heading of behavioural effects.

What flavours do we see?

1 **Anti-aid backlash.** An external intervention is met with suspicion about the ulterior motives of the aid actor. This suspicion often has historical origins. If implemented clumsily, the intervention itself can fire up latent discontent about foreign support, and local leaders can stir up discontent if it serves them. The backlash against aid reduces the effectiveness and sustainability of the intervention.

2 **Anti-foreign values backlash.** Values that external actors promote clash with the mainstream values present in a society. The anti-foreign values backlash shares many of the characteristics of the anti-aid backlash, but finds its origins in the cultural distance between aid actors and societies where they operate rather than discontent about ulterior motives.

In which instances have backlash effects been observed? Two examples:

1 Anti-aid backlash: angry citizens in Guinea and in the DRC attacked Ebola treatment centres because of a widespread belief that the health workers were spreading the disease.

2 Anti-foreign values backlash: in Uganda, the internationally supported campaign for Lesbian, Gay, Bisexual, Transgender, and Queer + (LGBTQ+) rights led to a backlash as leaders of the country seized the opportunity to crack down on these rights, leading to extra violence against LGBTQ+ people.

Key concepts from complexity thinking that help in understanding backlash effects:

1 Feedback loops. Whether it is the anti-aid or the anti-foreign values backlash, in all cases external inputs create certain outputs that set in motion a counter-reaction from governments and populations. By only looking at the primary effects, and

DOI: 10.4324/9781003356851-3

This Chapter has been made available under a CC-BY-NC-ND license.

not the ultimate results after the feedback loop, the perception of the result of an intervention is distorted.
2 **Adaptive agents.** Leaders understand the sentiment within their societies, and understand that they can benefit by orchestrating a backlash. They subsequently adapt their language (into more homophobic or anti-Western) to advance their interests.

Figure 3.1 Backlash effects in action.

Source: Maarten Wolterink.

While this chapter will treat two instances of the backlash effect, they share a common origin. Since external (Western) actors often overlook the origins of the backlash against them, let me get straight to it: the backlash effect often finds its roots in anti-colonialism.

There is a strong desire for self-determination across the globe. People prefer to be led and protected by their own people. Just like development cooperation is some offspring of colonialism,[1] albeit a progressive one, the backlash against aid is often the progeny of anti-colonialism. Centuries of dispossession and exploitation under the guise of 'progress' have led to a deep-seated suspicion of foreign (especially Western) interference, which is passed on from generation to generation. Regardless of how well-intentioned they might be, international development efforts touch this nerve. Foreigners often insufficiently understand this sensitivity. Local leaders understand this better and whip up discontent with development aid (Section 3.1) and the (perceived) imposition of foreign values (Section 3.2).

Many of my colleagues from the Global South – who work in development – share this suspicion. They point to the hypocrisy underpinning contemporary international development efforts. They criticize the lack of *ownership* in aid, in which (I make a caricature here) priorities are conceived in Western capitals, and executed by agencies dominated by white people in fancy cars and large compounds. They also chastise the *double standards* in which donors lecture some governments about human rights, but finance other governments with similar human rights records (who happen to be important in the fight against terrorism or illegal migration). Lastly, they criticize the *double agendas* of donors. Western governments and companies boast about vaccine donations and humanitarian aid, but simultaneously block patent reform (essential for vaccines) and arms export treaties (to prevent humanitarian emergencies). While colleagues were often recognizant of the aid being provided to deal with extreme weather events, they wondered rightfully if a stronger reduction in luxury emissions in the Global North wouldn't be more important. These often very legitimate grievances and suspicions can fuel an anti-aid backlash, to which I now turn.

3.1 Anti-aid backlash: 'you call it international cooperation, we call it international exploitation'

Every Friday I left the comfortable air-conditioned embassy compound in Kinshasa and drove to the other side of the town to the Catholic University. I was teaching the class 'International cooperation,' exploring with them topics such as foreign debt, international peacekeeping, and aid effectiveness. In general, the students were interested in my classes but they were critical right from the start. One student raised her hand during the first session and asked: 'Can I make a suggestion, can we change the title of your course? Instead of calling it "international cooperation", can you change it to "international exploitation"?' If you have read the excellent book *Born in Blackness* by Howard French you will fully comprehend the historical roots of her question, as exploitation of Africa by the West has been the defining feature of the relationship for centuries, often with an altruistic sauce poured over it.[2]

While the actual temperature in the classroom was already tropical, the perceived temperature often rose to boiling point during my lectures. There I stood as a white professor, sweating and proclaiming that without the peacekeeping missions, debt relief, and other interventions of the West the DRC might face more instability and poverty. My students believed the opposite: the West only exploits them. According to one of my students, Irène, the West was only interested in Congolese mineral resources, 'they send people like you as band aid.' While I argued that the international community is doing too little cooperation with the DRC, the students claimed that there is too much foreign interference.

I tried to convince them of my position by pointing out the composition of the UN peacekeeping mission MONUSCO in Congo. While that mission counts thousands of troops, only a handful of Western blue helmets are amongst them. How can my students maintain that 'we' as the West are doing everything possible to get a grip on Congolese mineral resources, if we are not even prepared to send our own soldiers? Most of my students, who normally never agree, were on the same page for once: 'That's just a masquerade. Your true intentions and hidden agenda (for instance, access to our resources) would be too clear if you send your own soldiers as you do in Afghanistan. You have learned that there is too much resistance from the local population. That is why you are sending soldiers from other poor countries here.'

Normally I can hold my own in discussions, but now I am knocked out. There is no point in going against them, because many students see me as part of the problem. What I didn't understand then, but get now, is that they were voicing their opposition to global white privilege. A more just and prosperous world meant for them a world without Western supremacy. They expressed the views Chandara Nair later expressed so eloquently in his book *Dismantling Global White Privilege*.[3] I wiped off some sweat and suggested moving on to the next, slightly more neutral topic: global warming. Given the scorching heat in the lecture hall, the students and I finally agree: this is a shared challenge that must be addressed.

Yet the question still haunts me: why is there so much critique amongst citizens in the DRC on international cooperation efforts? Why is this also the case in countries as diverse as Mali, Afghanistan, and Haiti? How does this impact the work of development practitioners? The DRC is on the receiving end of international cooperation in almost every conceivable area, but there remains a persistent mistrust of Western aid.

This mistrust seriously affects aid effectiveness, as becomes clear in the response to the Ebola epidemic in the DRC. The international response was quick as Ebola erupted in the eastern DRC in 2018. In collaboration with the government, the World Health Organization and Médecins Sans Frontières (MSF) set up treatment centres. But the

Figure 3.2 Burnt down Ebola treatment centre in the DRC.

Source: MSF.

rumour that the international aid agencies were actually intentionally bringing Ebola to the country to earn money in the response was rife.[4] Many centres were attacked by angry local mobs and burned to the ground. In one site in Butembo, 50 patients and 60 staff members had to flee during the attack and hide in nearby buildings.[5] Many of the infected patients could not be found afterwards. In the end, thousands of Congolese died because of Ebola, many more than necessary if the international agencies could have avoided the backlash. One quote from a Congolese staff member of MSF provides more insight into the Congolese backlash, even from people working for the aid agencies:

> *I have had three children die of malaria. No international organization has ever come to work in this area to make sure we have healthcare or clean water. But now Ebola arrives and all the organizations come, because Ebola gives them money.*[6]

The quote illustrates what many of my students also said: international actors have ulterior motives and are there for their personal profits.

3.1.1 The backlash against foreign aid in Afghanistan

The Ebola response is just one case of anti-aid sentiment across the world. Take Afghanistan: in the few instances that ordinary Afghans were asked,[7] they showed on average a large disillusionment with the international aid actors. According to some residents, the local populations had hoped for large infrastructure projects and jobs, but the NGOs were providing 'small NGO rehabilitation projects' that 'we can do ourselves.'[8]

This quote highlights but one side of international development efforts in Afghanistan: the positive effects are unmistakable. Foreign aid helped build about 20,000 elementary schools, and the number of universities also grew sharply. There were no female college students in 2001, but there were 54,861 in 2019. Largely because of international aid in the health sector, life expectancy rose over the two decades by about a decade, to 64.8 years in 2019, according to the World Bank.[9] In short, there has been huge social progress in Afghanistan during the twenty years of Western presence. But interestingly enough, the local populations often did not credit the aid agencies for this.

The international aid sector became the villain in a couple of years in Afghanistan, as one Afghan explains: 'We deserved better from the international community, but the Americans are only interested in Al Qaeda, not in the development of our country; that is why we are only getting small NGO projects that are totally unsustainable.'[10] There was no difference between the aid agencies and the international soldiers for the local population. Secretary of State Colin Powell had said that the international aid agencies were 'force multipliers,' part and parcel of the American military effort. Most Afghan people shared this view, of course in less positive terms. While the aid agencies said they were impartial or neutral, the local population did not view them as such. Many people, even staff of the agencies themselves, thought they were collecting intelligence for foreign powers.[11] For some, this legitimized Taliban attacks against them.

The Afghan government fuelled the lingering feeling of discontent with aid agencies amongst the local population. The Minister of Planning in Kabul once said that 'NGOs are worse than thieves' and President Karzai lambasted NGOs publicly stating that 'NGOs are squandering the funding that Afghanistan has received for Afghanistan.'[12] President Ghani thought nationals instead of internationals should spend more of the aid, making the backlash quite explicit. In a BBC interview in 2007 (before becoming president), he said: 'When we build a school by Afghans, the maximum cost is about $50,000. But when it is built by our international partners the cost can be as high as $250,000.'[13] According to him, the difference was caused by the fact that contractors, many of them foreign, took overhead costs: 'It's totally legal, but is it not corrupt?'

To answer President Ghani's question, whereas there are certain sick elements in the international development sector, it does not constitute one monolithic system that can be labelled corrupt as a whole. For instance, it is important to see the difference between for-profit multi-billion aid contractors and bottom-up international solidarity initiatives. American foreign aid contractors made enormous profits in Afghanistan during the two decades following the overthrow of the Taliban. Profit margins on reconstruction contracts for international and Afghan contractor companies were often 20 per cent and could be as high as 50 per cent. Most full-time expatriate consultants, working in private consulting companies, cost USD 250,000–500,000 a year.[14] This is in sharp contrast to Afghan diaspora initiatives supported with limited official development assistance. The initiatives were often effective, efficient, and supported by the Afghan population.[15]

There are so many 'ifs' here, but 'if' the international aid system would have collectively strengthened the Afghan state, instead of bypassing it as some did, would it have allowed the state to face off the backlash, instead of feeding it? If the aid agencies would have remained (even) more at a distance from the military, could they have avoided the backlash against them? Would the population have resisted the advance of the Taliban in that case? Unfortunately, we will never know. The only thing that we now know is that girls in Afghanistan are no longer allowed to enter secondary school and have to wear the Burqa again.

3.2 Anti-foreign values backlash

In October 2010, an Ugandan newspaper published the picture and address of gay activist David Kato and other gay people on the front page with the text 'hang them.' David was killed three months later, hammered to death in front of his house. In the same period, various anti-gay protests and vigils were held in Kampala.

What has aid got do with this? When many of the objectives that Western LGBTQ+ activists aimed for had been achieved in their respective countries, they started to branch out internationally. LGBTQ+ organizations in the West started international departments and received massive funding. In 2021 alone, the small country of the Netherlands invested EUR 69 million in aid funding in LGBTQ+ communities in 28 countries worldwide.

> Around the time of the killing of David, I was teaching a development course in a country neighbouring Uganda, the DRC. Lecture 1 of my course dealt with the definition of development. I explained to them that there are different definitions of development, but the most common today is that 'people have the opportunity to live their lives the way they want to.' My students agreed and I saw them nodding. My students agree that everyone should have the same rights; otherwise, some people can achieve their aspiration, while others cannot. I continued that, for most European countries, this means homosexuals should have the same rights as heterosexuals. Gays should also be able to live their lives however they want. The students fall silent and I see some frowns. I continued: with us, we consider it progress that gays can marry with each other and adopt children. Now most of the students were making dirty faces

and expressing their disagreement: 'That's not development, that's regression! These kids need to be protected against them. We really don't want that in our country!' When I hear about the discontent in neighbouring Uganda about the internationally supported emancipation struggle for LGBTQ+ people there, I often have to think about these discussions with my students.

3.2.1 'Immunization against the worldwide gay epidemic'

What passions me is understanding why norms change, or do not, over time and whether international activism can explain this. It is too simplistic to say that African countries are anti-gay: in Kenya the percentage of people who approved of gay relationships increased from 1 to 14 per cent in less than two decades.[16] However, in Uganda, where so much international attention went to promote gay rights, the rate of public rejection has increased from 95 per cent in 2002 to 96 per cent in 2013.[17] How is it possible that those two neighbouring countries display such different trajectories?

Nuñez-Mietz and García Iommi argue that the Ugandan government 'immunized' its population against the worldwide gay-epidemic, and the Kenyan government did not. When they talk about immunization, they do not mean the actual inoculation, but 'norm immunization': the creation of legal barriers that fend off a norm being transmitted internationally by blocking its local advocacy. Museveni, the president of Uganda, aimed to stop this gay 'contagion' and claimed their country was under siege. Subsequently, he adopted restrictive NGO laws and anti-gay legislation, under the guise that 'homosexuality is un-African.'

UK Prime Minister James Cameron responded in 2012 to the Malawian anti-gay law by stating that it would cut aid to countries not respecting the rights of gay people. One of his officials stated, 'If countries can afford to prosecute and imprison people for consensual relations, then they can clearly afford to lose aid.'[18] Parliamentarians across the Global North demand these public statements from government executives. Paradoxically, these kinds of statements play into the hands of conservative leaders in countries such as Malawi and Uganda. President Museveni, tapping handily into pre-existing anti-Western sentiments, signed the anti-gay bill into law, strengthening his position. Indeed, according to a government spokesperson, the president chose to sign the bill in public to 'demonstrate Uganda's independence in the face of Western pressure.'[19] A proponent of the anti-gay bill in Uganda happily denounced the (Western-funded) NGOs: 'the NGOs are hugely involved in recruiting and giving money to our young children with the intention of swaying them into this evil practice. But Uganda will never exchange her dignity for money.'[20] Western activists and politicians thus ended up giving Ugandan leaders an excuse to further marginalize LGBTQ+ people, with conservatives framing LGBTQ+ rights as a foreign cultural attack on the nation.[21]

While Western human rights groups, such as Human Rights Watch, found the statements of Western leaders as a reaction to these anti-gay laws too weak,[22] local LGBTQ+ groups opposed the tying of aid to the respect of gay rights for three reasons. First, conditional aid reinforces the argument that this type of sexuality is a Western construct.[23] Second, it distracts attention from oppressions that affect all Africans as it needlessly pits people experiencing poverty (who are in need of aid) against the gay (who are seen to be blocking aid). Lastly, local advocates are easily identifiable and often face extra stigmatization and violent public reactions, as the case of David Kato illustrates.[24] Statistical research shows that the local LGBTQ+ groups were probably right: the strong statements by Western leaders were often counterproductive. Someone who experienced just how dangerous this 'megaphone diplomacy' can be is François, who shares his testimony.[25]

Testimony by François: when a letter on inclusion backfired

Figure 3.3 François Ndoye.

'*It was even snowing yesterday!' François is sitting in a simple room in his new home in Stockholm. Originally from Senegal, he explains that adapting to his new surroundings takes some time. Especially to the cold weather, the different culture, and the difficult language.*

A wave of anti-gay sentiments

It was a few years ago when François's life changed completely. In July 2019, a so-called 'love letter' was shared by a large international NGO with all employees of their local office in Senegal. Its core message was: if you don't adhere to the inclusion of LGBTQ+, you don't have a place in our organization. At the time, François was living as a regular 33-year-old in Senegal, enjoying going out to the cinema, listening to music, and being with his family. He was also working for one of the LGBTQ+ organizations in Senegal, when the letter meant to promote inclusion set in motion a wave of anti-gay sentiments that washed over the country. It was used by a disgruntled staff member and conservative groups to stage a media war against 'foreign influence' and LGBTQ+ individuals. Pictures and full details of François and his colleagues as 'LGBTQ+ activists' started circulating. Soon, it became too dangerous for François to stay and he and three colleagues left the country and ended up in Sweden.[26]

Behind closed doors

'The message in the letter itself was not the problem,' says François. The fact that it was published so openly made it easy for conservative groups and politicians to use it to make name for themselves. A common phenomenon in Senegal, according to François. For him, more than ever the international community has a role to play in supporting LGBTQ+ groups in Senegal. 'My organization was supported by international agencies, which didn't make much noise, and that helped.' But the support must be provided in a way that doesn't allow opportunist forces to frame the discourse. 'People say that Senegalese are homophobes, but that's not true. You have to talk with people behind closed doors and you can achieve a lot.'

Changing strategy

In the meantime, the situation for LGBTQ+ people in Senegal is deteriorating. A law is in the making to criminalize homosexuality. François: 'There are no organizations left that can lobby against this law.' Out of fear of being attacked, organizations that previously focussed on advocating for equal rights have returned to service delivery for HIV. François is disappointed about this. 'If you're going to do service delivery, then at least support homosexuals who are beaten up. Strengthen the support for victims of homophobia at the local level.'

And the future?

François hopes to one day return to Senegal, but first there are some barriers to overcome. Social media is tenacious. As long as images of him keep circulating, François can't safely return. So from his new home in Sweden, he persistently reaches out to social media platforms to have hate speech targeting him removed. To make matters worse, there is no family to welcome him home, as they have publicly denounced him.

Despite everything, François stays positive. At least he has a few of his Senegalese friends and colleagues in Stockholm that he can talk to. 'In Senegal, we love to discuss a lot.'

The support for gay rights by foreign donors is just one area where the values and hence interests of the Western public and the public opinion in many countries in the Global South don't overlap: so the backlash against aid, and even the popularity payout it creates, can also materialize on different themes. For example, while Western donors prioritize climate change in their aid (e.g. no more support for gas and coal installations overseas), in many low-income countries, access to energy (no matter which source) is the first priority. While Western donors might favour national parks for tourism and biodiversity in low-income countries, these countries might prioritize livelihoods. While many donors might favour birth control, many families do not want other countries to tell them how many kids they should have. While many donor countries would like to reduce irregular migration, most recipient countries would prefer to increase remittances. In short, preferences often do not align, and by adopting a moralizing language (and often practices), donors feed their resistance.

3.3 Conclusion: why are we so ill-equipped to detect the backlash effect and what can be done?

The consequences of the backlash effect are dire. Ebola patients are forced to flee treatment centres and the virus can spread more readily. Gay activists, supported by the international community, are beaten to death, and anti-gay laws are adopted. More recently, testing campaigns against COVID-19 had to be stopped because of a backlash.[27]

Since backlash can be so strong, we should be vigilant in picking up the signs of resistance. However, in evaluations of international donors it rarely surfaces. In fact, in an assessment of 700 evaluation documents of Dutch aid, it wasn't mentioned a single time.[28] That is why this type of unintended effect is the book's first chapter: we are not very good at identifying signs of impending backlash. Why is that the case? The incentives in the international development system are stacked against these early warning signals, as one disappointing experience of a diplomatic colleague of mine shows.

3.3.1 *An international development system stacked against early warnings of a backlash*

A couple of years ago I got a phone call from a colleague based in our embassy in Mali. 'I have written a book about Mali. I did it in a personal capacity, but I shared a copy of the manuscript with the ministry for their information. They now want me to delete the last couple of chapters. They think that it gives too much space to local voices that are critical of the donor community. Can you please have a look at my draft book and say what you think I should do?'

Those last chapters of the book were my favourites. This is where she shows how large parts of the population felt that their government was elitist and that collusion with foreign donors enabled their lavish lifestyles. There is also a chapter in which she gives voice to some Malian youth, who are very critical about the 'foreign interference' in the country. At the end of the book, she predicted that this disgruntlement of the population would soon boil over, unless donors radically changed their course and aligned themselves more with the general population than with the disconnected elites of the country.

Unfortunately, the pressure she experiences is too high; she virtually deletes this most interesting chapter from her book and resigns, disillusioned with the Ministry. Fast forward four years later, to 2021: massive demonstrations rock the capital in favour of a coup by army colonels. The demonstrators hold cardboards saying 'Mali belongs to the Malians and not to the International Community.' The coup leaders vow to change the country's relationship with Europe, specifically France. Three months later the French ambassador is expelled, and the French troops have left Mali six months later. Popular support for the coup plotters was now higher than ever, and they invited

Russian mercenaries to restore order. This is a classic example of the backlash effect. My colleague saw it coming, but was effectively silenced.

3.3.2 *Two opposing tales of foreign aid: the two Haitis*

It appears that there are two Haitis – one as seen by the Haitians and one by the international community. Which news you follow is important. If you follow Radio France Internationale or CNN, like most diplomats and aid workers, less than a quarter of the publications you read are negative about the United Nations (23 per cent). However, if you follow the grassroots media in Haiti (Haiti has a tradition of participatory and citizen journalism), this percentage of negative reporting rises to 78 per cent![29] In the local news, stories about the history (from foreign occupation to manipulation – see textbox below) are often repeated. The internationally mobile aid workers are largely unaware of this fraught past, or are hesitant to integrate it into their conversations. Anthropologist Mark Schuller goes as far to conclude that 'Unfortunately, this silencing of the past is a major reason why these aid agencies fail in countries such as Haiti.'[30] This silence contributes to the emergence of two opposing narratives of the same foreign aid phenomenon, as shown by the textbox. It becomes very difficult to learn once you are inside a certain narrative and advocacy group. That is why I coined the term 'bounded policy learning' in Chapter 2, and that is what seems to be happening in Haiti. As Table 3.1 shows, it's almost as if international aid agencies and the people of Haiti seem to live in a completely different Haiti!

3.3.3 *Hopeful examples to avoid a backlash: when Catholics start to distribute condoms*

As the repeal of abortion rights in the United States shows so clearly, few issues can provide more backlash than sexual and reproductive rights. A Catholic NGO, Cordaid, was successful however in integrating condom distribution by their Catholic partners in Africa without a big backlash. This despite parts of the Catholic establishment being vehemently opposed to it. How did they do it? A careful reconstruction shows that key elements were (1) organizing local consultations with experts, (2) engaging seriously in religious and spiritual debates, and (3) including testimonies from other actors in the Global South in the discussion. In short, they prevented a backlash by respectful dialogues.[31]

And instead of distributing the condoms with much fanfare in front of the churches, they used more discrete methods to allow all actors to save face. By continuing to work with the local structures, Cordaid could build on networks of thousands of volunteers deeply embedded in the societies where they intervened. Instead of creating 'spaces of aid' (the cars and compounds that create a division between the local and the international, and can contribute to a backlash), they invested in a locally led response.[32]

I understand if this first chapter might be a bit off-putting, as the challenges to effective international solidarity appear plentiful, and the remedies cumbersome. However, as you progress in this book you will see that for some unintended effects much more action has already been taken, for instance, concerning conflict effects, on which we focus in the next chapter.

Table 3.1 Two tales of the same foreign aid and intervention: case of Haiti

	Mainstream Haitian view	*Mainstream development sector view*
Distant past	• Colonialism (first French, then American) • Slavery • Successful uprising against foreign domination under national hero Toussaint Louverture	• Nearly non-existent; little knowledge by humanitarian workers of historical and cultural context[33]
Recent past (since 1980s)	• CIA-led coup against democratically elected popular Prime Minister Aristide[34]	• Local corruption is endemic • Viewed from the aid sector, local politics looks complicated[35]
Reasons for high levels of poverty	• Foreign exploitation before, during, and after the Cold War • Foreign powers loaned money to corrupt Duvalier regime, and ordinary Haitians had to pay back • Forced liberalization, leading to an influx of dumped agricultural products such as rice, destroying local livelihoods[36]	• Haiti doesn't make use of the long-term aid that is given because of political instability, economic failure, violence, corruption, and high insecurity[37]
Reasons for low state and organizational capacity	• International donors have set up a parallel state, the international NGOs, in order to weaken the Haitian state[38]	• Because of a culture of laziness, dependence, and fatalism, local capacities remain weak[39]
Peacekeeping mission	• It is a foreign occupation, leading to increased costs of living • Cholera, brought by the peacekeepers (some say 'on purpose), killed thousands of compatriots[40]	• Overall, it has been a force for good, contributing to the stability of the country[41]
Impact of aid	• It serves the interest of the aid agencies and the aid workers, not the ordinary Haitians • Ordinary Haitians are not consulted on how the aid funding is spent and there is a lack of transparency as to where and how it is spent[42]	• While the long-lasting effects of aid have been disappointing, it has helped in the recovery after, for instance, the earthquake and HIV-AIDS reduction • There are some excesses by aid agencies (e.g. the Oxfam sex scandal), but these are being addressed[43]
Impact of narrative	• Tendency to try to obtain personal benefit of aid • Anti-foreign sentiments and nationalism strengthened[44]	• International actors see no other option than continuing what they have always done: provide emergency aid through international NGOs[45]

How to tackle backlash effects

Policymakers (and politicians)

- **Try to have no ulterior motives and be cognizant of them if they're present.** Since a backlash is often related to suspicion about ulterior motives of aid and development (the concerns about double agendas and double standards), it makes most sense to have no ulterior motives. Giving aid should hence be really about aiding.
- **If ulterior motives do exist, at least communicate openly about them.** Since other motivations are likely to continue to play a role in foreign aid (export promotion, migration management, etc.), it makes sense to communicate openly about it. By being explicit about other objectives, also more equitable partnerships can emerge.
- **Localize aid.** Another driver for discontent is the lack of ownership. Western governments, agencies, and individuals are still too much in the driver's seat. A respectful dialogue about divergent values is lacking. 'Localization' of aid (the process in which more use of local actors and structures is used and the local voices shape the aid) is important. Localization doesn't mean setting up a local office of an international NGO, which often means de-localization.
- **Engage in silent diplomacy.** If there is a risk of backlash against foreign public statements, try to bridge local differences by bringing groups together behind the scenes instead of engaging in megaphone diplomacy.

Practitioners

- **Programme in an adaptive way.** Adaptive programming appears key to respond to early signs of a backlash. A pause or change in programming can be needed if a backlash is forming. If security (of, for instance, local partners) is at risk, organizations must always be willing to pull out.
- **Know your context and diversify information sources.** A more diverse information base in the development sector is required. Expatriates need to improve their awareness of the undercurrents in the society in which they are working. Aid workers need to get out of their compounds, they need to exchange more informally with local staff and the population, they need to speak local languages and consume local news. They need to understand better local grievances against foreign aid and guidelines, which are often rooted in a deep-seated (and often justified) mistrust of foreign 'aid.'
- **Work under the radar where relevant.** Especially if they work on sensitive issues, it is often better to work with local partners and not brag publicly about successes.

Evaluators (but basically everybody)

- **Do not engage in (self-)censorship.** Operators in the aid sector should neither engage in self-censorship nor allow others to censor them. Backlash is a normal phenomenon; ignoring it doesn't make it disappear. Support evaluators and aid workers who dare to research and better understand it, instead of aiming to silence them.

Notes

1 Robtel Neajai Pailey, 'De-centring the "White Gaze" of Development,' *Development and Change* 51, no. 3 (2020): 729–745, https://doi.org/10.1111/dech.12550.

2 Howard W. French, *Born in Blackness: Africa, Africans, and the Making of the Modern World, 1471 to the Second World War* (New York: Liveright, 2021).

3 Chandran Nair, *Dismantling Global White Privilege: Equity for a Post-Western World* (Oakland, CA: Berrett-Koehler Publishers).

4 Kasereka Masumbuko Claude, Jack Underschultz, and Michael T. Hawkes, 'Social resistance drives persistent transmission of Ebola virus disease in Eastern Democratic Republic of Congo: A mixed-methods study,' *PloS One* 14, no. 9 (2019): e0223104, https://doi.org/10.1371/journal.pone.0223104

5 Médecins Sans Frontières, 'After the fire–how we could have better managed the DRC Ebola outbreak,' 11 March 2020, www.msf.org/after-fire-how-we-could-have-better-managed-drc-ebola-outbreak

6 Ibid.

7 Antonio Donini, Larry Minear, Ian Smillie, Ted van Barda, and Anthony C. Welsh, *Mapping the Security Environment: Understanding the Perceptions of Local Communities, Peace Support Operations, and Assistance Agencies* (Medford and Sommerville: Feinstein International Famine Center, 2005).; Antonio Donini, 'Local perceptions of assistance to Afghanistan,' *International Peacekeeping* 14, no. 1 (2007): 158–172, https://doi.org/10.1080/13533310601114376

8 Ibid., 164.

9 Mohammad Qadam Shah, 'What did billions in aid to Afghanistan accomplish? 5 questions answered,' *The Conversation*, 26 October 2021, https://theconversation.com/what-did-billions-in-aid-to-afghanistan-accomplish-5-questions-answered-166804

10 Donini, 'Local perceptions,' 168.

11 Ibid., 163.

12 Donini et al., *Mapping Security Environment*, 11.

13 BBC, 'Who is Ashraf Ghani? The technocrat who sought to rebuild Afghanistan,' 26 September 2019, www.bbc.com/news/world-asia-27142426

14 Matt Waldman, *Aid Effectiveness in Afghanistan* (Kabul: Agency Coordinating Body for Afghan Relief, 2008), www-cdn.oxfam.org/s3fs-public/file_attachments/ACBAR_aid_effectiveness_paper_0803_3.pdf

15 Nasrat Sayed, Caitlin Masoliver, and Bob van Dillen, *Diaspora Engagement in Afghanistan: A Policy Agenda for Sustainable Development* (The Hague: Cordaid, 2021), www.cordaid.org/en/wp-content/uploads/sites/7/2022/11/210330-Policy-Brief-Diaspora-Sustainable-Development-Afghanistan.pdf

16 Jacob Poushter and Nicholas Kent, 'The global divide on homosexuality persists,' *PEW Research Center*, 25 June 2020, www.pewresearch.org/global/2020/06/25/global-divide-on-homosexuality-persists/

17 Fernando G. Nuñez-Mietz and Lucrecia García Iommi, 'Can transnational norm advocacy undermine internalization? Explaining immunization against LGBT rights in Uganda,' *International Studies Quarterly* 61, no. 1 (2017): 196–209, www.jstor.org/stable/44510874

18 Adam J. Kretz, 'Aid conditionality as (partial) answer to antigay legislation: An analysis of British and American foreign aid policies designed to protect sexual minorities,' *ICL Journal* 7, no. 4 (2013): 489, https://doi.org/10.1515/icl-2013-0404

19 Nuñez-Mietz and Iommi, 'Can transnational norm advocacy,' 206.

20 Ibid., 206.

21 Interestingly, also the opponents of gay rights were receiving international support, especially from American evangelical organizations: Caleb Okereke, 'How U.S. Evangelicals Helped

Homophobia Flourish in Africa,' *Foreign Policy*, 19 March 2023, https://foreignpolicy.com/2023/03/19/africa-uganda-evangelicals-homophobia-antigay-bill/

22 Ciara Bottomley, 'Unintended consequences of international human rights advocacy in Uganda,' *SOAS Law Journal* 2 (2015): 49, https://vlex.co.uk/vid/unintended-consequences-of-international-847575296

23 Crystal Biruk, '"Aid for gays": The moral and the material in "African homophobia" in post-2009 Malawi,' *The Journal of Modern African Studies* 52, no. 3 (2014): 447–473, www.jstor.org/stable/43302934

24 What we should have realized, however, is that the aid conditionalities did not unfold as predicted. Despite all the speeches on the importance of gay rights in recipient countries by Secretary Clinton, President Obama and Prime Minister Cameron, the aid cuts did not materialize. As we have seen in the past, it is difficult for donors to live up to their own conditionalities, as the funding pressure remains. While the threats were not real, the anti-gay legislation was, and after Malawi and Uganda, Nigeria and Ghana started to 'immunize' their societies.

25 Kristopher Velasco, 'A growing queer divide: The divergence between transnational advocacy networks and foreign aid in diffusing LGBT policies,' *International Studies Quarterly* 64, no. 1 (2020): 120–132, https://doi.org/10.1093/isq/sqz075

26 Charles Senghor, 'Oxfam under attack in Senegal for defending LGBTI people,' *LaCroix International*, 16 July 2019, https://international.la-croix.com/news/%20ethics/oxfam-under-attack-in-senegal-for-defending-lgbti-people/10536

27 BBC, 'Coronavirus: Ivory Coast protesters target testing centre,' 6 April 2020, www.bbc.com/news/world-africa-52189144

28 Koch et al., 'Assessing international development cooperation.'

29 Cadey Korson, 'Framing peace: The role of media, perceptions, and United Nations Peacekeeping Operations in Haiti and Côte d'Ivoire,' *Geopolitics* 20, no. 2 (2015): 365, https://doi.org/10.1080/14650045.2015.1006362

30 Mark Schuller, *Killing with Kindness: Haiti, International Aid, and NGOs* (New Brunswick, NJ: Rutgers University Press, 2012).

31 René Grotenhuis, 'Sexual and reproductive health in the practice of the Dutch Catholic development agency Cordaid,' *The Heythrop Journal* 55, no. 6 (2014): 1056–1068, https://doi.org/10.1111/heyj.12211

32 Lisa Smirl, *Spaces of Aid: How Cars, Compounds and Hotels Shape Humanitarianism* (London: Zed Books, 2015).

33 Ibid.

34 Ibid.

35 Loukie Molenaar, *Opportunities and Obstacles Concerning Local Partnership in Cordaid's Post-Earthquake Aid Mission in Haiti*, master's thesis (Wageningen: Wageningen University & Research, 2012), https://edepot.wur.nl/194882

36 Schuller, *Killing with Kindness*.

37 Vijaya Ramachandran and Julie Walz, 'Haiti: Where has all the money gone?,' *Journal of Haitian Studies* 21, no. 1 (2015): 26–65, www.jstor.org/stable/24573148

38 Grace Everest, 'NGOs in Haiti: Caught in an aid worker bubble,' *E-International Relations*, 5 October 2011, www.e-ir.info/pdf/14509.

39 Molenaar, *Opportunities and Obstacles*, 58.

40 Georgia Fraulin, Sabine Lee, and Susan A. Bartels, ' "They came with cholera when they were tired of killing us with bullets": Community perceptions of the 2010 origin of Haiti's cholera epidemic,' *Global Public Health* 17, no. 5 (2022): 738–752, https://doi.org/10.1080/17441692.2021.1887315

41 Robert Muggah, 'The effects of stabilisation on humanitarian action in Haiti,' *Disasters* 34 (2010): S444–S463, https://doi.org/10.1111/j.1467-7717.2010.01205.x

42 Abigail St. E. Bilby, 'Local perceptions of NGOs in Montrouis, Haiti,' presented at *The National Conference of Undergraduate Research*, Montana State University, Bozeman, 26–28

March 2020, http://libjournals.unca.edu/ncur/wp-content/uploads/2021/01/3367-Bilby-Abig ail-FINAL.pdf; Meg Sattler and Jessica Alexander, 'There's a wide gap between aid's promise and reality, Haitians say,' *The New Humanitarian*, 4 April 2022, www.thenewhumanitarian. org/analysis/2022/04/04/haiti-wide-gap-between-aid-promise-and-reality
43 Although it is acknowledged that more transparency is needed, see, for example, Ramachandran and Walz, 'Haiti.'
44 Lonzozou Kpanake, Ronald Jean-Jacques, Paul Clay Sorum, and Etienne Mullet, 'Haitian people's expectations regarding post-disaster humanitarian aid teams' actions,' *Developing World Bioethics* 18, no. 4 (2018): 385–393, https://doi.org/10.1111/dewb.12158; Molenaar, *Opportunities and obstacles.*
45 Ibid.

Further reading

Autesserre, Séverine. *Peaceland: Conflict Resolution and the Everyday Politics of International Intervention.* Cambridge: Cambridge University Press, 2014.
BBC. 'Coronavirus: Ivory Coast protesters target testing centre.' 6 April 2020. www.bbc.com/ news/world-africa-52189144
BBC. 'Who is Ashraf Ghani? The technocrat who sought to rebuild Afghanistan.' 26 September 2019. www.bbc.com/news/world-asia-27142426
Bilby, Abigail St. E. 'Local perceptions of NGOs in Montrouis, Haiti.' Presented at *the National Conference of Undergraduate Research*, Montana State University, Bozeman, 26–28 March 2020. http://libjournals.unca.edu/ncur/wp-content/uploads/2021/01/3367-Bilby-Abigail-FINAL.pdf
Biruk, Crystal. '"Aid for gays": The moral and the material in "African homophobia" in post-2009 Malawi.' *The Journal of Modern African Studies* 52, no. 3 (2014): 447–473. www.jstor. org/stable/43302934
Bottomley, Ciara. 'Unintended consequences of international human rights advocacy in Uganda.' *SOAS Law Journal* 2 (2015): 49–75. https://vlex.co.uk/vid/unintended-consequences-of-intern ational-847575296
Donini, Antonio. 'Local perceptions of assistance to Afghanistan.' *International Peacekeeping* 14, no. 1 (2007): 158–172. https://doi.org/10.1080/13533310601114376
Donini, Antonio, Larry Minear, Ian Smillie, Ted van Barda, and Anthony C. Welsh. *Mapping the Security Environment: Understanding the Perceptions of Local Communities, Peace Support Operations, and Assistance Agencies.* Medford and Sommerville: Feinstein International Famine Center, 2005.
Everest, Grace. 'NGOs in Haiti: Caught in an aid worker bubble.' *E-International Relations*, 5 October 2011. www.e-ir.info/pdf/14509
Fraulin, Georgia, Sabine Lee, and Susan A. Bartels. '"They came with cholera when they were tired of killing us with bullets': Community perceptions of the 2010 origin of Haiti's cholera epidemic.' *Global Public Health* 17, no. 5 (2022): 738–752. https://doi.org/10.1080/17441 692.2021.1887315
French, Howard W. *Born in Blackness: Africa, Africans, and the Making of the Modern World, 1471 to the Second World War.* New York, NY: Liveright, 2021.
Grotenhuis, René. 'Sexual and reproductive health in the practice of the Dutch Catholic Development Agency Cordaid.' *The Heythrop Journal* 55, no. 6 (2014): 1056–1068. https://doi. org/10.1111/heyj.12211
Koch, Dirk-Jan, Jolynde Vis, Maria van der Harst, Elric Tendron, and Joost de Laat. 'Assessing international development cooperation: Becoming intentional about unintended effects.' *Sustainability* 13, no. 21 (2021): 11571. https://doi.org/10.3390/su132111571

Korson, Cadey. 'Framing peace: The role of media, perceptions, and United Nations Peacekeeping Operations in Haiti and Côte d'Ivoire.' *Geopolitics* 20, no. 2 (2015): 354–380. https://doi.org/10.1080/14650045.2015.1006362

Kpanake, Lonzozou, Ronald Jean-Jacques, Paul Clay Sorum, and Etienne Mullet. 'Haitian people's expectations regarding post-disaster humanitarian aid teams' actions.' *Developing World Bioethics* 18, no. 4 (2018): 385–393. https://doi.org/10.1111/dewb.12158

Kretz, Adam J. 'Aid conditionality as (partial) answer to antigay legislation: An analysis of British and American foreign aid policies designed to protect sexual minorities.' *ICL Journal* 7, no. 4 (2013): 476–500. https://doi.org/10.1515/icl-2013-0404

Masumbuko Claude, Kasereka, Jack Underschultz, and Michael T. Hawkes. 'Social resistance drives persistent transmission of Ebola virus disease in Eastern Democratic Republic of Congo: A mixed-methods study.' *PloS One* 14, no. 9 (2019): e0223104. https://doi.org/10.1371/journal.pone.0223104

Medecins Sans Frontières. 'After the fire–how we could have better managed the DRC Ebola outbreak.' 11 March 2020. www.msf.org/after-fire-how-we-could-have-better-managed-drc-ebola-outbreak

Molenaar, Loukie. *Opportunities and obstacles concerning local partnership in Cordaid's post-earthquake aid mission in Haiti.* Master's thesis. Wageningen: Wageningen University & Research, 2012.

Muggah, Robert. 'The effects of stabilisation on humanitarian action in Haiti.' *Disasters* 34 (2010): S444–S463. https://doi.org/10.1111/j.1467-7717.2010.01205.x

Nair, Chandran. *Dismantling Global White Privilege: Equity for a Post-Western World.* Oakland, CA: Berrett-Koehler Publishers.

Nuñez-Mietz, Fernando G., and Lucrecia García Iommi. 'Can transnational norm advocacy undermine internalization? Explaining immunization against LGBT rights in Uganda.' *International Studies Quarterly* 61, no. 1 (2017): 196–209. www.jstor.org/stable/44510874

Okereke, Caleb. 'How U.S. Evangelicals helped homophobia flourish in Africa.' *Foreign Policy*, 19 March 2023. https://foreignpolicy.com/2023/03/19/africa-uganda-evangelicals-homophobia-antigay-bill/

Pailey, Robtel Neajai. 'De-centring the "white gaze" of development.' *Development and Change* 51, no. 3 (2020): 729–745. https://doi.org/10.1111/dech.12550

Poushter, Jacob, and Nicholas Kent. 'The global divide on homosexuality persists.' *PEW Research Center*, 25 June 2020. www.pewresearch.org/global/2020/06/25/global-divide-on-homosexuality-persists/

Ramachandran, Vijaya, and Julie Walz. 'Haiti: Where has all the money gone?' *Journal of Haitian Studies* 21, no. 1 (2015): 26–65. www.jstor.org/stable/24573148

Sattler, Meg, and Jessica Alexander. 'There's a wide gap between aid's promise and reality, Haitians say.' *The New Humanitarian*, 4 April 2022. www.thenewhumanitarian.org/analysis/2022/04/04/haiti-wide-gap-between-aid-promise-and-reality

Sayed, Nasrat, Caitlin Masoliver, and Bob van Dillen. *Diaspora Engagement in Afghanistan: A Policy Agenda for Sustainable Development.* The Hague: Cordaid, 2021. www.cordaid.org/en/wp-content/uploads/sites/7/2022/11/210330-Policy-Brief-Diaspora-Sustainable-Development-Afghanistan.pdf

Schuller, Mark. *Killing with Kindness: Haiti, International Aid, and NGOs.* New Brunswick, NJ: Rutgers University Press, 2012.

Senghor, Charles. 'Oxfam under attack in Senegal for defending LGBTI people.' *LaCroix International*, 16 July 2019. https://international.la-croix.com/news/%20ethics/oxfam-under-attack-in-senegal-for-defending-lgbti-people/10536

Shah, Mohammad Qadam. 'What did billions in aid to Afghanistan accomplish? 5 questions answered.' *The Conversation*, 26 October 2021. https://theconversation.com/what-did-billions-in-aid-to-afghanistan-accomplish-5-questions-answered-166804

Smirl, Lisa. *Spaces of Aid: How Cars, Compounds and Hotels Shape Humanitarianism.* London: Zed Books, 2015.

Velasco, Kristopher. 'A growing queer divide: The divergence between transnational advocacy networks and foreign aid in diffusing LGBT policies.' *International Studies Quarterly* 64, no. 1 (2020): 120–132, https://doi.org/10.1093/isq/sqz075

Waldman, Matt. *Aid Effectiveness in Afghanistan.* Kabul: Agency Coordinating Body for Afghan Relief, 2008. www-cdn.oxfam.org/s3fs-public/file_attachments/ACBAR_aid_effectiveness_paper_0803_3.pdf

4   Conflict effects

Fighting over and with aid

Unintended conflict effects occur when the external intervention strengthens rebel groups or increases tensions between individuals, (ethnic) communities, or recipients and non-recipients.

What flavours do we see?

1 **Direct conflict effects.** Rebel groups siphon off the services or products provided by the external intervention (often by violent means) and aid strengthens these groups. The refugee warrior effect is a subtype of the direct conflict effect. In this case, refugees and internally displaced people become soldiers because of the aid.
2 **Indirect conflict effects.** The services or products provided by the external intervention are associated with increased conflict between communities, ethnic or other groups, and/or between recipients and non-recipients: fighting because of aid or made possible by aid. Indirect conflict effects also comprise staff welfare effects related to conflict.

In which instances have unintended conflict effects been observed? Two examples:

1 Direct conflict effects: from Chechnya to the Sahel, aid workers face the risk of kidnappings. Kidnapping is becoming an increasingly profitable industry for rebel groups and insurance companies. An example of the refugee warrior effect has been observed in the refugee camps in the eastern DRC in 1994 and 1995, which former genocidaires were using as their base to launch attacks into Rwanda.
2 Indirect conflict effects: the recruitment policies of aid agencies have contributed to violent antagonism between the local population and the international community, for instance, in South Sudan. The local population resented non-local staff as they felt that 'their' jobs had been stolen, contributing to violent protests.

Key concepts from complexity thinking that help in understanding conflict effects:

1 **Non-linearity.** If aid structurally benefits (or disadvantages) one group over another, this can lead to a build-up in tensions. This tension continues to grow under the surface for a long time, until violence at one point suddenly erupts.

DOI: 10.4324/9781003356851-4

This Chapter has been made available under a CC-BY-NC-ND license.

2 **Adaptive agents.** Rebel leaders are flexible when it comes to where they get their resources. When there is an increase in foreign aid, they focus on how they can maximize their revenue from this resource, be it kidnapping or siphoning material aid.

Figure 4.1 Conflict effects in action: kidnapping aid workers is one way of keeping the war and rebel economy going.

Source: Maarten Wolterink.

With some books, I have developed quite an intense love–hate relationship. Having a love–hate relationship with a book, is that even possible? With the book *Famine Crimes* of Alex de Waal, it apparently is.

I had to read the book in the year 2000, back when I was a student. I first admired the book because it turned my spoon-fed ideas about hunger and famine upside down. I was raised by the ads of aid agencies with the idea that hunger in Africa resulted from droughts, locusts, and crop failure and that aid agencies – if we donated – could solve this problem. The book rejects this view and shows how hunger in Darfur in the 1980s was human-made, used as a weapon of war. More importantly, it also shows how aid agencies, intending to do well, ended up prolonging the conflict. Being a starting academic, I loved the book for showing the complex effects of humanitarian aid.

When I became a policymaker, I started to dread the book. In 2003, conflict and famine resurged in Darfur. How could we ever choose between aiding conflict and simply letting people starve? The question resurged in Syria in 2014: should we let the internally displaced Syrians in government-controlled areas starve for fear of supporting the Assad regime? I loathed the book for highlighting a problem without posing a solution.

Currently, I am in the phase where I love and hate the book simultaneously. I have my students, and I use the book to teach them how well-intentioned efforts can have adverse effects. I don't come up with easy solutions either. Nevertheless, the operational typology of unintended effects can serve as an assessment framework to take the 'should I stay or should I go' decision more informedly (see Section 13.1). This chapter deals with the direct and indirect conflict effects of aid and the remarkable progress in the sector to learn from its mistakes: the uptake of a conflict-sensitive way of working by the sector.

4.1 Direct conflict effects: those with guns never go hungry

Humanitarian aid is particularly easy for armed factions and opposition groups to appropriate since unarmed personnel must transport it physically over long distances, often through disputed territories.[1] Even when aid reaches its intended recipients, it can still be appropriated or 'taxed' by armed groups or rogue parts of the regular army, against whom the recipients are typically powerless. This misappropriated aid (together with other resources gathered by rebels) is then used to fund conflict. Over the past decades, the stealing and taxing of humanitarian aid by armed actors has been documented in Ethiopia, Sudan, Afghanistan, and many other countries.[2] When rebel groups start stealing and diverting aid to wage war, I speak of direct conflict effects.

One way of diverting aid money is to kidnap aid workers, and according to Reuters aid worker kidnappings are becoming 'big business.'[3] With tight security guidelines for large international agencies and expatriates (such as the United Nations), security risks have been largely outsourced to local agencies and staff originating from the countries of operations. This becomes visible when analysing the data on kidnapping and attacks on aid workers: over 98 per cent concerns staff originating from the countries of operations.[4] As explained in the introduction, unintended effects are unequally distributed, with less powerful groups – in this case staff operating in the countries they originate from – bearing the brunt of the negative ones (abduction). When debating racism in the sector, we need to talk about outsourcing risk to people of colour.

Despite – or maybe because – aid workers from the Global North face much lower risks of violence and kidnapping, they get all the more press attention when something does happen. These cases give us an insight into the scale of the kidnapping business. Take the story of the kidnapping of Arjan Erkel in Dagestan from 2002 until 2004. A legal dispute arose between the Dutch section of Médecins Sans Frontières (his employer) and the Dutch state, which advanced the ransom. Normally, governments always deny that they have paid a ransom, as to avoid providing incentives for other kidnappers, but this time the ransom news leaked: the government wanted to 'go Dutch' for the ransom and split the bill between the employer and the state, but the NGO refused (even when it comes to paying a ransom, we Dutch people can be stingy!). Because of the court cases we know that a ransom of EUR 1 million has been paid to the Chechen rebels.[5] Rebel groups fill their war chest through kidnappings: that's why these abductions are direct conflict effects.

Arjan Erkel was leading the operations for Chechnya Internally Displaced Persons in neighbouring Dagestan in 2002 when one night he was taken hostage by four terrorists. He was put in a hole under the ground for 607 days. Pressure on the Dutch prime minister to ensure his release was tremendous, especially when the kidnappers released photos of a suffering Arjan. In the end, the Dutch government 'advanced' EUR 780,000 to Médecins Sans Frontières, which channelled the funding to the rebels. Arjan was released, 18 kilos lighter than we he was captured. He received a hero's welcome in the Netherlands, and the Dutch government received a boost for rescuing its citizen. Regrettably, not just the Dutch government got a boost, but also the extremist militiamen.

There are over a hundred people like Arjan Erkel every year, just showing how lucrative this has become. We don't hear about this often, because now 98 per cent of the hostages originate from the countries where they operate. Rebels are using this successfully to raise millions for their bloodshed from Burkina Faso to Myanmar and many places in between. While NGOs claim that they don't pay a ransom, they are simultaneously using the kidnap & ransom (K&R) insurance of providers.[6]

Why don't we know about the K&R insurances by NGOs and aid agencies? I once asked my wife, who was the international programme director of an international NGO, if she had such a ransom insurance, and she looked into the air: once the NGO has such a K&R insurance, one of the clauses is that they are not allowed to mention that anywhere, as this might drive up the ransom requested. As one of many, the insurance company Clement has special K&R insurance policies for NGOs and non-profits: 'Being prepared with the right kidnapping insurance can save lives. Clements Worldwide Kidnap and Ransom Insurance provides financial indemnification and expert crisis management in case of a kidnapping for ransom, wrongful detention, and/or extortion.' For these kinds of insurance companies, K&R is very profitable: '[I]n an unintentional conspiracy, the terrorist, the victim, and the insurance companies have found a level at which they are all prepared to work. The kidnappers get their cash, the victims have insurance, and the insurance companies get their premiums.[7]

International aid agencies, especially humanitarian aid agencies, hence face tough dilemmas. How much are they willing to pay to get access to the target population, both in terms of human risks and in strictly monetary terms? The question is often not *if* organizations pay, but more so *how* they pay.[8] If they pay cash, which is not standard practice, they need to worry about how they enter it into their cash registers, so that the costs won't be disallowed. Instead of cash, just handing over a part of the food and non-food items is another way of getting access. The sector is dealing with the direct conflict effect daily, even though these dilemmas are hardly discussed openly.

I started with the question of how to choose between aiding rebels and letting people starve. I will not give any answers, but rather provide the tools for analysing these dilemmas. In the conclusion (Section 13.1) on humanitarian aid to South Sudan, it becomes clear that conflict effects (both direct and indirect effects) don't come alone. Elite capture, democratization, tax, and corruption effects accompany them. To answer the question of whether or not to provide aid, all these various side effects need to be integrated into a decision framework, beyond just the question of how much money is siphoned off by rebel leaders.

Unfortunately, this integral way of decision-making is often lacking in the humanitarian sector, in part because of a dogmatic belief in the humanitarian principle of neutrality. This principle, that neither side of a conflict should benefit from aid, is important in theory, but often not realistic in practice. However, since many humanitarians have been taught that this is how humanitarian aid should be, they often work with blinders on. Often they have ideological boundaries to learning, as they conflate what *is* with what *should be*. Observations that don't tally with neutrality are all too often overlooked. For a more nuanced appraisal of how the humanitarian sector should move on with the principle of neutrality in the 21st century, Hugo Slim – a veteran humanitarian – champions the view that also non-neutral actors should be considered humanitarians, as long as they contribute to the welfare of the groups they work in solidarity with (even if that is a rebel group). This more pragmatic take on the role of neutrality opens the space to discuss the side effects of humanitarian aid, which is hardly possible with a dogmatic view that argues that an organisation that doesn't stick to 100 per cent neutrality is unprofessional.[9]

Without wanting to avoid the 'should I stay or should I go question,' the question could also be rephrased into '*how* can I stay?' Many aid agencies have become creative in reducing the bait. The days of air droppings of food, such as that done by Operation Lifeline in the 1990s in Sudan, are over. Food aid (easily siphoned off) is increasingly being replaced by monetary aid on credit cards and phones (harder to be extorted during transport). By taking the blinders off, looking for alternatives that do less harm can start in earnest.

4.1.1 A special type of direct conflict effects: the refugee warrior effect

Walking through the internally displace persons camp Mugunga on the outskirts of Goma, DRC, I was impressed by its liveliness: small shops, bars, and hairdressers lined the neat grid of alleys. I was posted at the Dutch embassy in Kinshasa from 2008 until 2011, overseeing Dutch humanitarian funding in the DRC. This included frequent visits to internally displaced persons camps such as Mugunga, where hundreds of thousands stayed.[10] Wandering through these alleys, my thoughts also started wandering off. Fifteen years ago, displaced persons were also reenergizing and planning their next moves in these camps. At that time, these displaced persons were not Congolese, but also Rwandan refugees, including many *génocidaires*. Hutu militias, chased from Rwanda, rapidly took control of the camps in Zaire, using them as a base for arms smuggling and military operations. They extorted and appropriated aid resources in considerable quantities, terrorizing and assaulting refugees and humanitarian agency staff, and assassinating refugees who refused their demands.

As I listened to technical briefings by the camp managers, my eyes fell on groups of men sitting in front of the small houses: could they also be 'refugee warriors'?[11] Were they benefiting from the humanitarian aid system to muster their strength to launch another rebel offensive? I suddenly felt deeply connected to my predecessors and their impossible dilemmas fifteen years ago. The humanitarian imperative obliged them to rescue the refugees from cholera (which killed 50,000 refugees in a matter of weeks in 1994). They were successful in combating cholera, but the extremist Hutu ringleaders also took huge advantage of the aid. As MSF reported honestly in a review of their intervention in the eastern DRC, 'humanitarian aid was being massively misappropriated by extremist leaders … we were unintentionally supporting a militarized system run by perpetrators of genocide.'[12]

The Hutu extremists in 1994 were refugee warriors. The big question is whether they are the exception or the rule: are revengeful refugees and displaced persons from Somalia, Syria, Afghanistan, and Palestine using the camps and the aid to prepare a violent comeback?

With hindsight, it becomes clear that aid benefitted warriors amongst the refugees on multiple occasions, sometimes even not wholly unintended. A clear example is the anti-communist Mujahedeen on the border between Pakistan and Afghanistan in the 1980s and 1990s. Western countries wanted to get food aid to the displaced populations under their control: not just 'needs' were an important criterion, but also their anti-communist stance. The entire country was hungry, but the food aid went virtually exclusively to the east of the country, where the Mujahedeen were strongest.[13] Clearly, 'our' warlords were benefiting as humanitarians made deals with local commanders to obtain security. Taxation of aid transport (at gunpoint if needed) was also common.[14] Some donors accepted 'wastage levels' of up to 40 per cent on cross-border programmes.[15] But since the refugee warriors were 'our' refugee warriors under the Cold War logic, the donors were willing to turn a blind eye.[16] While aid agencies might successfully achieve 'neutrality' at the tactical level (target people in the intervention area based on needs), it is harder for them to be neutral in selecting the intervention itself, which is more often a political choice.

It was not just in the geopolitical hotspot of Afghanistan where refugee warriors were supported. In Sri Lanka, the Tamil Tigers erected the Tamil Relief Organization (TRO). They were successful in pushing international agencies who wanted to operate in areas under their control to work through this agency.[17] Agencies such as the United Nations International Children's Emergency Fund (UNICEF) had to sign partnership agreements with the TRO, and when the Tsunami hit Sri Lanka, this enabled the TRO to fill their (violent) campaign coffers.[18]

Stedman and Tanner have written extensively on what they call 'refugee manipulation' in refugee camps and concur that 'separating soldiers from refugees' is a useless suggestion.[19] In their view, in many of the instances where the refugee camps were feeding the warriors, this was made possible – as the Pakistan example shows – as those refugees served the geopolitical interests of regional powers or global superpowers. Hence, focussing on 'separating warriors from refugees' (as the UNHCR proposes) will not happen as long as states use aid to further their security interests.[20]

Even more striking is that many 'refugee warriors' don't enter the camp as soldiers, but are recruited in the camps. Some refugee camps become a breeding ground for refugee warriors: the disillusioned men that constitute these camps are an important recruitment pool for militants to tap into.[21] Refugees are insufficiently integrated into the host country, receive little trauma/ psychological treatment, and are not allowed to work. Many of them risk becoming disillusioned, frustrated, and susceptible to narratives of fighting for some idealized community. After a military defeat at home, the warring party can use the suffering of refugees for its political purpose 'to siphon off aid, establish the international legitimacy of their cause, and, by manipulating access to them, ensure that they will not repatriate. As long as armies control refugee populations, they can demand a seat in negotiations.'[22]

While the percentage of displaced people residing in camps has declined to about 25 per cent, the overall number of displaced people is rising fast. For those active in providing services for displaced people, whether they are supporting (or breeding) 'refugee warriors' remains an important question. The 'neutrality blinds' also don't facilitate an open exchange. By not speaking up, humanitarians risk contributing to conflict in the long run. Aid workers are the antennas of the international community: if they do not include their field-level observations in the political debate, decision-makers will operate in a void.

4.2 Indirect conflict effects: when aid-funded programmes breed tension

It was the most stunning way in which I had ever woken up and will ever wake up. The sun was rising and colouring the Kilimanjaro and its snowy top in beautiful and ever-changing colours. Between the Kilimanjaro and us was a quiet savannah with elephants having breakfast at the edges of our lodge. I lived in Nairobi at the time with endless traffic jams and poor air quality, so I felt that my batteries were recharging here in Amboseli National Park. Yet, an uneasy feeling also started to nag at me. Questions started to pop up into my head: What had happened to the local population, the Maasai, who used to live here? We had chosen to stay at a 'sustainable' eco-lodge which promised to 'do no harm,' but maybe the harm had already been done? What happened to the rights of the Maasai when the World Bank turned this place with the Kenyan government into a national park in the 1970s?

Making use of the Wi-Fi in the lodge, I could find out that about 6,000 Maasai people were living in the area that is now Amboseli National Park. Then, the national government decided to turn first the area in a reserve (meaning the Maasai could still live there, but not hunt, which they hardly did anyway). Subsequently, they turned it into a park, meaning the Maasai would have to leave. In retaliation, the Maasai began killing rhinos and other wildlife as a form of political protest and in fear that Amboseli would be officially declared a National Park.[23] The World Bank co-financed a compensation scheme for the Maasai, including additional access to water outside the park and a revenue disbursement mechanism.[24] This worked reasonably well, and while there were occasional protests, especially when the promised funds did not get through, no violent clashes took place. Relatively assured on the Amboseli situation, I kept on reading on wildlife protection in Kenya, only to find out that in other parks the foreign-backed conservancies have contributed to – often-deadly – conflict.

The conflict around the Maasai in Amboseli is an example of an indirect conflict effect. I dub something an indirect conflict effect if an external intervention is associated with increased conflict between recipients and non-recipients or, for example, between class, gender, or ethnic lines. Rather than directly supporting conflict like direct conflict effects, these effects indirectly contribute to tensions. Unfortunately, the case of Amboseli doesn't stand alone as an indirect conflict effect, as it became clear when I researched the establishment of another nature conservancy in Kenya.

According to Greiner, conservancies can contribute to conflict in two ways: by increasing the value of these environmental resources (extra money coming in) and by re-regulating access and control entitlements.[25] The establishment of the Ltungai Conservancy, for instance, makes clear how internationally backed conservation methods can go horribly wrong. This Ltungai conservancy unintentionally contributed to increased tensions between the Pokot and Samburu ethnic groups, which contributed to a violent spiral leading to the death of more than five hundred people in 2006 and 2007. This newly established conservancy was a 'community' conservancy. Instead of the top-down conservancy of the 1970s (such as Amboseli), communities could now start them and attract international funding and tourists directly. However, in this case one ethnic group declared a sanctuary on the land of another community, or at least on contested territory.[26] The NGO that supported the programme did not do a conflict scan beforehand and was not aware of the contestation. More conflict sensitivity is needed to prevent this from happening, and when I was widening my search, it become clear that this doesn't only hold for conservancies, but also for other forms of environmental programming, such as the payment for environmental services programmes.

Over the last decade, the Payment for Environmental Services (PES) programmes have increased tremendously, partly because of the huge increase in financing related to climate and environment. Organizations such as the World Bank are now investing hundreds of millions into these PES programmes, especially for forest protection. The idea of PES is that titleholders of forests can get compensation for not cutting trees. A comprehensive academic literature by colleague Marloes Verholt indicated that conflict effects were a prevalent unintended effect of these types of programmes. PES programmes appear to be subject to the same mechanisms that make conservancy programmes contribute to conflict. The arrival of compensation payments suddenly makes it important to clarify to whom the forest belongs. Constructive ambiguity ceases to exist. Frozen conflicts about unclear boundaries can suddenly resurface, with examples as diverse as Vietnam, the DRC, and Mexico.[27]

To deal with the conflicts surrounding biodiversity efforts (amongst other problems), a global 'Convivial Conservation Coalition (CCC)' has been set up. The CCC criticizes the 'green violence' in and around so-called 'fortress conservation parks,'[28] where rangers are perpetrating often excessive violence against rural dwellers. They propose radical post-capitalist strategies, such as the Conservation Basic Income: a stipend allowing people living close to protected areas to sustain biodiversity-friendly livelihoods without competing within a ruthless global marketplace in ways that undermine the ecosystem.[29]

But conservation and environmental programming is only one example of indirect conflict effects. A classic work on indirect conflict effects is the book *Aiding Violence* by Peter Uvin.[30] He shows how donors in Rwanda colluded with the Hutu regime in the 1980s, enforcing a system of structural violence against the Tutsi. In a sense, they were setting the scene for the genocide. While it is difficult to prove this causal relationship, he is right in stating that donors and aid agencies should ask more often: are we indirectly contributing to conflict by supporting particular partners or policies?

The good news is that agencies are increasingly asking questions on the link between aid and violence, as the fast rise of conflict-sensitive programming in the sector demonstrates. Before we turn to that, I would like to acknowledge the consequences of working in conflict areas on the welfare of aid agencies' staff. Research by Daniella Vento shows that aid workers, especially local staff members, are mentally negatively affected by the conflicts in which they have to work. She also found that care for these local staff members leaves much to be desired, as also the testimony of Mary, working in north-eastern Nigeria (see textbox) makes clear.[31]

Testimony by Mary: the humans providing humanitarian aid

Figure 4.2 Mary.

My name is Mary. I have about seven years' experience working in the humanitarian context. A large part of my work is supporting the reintegration of women and children survivors of Boko Haram in the northeast of Nigeria.

Fighting back the tears

As aid workers, we facilitate dialogue sessions to help people heal from their traumatic experiences. Part of this process is that people tell the stories of how their family members were killed. For me, it is a lot trying to battle with hearing those stories and not being emotional about them. I often have to fight back my tears and be strong for them. Often, in the evenings, I still remember what they said, I imagine their faces and what they must have gone through.

Secondary trauma

Working in this kind of conflict zone hurts me (for example dreaming about being attacked by Boko Haram while delivering my duties in the communities), and I also hear from other peacebuilders that they experience this kind of 'secondary trauma.' Since I started this job five years ago, there have been some trainings on trauma-informed care and mental health. It is a first step, but I don't think it's enough given the context's impact on the staff. Some good initiatives, such as a game room for staff to vent, never materialized because of insufficient funds. Even refresher trainings were not sustained. There seems to be donor fatigue regarding the north-east of Nigeria, which has shifted priorities away. New staff members now mostly do without psycho-social care training due to the shrinking funds.

Consideration for national staff

Organizations have to look at how to compensate staff working in those locations, with for example R&R (Rest & Recuperation) policies, especially for staff who are not from there, to be able to see their families and to change environment. I am from the north-central part of Nigeria, which is very different from the northeast. The roads are not safe and the alternative is to travel by air, which is expensive for some of us – considering what we are earning and the family responsibilities we have. Most can afford to travel back home only once a year.

The disparities between expats and national staff are also clear. While we are all impacted by the context, international staff are prioritized. The national staff should receive more consideration in terms of not just remuneration, but also in evacuation plans, for example.

The 'human' in humanitarian aid

Sometimes organizations can be a little hypocritical. We provide psycho-social aid, talk about dignity of human lives, and talk about many things, but we don't really live up to it within our organizations. That doesn't mean it's all bad: positive initiatives are being taken to ensure the welfare and safety of staff, but that has to be improved. Organizations must look at the balance between the people who need aid and those who provide it.

4.3 The rise of conflict-sensitive programming

The UK Foreign Commonwealth and Development Office (formerly DFID) has been one of the frontrunners concerning conflict-sensitive programming. Conflict sensitivity is an approach to ensure that interventions do not unintentionally contribute to conflict, but strengthen opportunities for peace and inclusion.[32] DFID was the first donor to require that all civil servants who are developing aid programmes develop conflict scans: 'for all interventions in fragile and conflict-affected countries, you should set out how intervening will make an important contribution to addressing conflict and/or fragility, and how doing harm will be avoided.' After DFID, many donors followed suit, and a similar requirement now holds for all civil servants working on EU interventions in fragile states.[33] In Germany, the Ministry of Development Cooperation and the Deutsche Gesellschaft für Internationale Zusammenarbeit (GIZ) established conflict units to increase conflict sensitivity.

This conflict sensitivity should cover all aspects of unintended conflict effects, be they direct or indirect. When I worked for the conflict transformation organization Search for Common Ground in the DRC, we did many conflict sensitivity mappings for agencies such as UNICEF and UNDP. I think it helped them tremendously to make sure that, for instance, they did not build schools on contested lands and that their hiring practices did not favour one group over another. Having said that, I noticed that while our conflict scans were open about the ethnic cleavages in communities, the donors were often reluctant to incorporate ethnicity-related considerations into their programmes. They feared that they would end up in political debates about ethnicity in those countries. Still, by ignoring this factor, donors are shooting themselves in the foot in the long term, as ethnic tensions also need to be addressed.

Evidence from Afghanistan also points in the direction that all the efforts of DFID to become more conflict-sensitive have helped. CARD-F was an agricultural programme in Afghanistan funded by DFID. The programme hadn't done a proper conflict analysis, which led to incidents such as milk collection points being built in areas favouring one group over another.[34] Then DFID invited CARD-F partners to conflict sensitivity training, and shared ideas for conflict analysis and mapping. CARD-F subsequently rolled out training for all of their staff, built complaints mechanisms into their projects, and started to share regular feedback with the donor about the way the programme was affecting the conflict and vice versa. Negative side effects were no longer swept under the carpet. As a result, the programme was able to track and mitigate where it was potentially contributing to harm.

How to tackle conflict effects

Policymakers

- **Realize that neutrality is often a myth.** A myopic focus on neutrality can reduce the degree to which humanitarian agencies consider different side effects, from conflict to marginalization and governance effects. Stimulate an open debate about this and modernize the principle of neutrality.
- **Promote providing material support that is less easily misappropriated.** Digital transfers can replace cash handouts, and stay away from air droppings.
- **Explore less coercive alternatives.** For agencies working in sectors that are most associated with conflict, such as environmental protection, ally yourself with new initiatives that seek more harmonious solutions to conservation, such as conviviality.

Practitioners

- **Work in a conflict-sensitive way.** For agencies not working yet in a conflict-sensitive way: step up your game. This includes conflict mapping before an intervention, continuous conflict monitoring during the intervention, as well as adapting the programming to signs of tensions and conflict. When planning, consider more sensitive issues, such as ethnicity, as they are often closely linked with conflict.
- **Realize that armed groups are highly adaptive agents**. Armed groups can rapidly shift their income strategies, and aid agencies are their prime target.
- **Be open about the chosen risk appetite.** For humanitarian workers operating in fragile environments: be more open about the dilemmas and the chosen risk appetite of the

organization and communicate more openly what this means for the likelihood of aid diversion, for instance.

- **Communicate openly about uneasy facts from the intervention area.** For humanitarian agencies: communicate the information received by operating at the field-level, such as rebel recruitment of refugees.

Evaluators

- **Acknowledge and measure the potential militarization of refugee camps and humanitarian aid.** Weigh short-term and long-term interests, and make careful decisions based on this analysis. Whenever possible, address militarization at the political level.
- **Tap into local contextual knowledge.** Locals often have a better idea of the conflicts in the area. Please give them the lead in mapping exercises of these conflict-sensitive areas (instead of flying in people from abroad to do the job).

Notes

1 Nathan Nunn and Nancy Qian, *Aiding Conflict: The Impact of U.S. Food aid on Civil War. Working Paper 17794* (Cambridge, MA: National Bureau of Economic Research, 2012), www.nber.org/papers/w17794

2 Linda Polman, *The Crisis Caravan: What's Wrong with Humanitarian Aid*, translated by Liz Waters (New York, NY: Metropolitan, 2010).

3 Emma Batha, 'Aid worker kidnappings "big business" as criminals wade in: Ex-hostage,' *Reuters*, 13 August 2019, www.reuters.com/article/us-global-aid-kidnapping-interview-idUSKCN1V31J6

4 Humanitarian Outcomes, 'Aid Worker Security Database,' n.d., accessed 1 February 2023, https://aidworkersecurity.org

5 Médecins Sans Frontières, 'MSF statement on the release of Arjan Erkel,' 15 June 2004, https://msf-seasia.org/news/8782

6 Kjell Lauvik, Lyn Snodgrass, and Thokozile Mayekiso, 'Hostage incident management: The dilemma of kidnap and ransom insurance for humanitarian aid workers,' *Africa Insight* 44, no. 2 (2014): 79–93, https://journals.co.za/doi/10.10520/EJC164283

7 Ibid., 89.

8 Ian Cobain, 'Aid charity facing scrutiny over payments to armed opposition group,' *Middle East Eye*, 10 February 2021, www.middleeasteye.net/news/aid-charity-facing-scrutiny-over-payments-armed-opposition-group

9 Hugo Slim, *Solferino 21: Warfare, Civilians and Humanitarians in the Twenty-First Century* (London: Hurst Publishers, 2022).

10 Gloria Nguya, *Livelihood Strategies of Internally Displaced Persons in Urban Eastern DRC*, doctoral thesis (Rotterdam: Erasmus University Rotterdam, 2019), https://repub.eur.http://hdl.handle.net/1765/117891nl/pub/117891. My Congolese PhD researcher Gloria Nguya demonstrated in her research how important these camps were for the internally displaced persons to reenergize and prepare for their next phase in their lives.

11 The term 'refugee warrior' is actually incorrect, since also internally displaced persons can militarize the aid.

12 Médecins Sans Frontières, 'Rwandan genocide 25 years on: MSF caught in spiral of extreme violence from Rwanda to Zaire,' 5 April 2019, www.msf.org/rwandan-genocide-25-years

13 Jonathan Goodhand, 'Aiding violence or building peace? The role of international aid in Afghanistan,' *Third World Quarterly* 23, no. 5 (2002): 837–859, https://doi.org/10.1080/0143659022000028620

14 Astri Suhrke, Kristian Berg Harpviken, Are Knudsen, Arve Ofstad, and Arne Strand, *Peacebuilding: Lessons for Afghanistan* (Bergen: Chr. Michelsen Institute, 2002), www.cmi.no/publications/file/831-peacebuilding-lessons-for-afghanistan.pdf
15 Goodhand, 'Aiding violence,' 843.
16 Antonio Donini, *United Nations Coordination in Complex Emergencies: Lessons from Afghanistan, Mozambique and Rwanda'*, *Humanitarianism and War Project* (Boston, MA: Brown University, 1995).
17 Shawn Teresa Flanigan, 'Nonprofit service provision by insurgent organizations: The cases of Hizballah and the Tamil Tigers,' *Studies in Conflict & Terrorism* 31, no. 6 (2008): 499–519, https://doi.org/10.1080/10576100802065103
18 To make the situation even murkier, what constitutes a freedom fighter for one group might be considered a terrorist by the other. The international community claims to always support the freedom fighters, but local perceptions are often different.
19 Stephen John Stedman and Fred Tanner, *Refugee Manipulation: War, Politics, and the Abuse of Human Suffering* (Washington, DC: Brookings Institution Press, 2004).
20 Ibid., 9.
21 Ibid., 3.
22 Ibid., 3.
23 Gabriela Schieve Fleury, *Lion and livestock conflict in the Amboseli region of Kenya*, bachelor's thesis (Harrisonburg, VA: James Madison University, 2014).
24 David Western, 'Amboseli National Park: Enlisting landowners to conserve migratory wildlife,' *Ambio* 115 (1982): 302–308, https://eurekamag.com/research/020/651/020651504.php
25 Clemens Greiner, 'Unexpected consequences: Wildlife conservation and territorial conflict in Northern Kenya,' *Human Ecology* 40, no. 3 (2012): 415–425, www.jstor.org/stable/41474671
26 Ibid., 424.
27 Koch and Verholt, 'Limits to learning.'
28 Fortress conservation parks are conserved areas where virtually all human activity is banned, except for regulated tourism. 'Green violence' refers to the violence that is perpetrated using the pretext of nature conservation.
29 Bram Büscher and Robert Fletcher, 'Towards convivial conservation,' *Conservation & Society* 17, no. 3 (2019): 283–296, www.jstor.org/stable/26677964.
30 Peter Uvin, *Aiding Violence: The Development Enterprise in Rwanda* (West Hartford, CT: Kumarian Press, 1998).
31 Daniella Vento and Dirk-Jan Koch, 'How to care for carers? Psychosocial care for local staff of humanitarian agencies' (unpublished manuscript, submitted to Disasters, 1 May 2023).
32 Canadian Agency for International Development, 'Conflict sensitivity tip sheet,' last modified on 22 September 2021, www.international.gc.ca/world-monde/funding-financement/conflict_sensitivity-sensibilite_conflits.aspx?lang=eng
33 Directorate-General for International Cooperation and Development, *Guidance Notes on Conflict Sensitivity in Development Cooperation–An Update and Supplement to the EU staff Handbook on 'Operating in Situations of Conflict and Fragility'* (Brussels: European Commission, 2021), https://europa.eu/capacity4dev/file/120184/download?token=LUzfP3sp
34 Ibid., 39.

Further reading

Batha, Emma. 'Aid worker kidnappings "big business" as criminals wade in: Ex-hostage.' *Reuters*, 13 August 2019. www.reuters.com/article/us-global-aid-kidnapping-interview-idUSKCN1V31J6
Büscher, Bram, and Robert Fletcher. 'Towards convivial conservation.' *Conservation & Society* 17, no. 3 (2019): 283–296. www.jstor.org/stable/26677964

Canadian Agency for International Development. 'Conflict sensitivity tip sheet.' Last modified on 22 September 2021. www.international.gc.ca/world-monde/funding-financement/conflict_sens itivity-sensibilite_conflits.aspx?lang=eng

Cobain, Ian. 'Aid charity facing scrutiny over payments to armed opposition group.' *Middle East Eye*, 10 February 2021. www.middleeasteye.net/news/aid-charity-facing-scrutiny-over-payme nts-armed-opposition-group

Collier, Paul, and Anke Hoeffler. 'Unintended consequences: Does aid promote arms races?' *Oxford Bulletin of Economics and Statistics* 69, no. 1: 1–27. https://doi.org/10.1111/ j.1468-0084.2006.00439.x

Directorate-General for International Cooperation and Development. *Guidance Notes on Conflict Sensitivity in Development Cooperation–An Update and Supplement to the EU Staff Handbook on 'Operating in Situations of Conflict and Fragility'*. Brussels: European Commission, 2021. https://europa.eu/capacity4dev/file/120184/download?token=LUzfP3sp

Donini, Antonio. *United Nations Coordination in Complex Emergencies: Lessons from Afghanistan, Mozambique and Rwanda', Humanitarianism and War Project*. Boston, MA: Brown University, 1995.

Flanigan, Shawn Teresa. 'Nonprofit service provision by insurgent organizations: The cases of Hizballah and the Tamil Tigers.' *Studies in Conflict & Terrorism* 31, no. 6 (2008): 499–519. https://doi.org/10.1080/10576100802065103

Fleury, Gabriela Schieve. *Lion and Livestock Conflict in the Amboseli Region of Kenya*. Bachelor's thesis. Harrisonburg: James Madison University, 2014. https://commons.lib.jmu.edu/honors201 019/409

Goodhand, Jonathan. 'Aiding violence or building peace? The role of international aid in Afghanistan.' *Third World Quarterly* 23, no. 5 (2002): 837–859. https://doi.org/10.1080/0143 659022000028620

Greiner, Clemens. 'Unexpected Consequences: Wildlife Conservation and Territorial Conflict in Northern Kenya.' *Human Ecology* 40, no. 3 (2012): 415–425. www.jstor.org/stable/ 41474671

Koch, Dirk-Jan, and Marloes Verholt. 'Limits to learning: The struggle to adapt to unintended effects of international payment for environmental services programmes.' *International Environmental Agreements: Politics, Law and Economics* 20, no. 3 (2020): 507–539. https://doi.org/10.1007/ s10784-020-09496-2

Lauvik, Kjell, Lyn Snodgrass, and Thokozile Mayekiso. 'Hostage incident management: The dilemma of kidnap and ransom insurance for humanitarian aid workers.' *Africa Insight* 44, no. 2 (2014): 79–93. https://journals.co.za/doi/10.10520/EJC164283

Médecins Sans Frontières. 'MSF statement on the release of Arjan Erkel.' 15 June 2004. https:// msf-seasia.org/news/8782

Médecins Sans Frontières. 'Rwandan genocide 25 years on: MSF caught in spiral of extreme vio- lence from Rwanda to Zaire.' 5 April 2019. www.msf.org/rwandan-genocide-25-years

Nunn, Nathan, and Nancy Qian. *Aiding Conflict: The Impact of U.S. Food aid on Civil War. Working Paper 17794*. Cambridge, MA: National Bureau of Economic Research, 2012. www. nber.org/papers/w17794

Gloria Nguya, *Livelihood Strategies of Internally Displaced Persons in Urban Eastern DRC*. Doctoral thesis. Rotterdam: Erasmus University Rotterdam, 2019. https://repub.eur.http://hdl. handle.net/1765/117891nl/pub/117891

Polman, Linda. *The Crisis Caravan: What's Wrong with Humanitarian Aid*. Translated by Liz Waters. New York, NY: Metropolitan, 2010.

Slim, Hugo. *Solferino 21: Warfare, Civilians and Humanitarians in the Twenty-First Century*. London: Hurst Publishers, 2022.

Stephen John, Stedman and Fred Tanner. *Refugee Manipulation: War, Politics, and the Abuse of Human Suffering*. Washington, DC: Brookings Institution Press, 2004.

Suhrke, Astri, Kristian Berg Harpviken, Are Knudsen, Arve Ofstad, and Arne Strand. *Peacebuilding: Lessons for Afghanistan.* Bergen: Chr. Michelsen Institute, 2002. www.cmi.no/publications/file/831-peacebuilding-lessons-for-afghanistan.pdf

Uvin, Peter. *Aiding Violence: The Development Enterprise in Rwanda.* West Hartford, CT: Kumarian Press, 1998.

Vento, Daniella, and Dirk-Jan Koch. 'How to care for carers? Psychosocial care for local staff of humanitarian agencies.' Unpublished manuscript, 1 February 2023.

Western, David. 'Amboseli National Park: Enlisting landowners to conserve migratory wildlife.' *Ambio* 115 (1982): 302–308. https://eurekamag.com/research/020/651/020651504.php

5 Migration and resettlement effects
Aid-induced displacement

Unintended migration and resettlement effects occur when an external intervention creates a movement of population, either towards or away from the intervention, which is different from the objective of the intervention. These movements can be either voluntary or involuntary.

What flavours do we see?

1 **Aid-induced resettlement.** Externally funded projects need land which people currently occupy, thus requiring their voluntary or involuntary resettlement.
2 **Migratory push effects.** Successful aid projects relax the budget constraint for beneficiaries, or their direct family, providing them the means to migrate.
3 **Migratory pull effects.** The external intervention incentivizes people in surrounding regions to migrate or temporarily move to the site of the aid intervention.

In which instances have unintended migration and resettlement effects been observed? Three examples:

1 Aid-induced resettlement: the construction of internally sponsored hydraulic dams has led to the resettlement (voluntary and involuntary) of millions of people over the last decades, for instance, in China. This resettlement is aid-induced if there is international development assistance involved substantially.
2 Migratory push effects: cash transfers to rural families providing them with the means to send one family member to an urban area, for instance, in South Africa.
3 Migratory pull effects: the incentives that stimulate people to migrate (or even flee) to project intervention areas can be for social, economic, or security reasons. Aid projects often provide one of few opportunities for formal employment in economically insecure regions, but aid organizations – especially peacekeeping missions – can also provide a protected area for civilians at risk, such as in South Sudan.

Key concepts from complexity theory that can help to understand migration and resettlement effects:

1 **Interconnectivity.** The borders between the target area and the surrounding area are porous. People move in and out, sometimes voluntarily and sometimes

DOI: 10.4324/9781003356851-5

This Chapter has been made available under a CC-BY-NC-ND license.

involuntarily. By ignoring these movements we can overestimate the impact of the intervention when those negatively affected by the intervention move out, just like we can underestimate its impact if those positively affected by it move out.

2 **Alternative impact pathways.** Often we assume that certain outputs (e.g. extra training) lead to certain outcomes (e.g. less unemployment in the target area, hence less outward migration), but it could also be that the same output leads to a different outcome (e.g. higher perceived job opportunities in foreign labour market, hence more outward migration).

Figure 5.1 Migration effects in action: resources obtained in regional refugee centres might lead to more migration.

Source: Maarten Wolterink.

5.1 Aid-induced resettlement: the blurred boundaries between voluntary and involuntary resettlement

5.1.1 What statistics can't show: the hidden costs of resettlement

A young woman was singing in the newly constructed school. The song was beautiful and chilling at the same time. While she was singing in a language that I could not comprehend, it was clear that she was singing about sorrow and resistance. I was looking around me and I saw that also the other members of the delegation were taken aback by the dramatic performance. I was leading a delegation of the Dutch government with Dutch energy firm CEOs and Dutch NGOs in my wake. It was an official fact-finding mission of the Dutch government, as we were importing a lot of coal from South Africa while also supporting the country to reduce the social costs of mining.

We were sitting in a newly constructed school, because the local population was resettled from a new coal mining area. The entire village was new and located in the coal-mining region of Mpumalanga, where so much coal is mined that it touches all your senses: you breathe it in the heavy air, you smell it in the alcoholic breaths of some of the (ex)-mineworkers you cross, and see it when climbing the mining pits.

The mining companies wanted us to visit the new village because it was a shining example of its internationally backed relocation scheme for affected populations. The NGOs wanted us to visit it, because it was a typical example that laid bare the differences between the glossy brochures highlighting the successes of the social turn in mining and the realities on the ground. The company claimed it was voluntary resettlement and had the signatures for it. The community, meanwhile, said it was involuntary: they were never given a proper choice, signature or not.

The newly constructed houses looked small but solid, the school was spacious and colourful, the road to the village wasn't paved, yet of good quality, so what was the problem? I was raised in a quantitative tradition, working as a statistical programmer at LSE's economics research centre. However, nowhere was the gap for me more clear between the rosy statistics and the lived realities than in Mpumalanga. It was not that the statistics were incorrect (e.g. the 'number of people with access to clean water' had indeed increased due to their resettlement); they were just inadequate to capture the population's wellbeing. The women, for instance, explained that they did not have access to the graves of their parents anymore, because these graves were still located on the land the coal mining companies acquired. They were in grief, as they could not honour them as they used to (showing the importance of having a broad definition of well-being).[1] I have browsed so many development indicator databases that I lost track, but I found nothing that remotely captures the spiritual dispossession I felt there. While the performance standards of the International Finance Cooperation require attention for 'cultural heritage,' which can include burial sites, these standards haven't reached the coal-mining areas in South Africa yet.

Involuntary resettlement poses a real development dilemma: if one farmer is resisting being resettled and this prevents a critical dam from being constructed that will provide energy to a million people, whose interests should prime? I am not of the school that involuntary resettlement is unacceptable under any circumstances: countries often have reasonable legal frameworks for it, including compensation. The questions that development agencies and financial institutions (and preferably governments) need to pose themselves are: has everything been done to achieve voluntary – instead of involuntary resettlement? Is the legal framework in the country reasonable and has it been followed? – Is the relation between individual costs and societal benefits reasonable? Answers to these questions are often subjective, as the example of Mpumalanga showed. This chapter analyses how major development banks have been dealing with this dilemma, and how the rise of Chinese development financing is changing the way this dilemma is being addressed.

5.1.2 International aid and (in)voluntary resettlement: two sides of the same coin

Resettlement is often considered unavoidable: villages are sometimes just literally 'in the way' of development. While resettlement is normally unintended (projects are not developed to resettle people), it is also anticipated. This speaks to the first myth we busted in the book's introduction (Myth 1: Unintended effects cannot be anticipated). Take, the case of Sarima, a village in northern Kenya, researched by Danish NGO Danwatch.[2] When I lived in Nairobi for a couple of years, the frequent blackouts were a sign that Kenya desperately needed more energy to transition to a middle-income country. The village of Sarima found itself in the way of solving that: it was located on a dirt road between a planned mega wind farm (350 turbines) in northern Kenya and the nearest city.[3] The dirt road had to become a major road to transport the 350 turbines, so the village had to move. The government considered that the enormous benefits of the mega wind farm, which would provide about 15–20 per cent of all energy in Kenya and was co-financed by various state-owned development banks, outweighed the costs. The side effects were taken for granted and it became just a matter of minimizing the 'collateral' damage of development.

There are thousands of towns like Sarima finding themselves in the way of development, from the almost one million Chinese living too close to the Three Gorges Dam in China to the thousands of poor families at the urban peninsula of Luanda.[4] Their 'choice' is often between leaving on their own accord or being 'bulldozed' away. According to the final report of the World Commission on Dams,[5] between 40 and 80 million people worldwide have been resettled by the construction of dams alone. This figure hence excludes (in)voluntary resettlement because of, for instance, urban re-development (the Luanda case) and wind energy projects (such as Sarima), in which donors often had an important hand.[6]

Resettlement is the daily bread and butter of international development projects, and will become increasingly so with the world population continuing to rise and the squeeze on land becoming increasingly tight. While many of the international development banks and export credit agencies have due diligence measures in place, this often goes wrong. An analysis by Kelebogile Zvobgo and Benjamin Graham of all the official complaints that are logged by communities that are affected by World Bank projects makes this clear.[7]

They analysed 250 complaints filed by affected communities at the inspection panel of the World Bank since its inception in 1993. Their overview of the 250 complaints reads like an encyclopaedia of the unintended effects in this book. Resettlement (both voluntary and involuntary) was, after environmental and economic damages, the third largest area of concern for plaintiffs: 25 per cent of the complaints concerned resettlement. The overview also shows that World Bank programmes in the transport and mining sector are particularly prone to negative side effects. The interventions by the inspection panel concerning the issues around (in)voluntary resettlement led in 33 per cent of the cases to a change in the project, in 30 per cent of the cases to compensation, and in 25 per cent of the cases to an acknowledgement of the harm caused.[8] This shows how important the resettlement issue is when dealing with unintended effects.

A key reason that we can track the (in)voluntary resettlement problems of World Bank programmes is that there are detailed guidelines and an independent and accessible complaints mechanism. If negative side effects don't surface in regular reporting (because of institutional pressures to showcase success) such an independent feedback loop can overcome these institutional boundaries to learning. In the testimony of Madame Messina, a fish trader who is experiencing first-hand the unintended effects of Western-funded development projects shares her story. This story would not have been known without the complaints mechanism.

Testimony by fish trader Mme. Messina: how a new dam means progress for Cameroon and worries for local inhabitants

Figure 5.2 Madame Messina.

It all sounds very promising. The development of a massive dam in the Sanaga River, Cameroon's largest river, will connect a part of the population to low-cost hydroelectric power. This so-called Nachtigal dam is funded by international financial institutions like the World Bank, the European Investment Bank (EIB), and the African Development Bank (AfDB), and will be completed in 2023. Yet, communities living around the river are sounding alarm bells. Building a dam in the river that is so important to people's livelihoods is causing several serious social, environmental, and economic issues, and locals feel they were insufficiently informed and consulted and compensated before construction started.

Mme. Messina is a community member living near the Sanaga River. She is 'economically displaced,' meaning she can't earn the income she did before.

Reduced to a life of poverty

I have four children and I'm even a grandmother already. I am a representative of the community of fishmongers. I sell smoked fish, or I should say: I used to sell, because now I can't anymore. Before the dam came, I was not miserable like today. We led an average village life and could afford the necessities. For example, we sent our children to school. Now, we cannot fish anymore and are reduced to a life of poverty.

The destruction of sacred sites, medicinal plants, and water resources

The area was sacred and reserved only for special spiritual leaders of the village. They organized essential rituals for the whole village where problems could be solved. In addition, great apes and reptiles, considered holy, used to cross the Sanaga River. There were also trees and other plant species used for medicine.

Efforts by the international community for compensation

The international organizations tried to come up with a compensation, but it took a very long time and was little. First they did a census of who was living in the area, but that went wrong, because many people got counted that don't live here. And when we got compensation, it helped us only for a short time and wasn't permanent.

What is your advice for the 'international community'?

International donors have most certainly contributed to development. But we are asking for more consideration for the local populations when these grand structural projects are set up. There should be policies in place that provide a solution for the immediate impact these constructions have. Also, the communities must be trained to be dynamic and economically profitable in the long term.

In the end, this project is good for the Cameroonian state's economy, but for our part we plunged into a suffocating misery.

In 2022, an official complaint was filed to the World Bank on behalf of the communities living near the Nachtigal Hydropower Project. In February 2023, the case was still in 'dispute resolution process' (all documents are publicly available).

5.1.3 Sliding backwards? From consent to consultation

In line with its shift from benefactor to banker, China has set up two development banks since 2014: the New Development Bank (NDB) and the Asian Infrastructure Investment Bank (AIIB).[9] These banks compete with the World Bank and other Western-dominated development banks financially and ideologically. Democratic control, also on (in)voluntary resettlement, is more limited for these banks.[10] Civil society organizations (a key driver of taking side effects seriously) have no formal access to these banks: the AIIB and the NDB do not even ensure consultation and exchange. Their access-to-information policies are less comprehensive than that of the World Bank, as they give member states the final say about which documents will be public and which ones will be classified. The NDB does not even give individuals or groups affected by its projects the right to file complaints. If we will see fewer complaints about the (in)voluntary resettlements linked to projects of these banks, it is not because there are no complaints, there is just a higher likelihood that they are swept under the carpet.

Guidelines for 'Free, Prior, and Informed Consent' (FPIC) are crucial for thousands of communities facing eviction because of internationally financed projects. The World Bank (following the International Finance Corporation guidelines) requires that their clients practice this. For indigenous populations, they follow the United Nations Declaration on the Rights of Indigenous Peoples:

> *Indigenous peoples shall not be forcibly removed from their lands or territories. No relocation shall take place without the free, prior, and informed consent [FPIC] of the indigenous peoples concerned and after agreement on just and fair compensation and, where possible, with the option of return.*

So what did the Chinese-dominated banks do to this powerful clause? They kept the acronym FPIC. They only changed the C from Consent to Consultation.[11] While the suffering of those displaced without consent doesn't compare to my woes, it feels as if my wife is warning me that from now on I am only allowed to join the family holidays if I won't bring my laptop, and dubbing this warning 'a consultation.' Luckily, we still use the 'consent' (instead of 'consultation') guidelines in our household, otherwise this book would have never seen the light of day!

Western international financial institutions have made important progress in strengthening safeguards for (in)voluntary resettlement, even though much can be improved, as the World Bank inspection panel shows. The incidence of 'aid accidents' is reduced. However, resettlement side effects might be on the rise again now that the Chinese rules of the game give less voice to those who have to be moved in the name of development. However, if the governments of countries where China invests have strong safeguards, the Chinese actors will tend to align their practices as they work with host governments' consent. To protect populations the most direct way might thus be to work with host governments to strengthen their safeguards.

We have just dealt with resettlement effects, relating to anticipated relocations of populations that are affected by development programmes. We now move to migratory side effects of development programmes. The academic literature increasingly pays attention to two opposing unintended effects concerning migration and finds strong evidence for both of them, depending on the situation.[12] The migratory effects that academics have reported are both push and pull effects. Let us start with the migratory push effect.

5.2 Migratory push effects: a heated debate

One school of thought postulates that aid programmes, especially economic empowerment programmes, can inadvertently stimulate outward migration. Economists argue that successful development programmes 'relax the budget constraint,' meaning people have more means to migrate. In Chapter 8 on behavioural unintended effects, I will write that aspirations to migrate increase once people get more schooling; but in this section, I will focus on the increased possibilities people have to migrate because of more financial means (the so-called 'hump effect').

The rather extreme migration story of a family friend in Kinshasa, Chantal, was a beautiful exemplification of the 'relaxation of the budget constraint' resulting from development programmes. Worldwide, there has been an absolute boom of micro-credit programmes financed by international agencies, also in the eastern DRC. The intended effect of these microcredit programmes is to stimulate local entrepreneurship, not to facilitate emigration, but this is what happened in the case of Chantal. She was a small-scale trader from Butembo in the eastern DRC, from the Nande ethnic group, well-known for their business acumen (and cheap potatoes). She was a trader in pota-toes and her business got a boost because of a microcredit loan. She decided to expand her business and start from Kinshasa, in dire need of potatoes in her view.

Alas, disaster struck: the plane she took from the eastern DRC to Kinshasa, with all her potatoes, crashed in a residential area in Goma just after take-off.[13] Dozens of people died, but she miraculously survived the plane crash. Unfortunately, all her potatoes were gone and she was broke. Since the airline, Hewa Bora, still owed her a plane ticket, she decided to move to Kinshasa regardless, this time without potatoes.

Once she had arrived in Kinshasa, she found herself a job at the microcredit agency from which she had borrowed money in the eastern part of the country. The wages in Kinshasa were much higher than in the east of the country, so she was excited about her move, and started sending money back to her extended family in Butembo when her income rose. Chantal's microcredit had enabled her to migrate. This was clearly an unintended but also a positive effect in the strict financial sense.

The story of Chantal hints at an important flaw of mainstream development pro-gramme evaluations. Her financial success would have remained unnoticed in a standard effect measurement of the Butembo microcredit programme. She would just be one of the beneficiaries that could not be traced. In contrast, her substantial finan-cial progress (and the money she is sending back to her family) can at least partially be attributed to the programme. Because of the tendency to evaluate 'against design' (what were the intended objectives), these types of issues are missed.

Academics have confirmed an increase in emigration and relocation of beneficiaries, and it has been well documented concerning 'cash transfers,' one of those other highly popular, newer forms of international development. The side effects of these cash transfers on prices will be discussed in Chapter 6 on price effects. But there are also unintended migra-tion effects to these cash transfers.[14]

International donors supported the new South African pension scheme in the late 1990s. The cash transfers aimed to reduce poverty amongst the elderly and it succeeded in that objective. However, it also had major migration effects on the prime-aged individ-uals living in those pensioners' households.[15] It significantly increased their propensity to migrate to other parts of the country and find jobs. In the meantime, the grandparents – often in the rural areas – would care for the grandchildren. Also in Mexico studies have shown that cash transfers can lead to an increase in migration, internal as well as inter-national (to the United States in the case of Mexico).[16]

5.3 Migratory pull effects: external intervention as a magnet for populations

An alternative hypothesis is that aid programmes and external interventions are a major pull factor and will attract people from wide and far. Sometimes this is through the employment opportunities that the programme offers. Do you remember the village, Sarima, in northern Kenya that had to be moved because of the road to the wind turbines in northern Kenya? Sarima, initially a village of around one thousand people, had nearly doubled in population during the peak of the construction works.[17] This influx in workers had all sorts of consequences, from linguistic (more Swahili and English), to cultural (more modern clothing and less beadwork for women), to social (an increase in divorce).

Large-scale building projects and the United Nations (UN) peacekeeping missions are prone to migratory pull effects. Take the example of Malakal, a military basis of the UN Mission in South Sudan (UNMISS) during the Sudanese Civil War (2013–2017). The intended objective of the military basis of the blue helmets was to provide a logistical hub for their soldiers, as well as a place to stay and from which patrols could be organized so that the South Sudanese could safely stay where they were living. However, many blue helmets had neither the equipment nor the political support to venture far away from their military bases to protect civilians. Subsequently, many South Sudanese simply thought, 'If the blue helmets won't come to us, we will come to them.' Initially unintentionally, hundreds of thousands of South Sudanese sought and found relative refuge in impromptu 'internally displaced people camps' (IDP Camps) next to these military bases. Sometimes these impromptu IDP camps even sprung up inside these bases after the IDPs entered the basis with force, such as in Malakal. The IDPs did not come to these bases for economic opportunities as was the case in Sarima, but because they

Figure 5.3 New road also creates new business in the village of Sarima, Kenya.

Source: Danwatch.

feared being killed. Some officials initially opposed these spontaneous camps as they might increase rates of displacement, but in the end, the UN supported these 'Protection of Civilians' sites as they offered better opportunities for survival. Even the reports and analyses that criticize UNMISS's failures highlight that many thousands of lives were saved via this ad hoc solution.[18] In the end, the unintended migratory pull effect saved the mission.

Humanitarian aid can also attract displaced populations and influence decisions of refugees and IDPs. I experienced that first-hand when visiting the virtually empty riverine border town of Dongo in the DRC that was ravaged by ethnic violence in 2011. We had to fly in a small humanitarian plane to the neighbouring country, the Republic of the Congo (RoC), to reach the town. After landing on the airstrip in the dense equatorial forest, we drove in a small bus for a couple of hours to the refugee camps established opposite the town of Dongo on the RoC side of the border. The refugees received their rations from the World Food Programme every week and were not hungry. The problem for the World Food Programme was that feeding the population in this remote location was expensive and the situation was now safe in Dongo, especially because peacekeepers were present. I was working for the organization Search for Common Ground. We had even mounted a radio station in Dongo, broadcasting messages to the other side of the border that the refugees could return. However, the refugees would not budge. Officially, that is.

In 2012, the UNHCR offered reintegration kits for those refugees who decided to return. I was in Dongo when the 'first' refugees came back with an official ceremony. They appeared happy when they received seeds and agricultural equipment, such as hoes, to 'restart' their lives. Official UN boats transported them and they were wearing orange life jackets. Traditional music and local dignitaries welcomed them. However, when I was looking across the river I saw quite some *pirogues* (local canoes dug out of tropical trees) shuttling back and forward. What was going on? After I talked to the local staff, it became clear that the 'refugees' had been commuting between their refugee camp (in the RoC) and their fish ponds and fields (in the DRC) all along. Suddenly, the entire ceremony felt fake, like a bad theatre play. The refugees had felt safe to come back for some time, almost daily; the food rations were keeping them officially across the border. The presence of the peacekeepers and the radio station were not enough to persuade them to come back. The movement back only started in earnest when the World Food Programme started to cut the rations it provided on the RoC side of the border.

Why hadn't I been reading about these informal cross-border movements in the official reports? I had been following the developments very closely! Why wasn't it made clear to us humanitarian workers that it wasn't so much because of the lack of safety in the DRC that people were not moving back, but largely because of the attraction of free food in the RoC? Once there is a narrative, donors and actors in the aid system are interested in keeping that narrative alive. Since so few people have a chance to see what is really going on, these narratives can be left unchecked: I only found this out because I was physically present there. Side effects can be turned a blind eye to, and success stories can be mediatized.[19] The remote monitoring trend accelerated by the coronavirus pandemic further exacerbates this effect.

External intervention can act as a pull factor, be it economic (Sarima), security (Malakal), or nutritional (Dongo). Academic research in countries as diverse as Malawi and Syria confirm this: people in need vote with their feet, and often the movement is towards the external intervention.[20]

5.3.1 Recap: migration and resettlement

If there is one thing that becomes clear from this chapter, it ought to be that migratory and resettlement effects are often part and parcel of international aid programmes. What strikes me is that migration effects are virtually always left out of evaluations. Of the almost 700 evaluation documents of the Operations and Evaluations Department of the Netherlands Ministry of Foreign Affairs between 2000 and 2020, only five documents paid attention to possible migration effects of aid programmes. Why are these effects so often overlooked?

When it comes to involuntary resettlement, large international players such as development banks have a stake in downplaying these unintended effects. It is already difficult enough for them to get all the financing and clearance needed to move forward with their mega projects. The more people officially recognized to be in need of resettlement, the more difficult it will become to get the project approved. No wonder that the Chinese-dominated banks have moved from 'free, prior, and informed consent' to 'free, prior, and informed... consultation.'

For the migration effects of aid (either inward or outward), a different mechanism is at play: it is just tough to measure it. In post-tests of development interventions (for instance, surveys administered to beneficiaries of aid programmes), researchers often note that they cannot find the same people as those that they had surveyed for the pretests. In technical terms, it is then noted that 'there has been quite a high level of attrition.' Subsequently, the findings are presented as the final and definitive results of a programme, excluding those who have left the programme.

But people who have 'left' the programme could often leave *because* of the said programme, thus greatly impacting the programme outcomes. Why does this matter? It matters because people that have left the programme area greatly influence the actual impact of the programme. Has their emigration been facilitated because of the programme? In that case, any additional income gains for them can also be credited to the programme. For instance, the cash transfers programme to low-income families in Mexico – which enabled their journeys to the United States – has clear positive multiplier effects, yet these are now overlooked. But the opposite can also be the case. An urban rehabilitation programme can lead to a higher measured income of the surveyed people in the rehabilitated area, but if this rehabilitation programme also involves the involuntary resettlement of slum dwellers from that area, who are not included in the final impact analysis, results will be grossly overestimated.[21] We often pretend that we know the impact of aid, but migratory effects all too often fall through the cracks of evaluation mechanisms.

How to tackle migration and resettlement effects

Policymakers

• Ensure strong and independent complaints mechanism for resettlement.

- **Stimulate a level playing field in safeguards (towards the highest common denominator):** with the entry of new actors in the international development scene (especially Chinese-dominated banks), it is important to check if they have high safeguards concerning unintended effects of their operation, for example, concerning forced resettlement. The most direct route is to strengthen the laws and policies of the recipient government in this regard.

Practitioners

- **Develop local independent research hubs.** Don't exclusively rely on remote monitoring, but always try to have people on the ground without a stake in the development intervention to understand what is actually going on.
- **Use a broad concept of well-being.** When analysing the well-being of affected populations, do not only look at quantitative socio-economic indicators, but also at qualitative changes in well-being (e.g. loss of cultural heritage).

Evaluators

- **Include migrants (both incoming and outgoing) in both pretest and post-test.** To detect unintended migration effects, post-tests need to be modified as to include those who have left the intervention area and the new arrivals as well.
- **Organize longitudinal studies.** These are needed to determine if – amongst others – the resettled populations have been successful in securing durable livelihoods.

Notes

1 J. Allister McGregor and Nicky Pouw, 'Towards an economics of well-being,' *Cambridge Journal of Economics* 41, no. 4 (2017): 1123–1142, https://doi.org/10.1093/cje/bew044.

2 Danwatch. 'A village in the way of progress.' 2016. https://old.danwatch.dk/undersogelseskapi tel/a-village-in-the-way-of-progress/

3 Agnieszka H. Kazimierczuk, *Tracing inclusivity: Contribution of the Dutch Private Sector to Inclusive Development in Kenya. Case Study of Unilever Tea Kenya Ltd., the Flower Sector and Lake Turkana Wind Power project* (Leiden: Leiden University, 2020), https://hdl.handle.net/ 1887/137215. Financial considerations play a role as well in these aid-induced resettlements: from a human (instead of financial) perspective, relocating the road instead of the village seems like the most ethical decision.

4 Brooke Mcdonald, Michael Webber, and Duan Yuefang, 'Involuntary resettlement as an opportunity for development: The case of urban resettlers of the Three Gorges Project, China,' *Journal of Refugee Studies* 21, no. 1 (2008): 82–102, https://doi.org/10.1093/jrs/fem052.; Juliette Garside and Jason Burke, '"It's all gone": community bulldozed at site of Isabel dos Santos "masterplan",' *The Guardian*, 20 January 2020, www.theguardian.com/world/2020/jan/20/fish ing-community-bulldozed-isabel-dos-santos-masterplan-luanda-leaks-angola.

5 World Commission on Dams, *Dams and Development: A New Framework for Decision-Making* (London: Earthscan, 2000), www.iied.org/9126iied.

6 Bogumil Terminski, *Development-Induced Displacement and Resettlement: Theoretical Frameworks and Current Challenges* (Stuttgart: Ibidem Press, 2015).

7 Kelebogile Zvobgo and Benjamin A. T. Graham, 'The World Bank as an enforcer of human rights,' *Journal of Human Rights* 19, no. 4 (2020): 425–448, https://doi.org/10.1080/14754 835.2020.1786358.

8 Ibid.
9 Alex Dreher, Andreas Fuchs, Bradley Parks, Austin Strange, and Michael J. Tierney, *Banking on Beijing: The Aims and Impacts of China's Overseas Development Program* (Cambridge: Cambridge University Press, 2022).
10 Eugénia C. Heldt and Henning Schmidtke, 'Global democracy in decline? How rising authoritarianism limits democratic control over international institutions,' *Global Governance: A Review of Multilateralism and International Organizations* 25, no. 2 (2019): 231–254, https://doi.org/10.1163/19426720-02502005; Mengqi Shao, May Tan-Mullins, and Linjun Xie, 'Asian Infrastructure Investment Bank (AIIB)'s sustainable safeguard mechanism on energy projects,' *Energy Strategy Reviews* 38 (2021): 100711, https://doi.org/10.1016/j.esr.2021.100711
11 Kate Geary, *Do No Harm? Recommendations for the Review of the Asian Infrastructure Investment Bank's Environmental and Social Framework* (Washington, DC: Bank Information Centre Europe, 2019), www.re-course.org/wp-content/uploads/2019/12/Do-no-harm-Recommendationsfor-the-review-of-the-AIIBs-ESF.pdf
12 Samik Adhikari and Ugo Gentilini, *Should I Stay or Should I Go: Do Cash Transfers Affect Migration? Policy Research Working Paper 8525* (Washington, DC: World Bank, 2018), https://papers.ssrn.com/sol3/papers.cfm?abstract_id=3238368
13 She confided me that she (and many others) had carried too much 'luggage' and had paid the ground personnel some money under the table to turn a blind eye to it.
14 If an international funded programme actually aims to reduce (irregular) migration but risks contributing to an increase in (irregular) migration, it falls in the category of rebound effects. We turn to that in chapter 8 on behavioural responses.
15 Cally Ardington, Anne Case, and Victoria Hosegood, 'Labor supply responses to large social transfers: Longitudinal evidence from South Africa,' *American Economic Journal: Applied Economics* 1, no. 1 (2009): 22–48, https://doi.org/10.3386/w13442
16 Jeronimo Cortina, 'Subsidizing migration? Mexican agricultural policies and migration to the United States,' *Policy Studies Journal* 42, no. 1 (2014): 101–121, https://doi.org/10.1111/psj.12044
17 Kazimierczuk, *Tracing inclusivity.*
18 Ralph Sundberg, 'UN Peacekeeping and Forced Displacement in South Sudan,' *International Peacekeeping* 27, no. 2 (2020): 210–237, https://doi.org/10.1080/13533312.2019.1676642
19 For example, UNHCR, 'UNHCR completes challenging repatriation of almost 120,000 Congolese refugees,' 5 August 2014, www.ecoi.net/en/document/1123955.html
20 Mauro Lanati, Marco Sanfilippo, and Filippo Santi, *Aid and Internal Migration in Malawi: Robert Schuman Centre for Advanced Studies Research Paper No. RSCAS 2021/18* (Florence: RSCAS, 2021), http://dx.doi.org/10.2139/ssrn.3804731; Shaza Loutfi, *The Impact of Humanitarian Aid on Internally Displaced Persons' Movement: A Case Study in Syria*, master's thesis (Chicago, IL: University of Illinois Chicago, 2017), https://indigo.uic.edu/articles/thesis/The_Impact_of_Humanitarian_Aid_on_Internally_Displaced_Persons_Movement_A_Case_Study_in_Syria/10846949
21 Cortina, 'Subsidizing Migration?'

Further reading

Adhikari, Samik, and Ugo Gentilini. *Should I Stay or Should I Go: Do Cash Transfers Affect Migration? Policy Research Working Paper 8525*. Washington, DC: World Bank, 2018. https://papers.ssrn.com/sol3/papers.cfm?abstract_id=3238368
Alex Dreher, Andreas Fuchs, Bradley Parks, Austin Strange, and Michael J. Tierney. *Banking on Beijing: The Aims and Impacts of China's Overseas Development Program*. Cambridge: Cambridge University Press, 2022.

Ardington, Cally, Anne Case, and Victoria Hosegood. 'Labor supply responses to large social transfers: Longitudinal evidence from South Africa.' *American Economic Journal: Applied Economics* 1, no. 1 (2009): 22–48. https://doi.org/10.3386/w13442

Cortina, Jeronimo. 'Subsidizing migration? Mexican agricultural policies and migration to the United States.' *Policy Studies Journal* 42, no. 1 (2014): 101–121. https://doi.org/10.1111/psj.12044

Danwatch. 'A village in the way of progress.' 2016. https://old.danwatch.dk/undersogelseskapitel/a-village-in-the-way-of-progress/

Garside, Juliette, and Jason Burke. ' "It's all gone": Community bulldozed at site of Isabel dos Santos "masterplan."' *The Guardian*, 20 January 2020. www.theguardian.com/world/2020/jan/20/fishing-community-bulldozed-isabel-dos-santos-masterplan-luanda-leaks-angola

Geary, Kate. *Do No Harm? Recommendations for the Review of the Asian Infrastructure Investment Bank's Environmental and Social Framework.* Washington, DC: Bank Information Centre Europe, 2019. www.re-course.org/wp-content/uploads/2019/12/Do-no-harm-Recommendationsfor-the-review-of-the-AIIBs-ESF.pdf

Heldt, Eugénia C., and Henning Schmidtke. 'Global democracy in decline? How rising authoritarianism limits democratic control over international institutions.' *Global Governance: A Review of Multilateralism and International Organizations* 25, no. 2 (2019): 231–254. https://doi.org/10.1163/19426720-02502005

Kazimierczuk, Agnieszka H. *Tracing Inclusivity: Contribution of the Dutch Private Sector to Inclusive Development in Kenya. Case Study of Unilever Tea Kenya Ltd., the Flower Sector and Lake Turkana Wind Power Project.* Leiden: Leiden University, 2020. https://hdl.handle.net/1887/137215

Lanati, Mauro, Marco Sanfilippo, and Filippo Santi. *Aid and Internal Migration in Malawi: Robert Schuman Centre for Advanced Studies Research Paper No. RSCAS 2021/18.* Florence: RSCAS, 2021. http://dx.doi.org/10.2139/ssrn.3804731

Loutfi, Shaza. *The Impact of Humanitarian Aid on Internally Displaced Persons' Movement: A Case Study in Syria.* Master's thesis. Chicago, IL: University of Illinois Chicago, 2017. https://indigo.uic.edu/articles/thesis/The_Impact_of_Humanitarian_Aid_on_Internally_Displaced_Persons_Movement_A_Case_Study_in_Syria/10846949

Mcdonald, Brooke, Michael Webber, and Duan Yuefang. 'Involuntary resettlement as an opportunity for development: The case of urban resettlers of the Three Gorges Project, China.' *Journal of Refugee Studies* 21, no. 1 (2008): 82–102. https://doi.org/10.1093/jrs/fem052

McGregor, J. Allister, and Nicky Pouw. 'Towards an economics of well-being.' *Cambridge Journal of Economics* 41, no. 4 (2017): 1123–1142. https://doi.org/10.1093/cje/bew044

Mengqi Shao, May Tan-Mullins, and Linjun Xie. 'Asian Infrastructure Investment Bank (AIIB)'s sustainable safeguard mechanism on energy projects.' *Energy Strategy Reviews* 38 (2021): 100711. https://doi.org/10.1016/j.esr.2021.100711

Sundberg, Ralph. 'UN Peacekeeping and Forced Displacement in South Sudan.' *International Peacekeeping* 27, no. 2 (2020): 210–237. https://doi.org/10.1080/13533312.2019.1676642

Terminski, Bogumil. *Development-Induced Displacement and Resettlement: Theoretical Frameworks and Current Challenges.* Stuttgart: Ibidem Press, 2015.

UNHCR. 'UNHCR completes challenging repatriation of almost 120,000 Congolese refugees.' 5 August 2014. www.ecoi.net/en/document/1123955.html

World Commission on Dams. *Dams and Development: A New Framework for Decision-Making.* London: Earthscan, 2000. www.iied.org/9126iied

Zvobgo, Kelebogile, and Benjamin A. T. Graham. 'The World Bank as an enforcer of human rights.' *Journal of Human Rights* 19, no. 4 (2020): 425–448. https://doi.org/10.1080/14754835.2020.1786358

6 Price effects

When aid drives prices up (or down)

Unintended price effects occur when an external intervention distorts prices in recipient or adjacent villages, communities, cities, or regions, or affects the exchange rates of local currencies.

What flavours do we see?

1 **Downward price effects.** An influx of externally provided and subsidized in-kind aid suppresses prices, undermining local producers and ultimately reducing local production capacities.
2 **Upward price effects.** An inflow of aid workers or externally provided cash aid contributes to (localized) inflation, pushing up the cost of living, especially for non-beneficiaries.
3 **The Dutch disease.** Aid inflows drive up the value of the local currency, rendering exports from the recipient country less competitive and reducing the long-term economic capacity of the recipient country to grow and develop economically.

In which instances have unintended price effects been observed? Three examples:

1 Downward price effects: food aid from outside depressed food prices, unintentionally creating a disincentive for local farmers in Zimbabwe to produce food, which can ultimately reduce local food production capacities as well as local resilience.
2 Upward price effects: cash transfers lead to a rise in food prices in the Philippines due to a large influx of cash into a community, ultimately exacerbating malnutrition amongst non-beneficiaries whose access to food is reduced.
3 The Dutch disease: Ghana was a 'donor darling' during the 1980s and 1990s, but the influx of aid led to exchange rate appreciation with various adverse consequences: (1) an increase in prices in the non-traded goods sector and higher inflation and (2) reduced access to credit because of a tighter monetary policy to offset the exchange rate appreciation and potentially reduced international competitiveness. However, other than Ghana, there are only a few convincing case studies of the Dutch disease.

DOI: 10.4324/9781003356851-6

This Chapter has been made available under a CC-BY-NC-ND license.

Key concepts from complexity thinking that help in understanding price and exchange rate effects:

1 **Alternative impact pathway.** The collection of second-hand clothing in the Global North to dispatch to people in the Global South also sets in motion an alternative impact pathway: it hurts the nascent apparel industry in various African markets.
2 **Interconnectivity.** There is an interconnectivity between beneficiaries and non-beneficiaries, as the example of the localized inflation induced by cash transfers indicates. This interconnectivity can offset gains achieved by the programme.

Figure 6.1 Price effects in action.

Source: Maarten Wolterink.

Driving through Goma, a major city in eastern Congo, a major unintended price effect struck me. It was not so much the number of white four-by-four land cruisers (I had gotten used to those), but more the houses where those cars were parked. They were large villas, actually–modern and spacious, dotted along the peaceful shores of Lake Kivu. Full disclosure: I also lived next to Lake Kivu, but on the other side in Bukavu.

Every time I went to Goma (I lived in the DRC from 2008 until 2013, and went back regularly to visit afterwards), I would visit my friend 'engineer Alain' (friends would call him *ingénieur*). The Congolese national electricity company had sent him to work in Goma. Every time I visited, he had moved house, and every time he moved, he went further from the lake. This was a shame for him, since the further you went from the lake, the worse the roads were, the less reliable the power supply and the trickier the security situation was. As we were chatting one evening, I asked him why he kept moving house. 'The rents are just crazy, partially because of all these expatriates,' he lamented. 'Local middle-class people can no longer afford to live near the lake anymore. We have to move to the outskirts of the city.' Rather wryly, he added: 'the United Nations peacekeeping mission was sent here to protect us, but partly because of them, we have to move out to the unsafe parts of the city. *Bizarre, n'est-ce pas?*

At first, I assumed that this effect was peculiar to Goma, where it is visible and well-documented.[1] But many cities where large groups of peacekeepers, aid agencies, and donors are based see urban reconfiguration. The arrival of international peacekeepers, aid workers, and diplomats brings more than just higher prices for houses, it also creates many demands and higher prices for services (guards, cooks, maids, etc.). This is good news for wages in the service sectors. It also creates a higher demand for

Figure 6.2 Nearly all plots next to Lake Kivu are now occupied by wealthy owners renting out international staff and local businessmen, leaving little access to the lake for the ordinary citizens of Goma.

Source: Miriam Berger.

particular goods, often luxury (e.g., cars, security equipment, and latte macchiato).[2] The arrival of the aid caravan has a host of price effects, on which this chapter focusses.

6.1 The downward price effect

6.1.1 How food aid programming successfully tackled unintended effects

A 2007 article in *The New York Times* spelled out the dilemma in stark terms:

> CARE, one of the world's biggest charities, is walking away from about USD 45 million a year in federal funding, saying American food aid is not only plagued with inefficiencies but may hurt some of the very poor people it aims to help.[3]

CARE had just decided to stop providing a certain type of food aid (known as 'monetized food aid,' which we will return to later) because of its unintended effects on local communities. At that time, other lesser-known NGOs were still more than willing to snap up the USD 45 million that CARE had declined. A decade later, this type of food aid, which United States (US) taxpayers used to spend more than a billion dollars a year on, finally went on the decline.

How can food aid for hungry people end up hurting 'some of the impoverished people it aims to help?' The main criticism came from the more activist NGOs such as Oxfam, which highlighted the 'price disincentive effect.' Oxfam described this in its report *Food Aid or Hidden Dumping?*, arguing that because of a sudden influx of US-grown staple crops, food prices had fallen and local producers had found themselves priced out of a livelihood.[4] They cited Malawi as an example: 'in 2002/2003 food aid donors over-reacted to a projected 600,000 metric ton food deficit in Malawi, causing a severe decline in cereal prices and hurting local producers.'[5] The main criticism was levelled against in-kind food aid, whereby donors send actual staple crops. In particular, they criticized monetized in-kind food aid (the type that CARE walked away from), whereby international NGOs must sell US-grown food on local markets as aid. Oxfam lashed out at NGOs still providing this kind of aid in a blog concluding with 'SHAME ON THEM.'[6]

Academics have also seriously criticized in-kind food aid, which all donors except for the US have discontinued. After 2005, studies noted disincentive effects in Zimbabwe[7] and Ethiopia.[8] In addition to disincentive effects, academics are almost unanimous in opposing in-kind food aid because of its inherent inefficiency: it often arrives too late, and it is very costly to ship huge quantities of food worldwide.[9]

The largest food aid agency in the world, the World Food Programme (WFP), has led the way in showing what getting serious about unintended effects means. In their case, it has meant overhauling their entire operation over the last decade. It used to receive a great deal of 'tied' in-kind food aid from countries such as Canada, meaning that it had to come from the donor country. Despite its obvious negative side effects, there has been strong pressure from donor countries such as Canada, to continue with in-kind food aid. Policy learning was severely bounded, as there were institutional pressures not to put lessons into practice. In-kind food aid had helped Canada to deal with domestic food surpluses, and the Canadian farmers' lobby was strong.[10] In effect, Canada's development aid budget paid for excess production by Canadian farmers.

After an advocacy coalition of NGOs (as the text by Oxfam showed) decried the old model, the WFP introduced a completely new business model in 2008. Instead of facilitating shipments of leftover food from the West, it set off to purchase food locally through introducing the Purchase for Progress programme. For this programme, the WFP united its donors around providing food aid through untied cash instead of tied in-kind contributions. One persuasive WFP executive director who argued for cash-based food aid was Josette Sheeran, who was crucial in advocating for local purchasing.[11] In addition, international norm-setting organizations, such as the Organisation for Economic Cooperation and Development and the World Trade Organization, did their best to cajole laggards such as Canada and the US into abandoning their tied practices and allowing organizations such as the WFP to purchase locally. The rise of local purchasing programmes has been phenomenal. It started in just a handful of countries in 2008, and by 2020 it had spread to 35 focusing on smallholders. The WFP now spends more than USD one billion yearly purchasing food from smallholders in developing countries. The school-feeding programmes have been particularly successful, especially when they have included requirements to buy food from local smallholders. This not only ensures that girls stay in school for longer and children are less hungry, but also that local food production capacity is strengthened. The example of the WFP shows that when an organization gets serious about unintended effects, it can transform negative effects into positive ones: purchasing locally is cheaper and faster, reduces adverse side effects, and creates positive spillover effects.[12] The testimony of Baylon Katsongo, a farmer in North Kivu, shows the positive impact on the lives of farmers when an aid agency starts to act on side effects.

Testimony by Baylon Katsongo: The big difference between Food Aid 1.0 and Food Aid 2.0

Figure 6.3 COOCENKI members now cultivating maize in the eastern DRC.

My name is Baylon Katsongo and I am a farmer in North Kivu, in the DRC, where I grow maize and manioc, but I also have sheep and goats. Next to my job I am also leading the union of cooperatives of farmers in North Kivu called COOCENKI.

About humanitarian aid 1.0

Food aid coming from the West used to be distributed in North Kivu free of charge, leading to all kinds of negative side effects for the population, but especially for us farmers. The people sometimes received food from abroad that didn't necessarily respond to their most pressing needs, but it was extra detrimental for us small-scale farmers. We were often displaced because of the insecurity, but when we returned, we couldn't sell our products anymore. I realized that the prices we got for our crops were too low because of the free food aid, as for us the costs of inputs were high and our yields were low. For us as a union of cooperatives, it was a hard time and our production figures remained low. There was no use for us to produce extra food and make a loss.

Dealing with side effects of aid

We then started a lobbying campaign in 2005 to ensure that the World Food Programme (WFP) would buy locally here in our province, instead of importing from abroad and dumping it on our market. You know, North Kivu is a very rich agricultural province, we grow everything: bananas, rice, manioc, beans, potatoes, and more! Initially, it was difficult to convince WFP since they are used to buying in very large quantities, but we convinced them in 2006. In 2007 we could start to sell to them. Now they are buying more and more foodstuff locally, such as maize and manioc. We can't sell our products easily yet, because it is still a competitive tender, and also farmers from Uganda and Rwanda can sell to them. And what I don't like is that we still have to sell to the WFP via private-sector intermediaries. I dream that in the future we can sell directly to WFP, with clear annual procurement targets.

Closing the loop locally: Food Aid 2.0

There is one new development that really excites me; it is called the 'school cantinas program.' In this programme school kids get a meal at school, and local farmers' associations produce this meal (often with beans and maize). I really like that these meals are not bought via intermediaries or enterprises but directly from the farmers' organizations, and COOCENKI is one of them. I see first-hand so many advantages: more schools can be reached because the food is cheaper, the kids get the food they really like and our farmers' organizations become stronger. So this is how we can get flourishing farmers, healthier kids, and stronger communities.

Although the WFP has turned the corner, various aid agencies continue to distribute a lot of Western-grown food around the globe. This is okay, as long as adequate pre-market scans are available and there is adequate monitoring of price effects. These market scans need to ensure that food aid does not lead to market disincentive effects. We now know that the likelihood of price disincentive effects is lower when the specific food crop type provided is not produced locally, and if it is targeted at poorer households and timed during the lean season.[13] The good news is that the US government now requires market assessments before food aid can be shipped. The bad news came with an audit of the United States Government Accountability Office, which concluded that these market assessments are not carried out properly and that even if the market scans indicate that food aid should be limited, this does not happen.[14] So even if an organization has taken on board the price disincentive effects of in-kind aid, this does not automatically mean that this side effect has been dealt with effectively.

> The prize disincentive effect does not only apply to food aid: other in-kind donations can have similar downward price effects, such as second-hand clothes donations. One of my tasks as a child was to bring the clothes that my brother, my parents, and I didn't use any more to the 'Humanitas' container in the village. On the container, I saw smiling children in Africa trying on new clothes, and I put the clothes in the container with a good feeling. What started as small-scale donations via churches and charities became a large-scale market in second-hand clothing. This cheap Western clothing was a boom for consumers in many low-income countries that had access to afford-able Western clothing, such as Zambia.[15] It also created some new jobs in the sorting and repair sector, which was beneficial for those countries that did not have an apparel industry to start with, such as Rwanda.[16] Yet, the warm glow I felt when donating the clothes might have been misguided.

While estimations vary, the decline of the apparel industry in many developing countries can partially be attributed to the huge influx of second-hand clothing to these markets. Used-clothing imports are found to hurt apparel production in Africa, explaining roughly 40 per cent of the decline in production and 50 per cent of the decline in employment in the sector over the period 1981–2000.[17] This can be seen in Ghana, where a study found that market liberalization in the 1980s had led to a sharp drop in textile and clothing jobs – from 25,000 people in 1977 to just 5,000 in 2000.[18] Of course, I am not attributing this uniquely to the efforts of charities in the Global North collecting second-hand clothes. While these charities have played a significant role in creating the second-hand clothing market, this market is now so big that they can no longer control the consequences. It has become a big business with large profit margins (and concomi-tant lobbying budgets).

Aware of the side effects of the second-hand clothes market, many low-income country governments have banned or are considering banning the import of second-hand clothes, including those donated by charities.[19] This is easier said than done, as the US – pushed by lobbying second-hand clothes exporters – threatens to cut off trade preferences for countries which increase tariffs on used clothing.[20] The garment industry will not grow automatically because of the import ban in these countries, since other industrial policies are needed for that.[21] Nevertheless, governments are getting serious about dealing with the potential downward price effects of the second-hand clothing market. This also explains why the picture of the smiling Africans on the second-hand clothes container has been removed in the village where I grew up: now the second-clothes are donated to homeless shelters in the Netherlands instead of shipped overseas.

Figure 6.4 A container to donate second-hand clothing for Africa.

Source: Wikimedia Commons.

6.2 The upward price effect: aid-induced gentrification

Price effects occur not only because of an influx of aid workers (as the example of Goma showed), but also because of an influx of aid funding. Let us look at one of the fastest-growing intervention methods of international development in recent years: cash transfers. The growth of cash transfers has been 'exponential,'[22] and seen as a silver bullet to eradicate poverty by the European Commission and other big parties.[23]

6.2.1 Cash transfers: the flip side of a success story

Cash transfers have transformed the face of anti-poverty programming in many low-income countries. It all started in Latin America in the 1990s, in countries such as Mexico and Brazil, and has by now reached hundreds of millions of people in low-income countries. Sometimes the cash transfers come with conditions attached (e.g. the children of the receiving household need to be sent to school or be vaccinated), but often they are unconditional. They have proven immensely successful in reducing poverty, not only in the current generation but also long-term. Girls whose parents received cash transfers twenty years ago have gone on to earn an average income 40 per cent higher than girls whose parents were not enrolled (after correcting for other factors).[24] In short, these cash transfers can have a truly transformational effect, often across generations. Well done!

As you can expect by now, I look not only at the effects on beneficiaries, but also on non-beneficiaries. A landmark study by Angelucci and De Giorgi, cited almost one thousand times (numbers I can only dream of), was the first to look at what they call 'indirect effects' (i.e. unintended effects of cash transfers on non-beneficiaries).[25] Their findings were positive: an increase of 100 pesos to recipient households leads to an increase in consumption of 11 pesos amongst non-recipient households. So how can we account for this increase in consumption amongst those who had nothing to do with the programme? Well, it turns out that non-participants received more gifts and loans from those receiving money from the programme. The programme reduced the 'price' of helping other people financially, so the entire community benefited. The good news does not stop here for the non-beneficiaries: there is also a multiplier effect (we focus more on that in Section 12.2 on catalytic spillover effects). This means that those who receive the money spend it on goods and services, and that those selling these goods and services will also buy additional goods and services, setting in motion a virtuous circle, at least in theory (in practice, this sometimes plays out differently, as we shall see). At any rate, to get a complete picture, Angelucci and De Giorgi propose that cash transfer programme results should be measured at the community level rather than the individual one.

The World Bank did not initially take this advice on board when it carried out an impact assessment of a cash transfer programme in the Philippines that it had helped to develop. After a couple of years of the intervention, the first positive results were starting to show up in the health of children whose parents were part of the programme. The children of participants saw an impressive 40 per cent reduction in stunting. In a somewhat self-congratulatory randomized control evaluation, the World Bank evaluators concluded that: 'the findings of the impact evaluation support administrative and other assessments that have found that Pantawid Pamilya is achieving most of its key objectives, with an additional four out of ten children following the standard lines.'[26] Worryingly, they stopped their assessment there and the programme was therefore marked down as an undisputed success.

But the reality was messier than this impact evaluation made it seem. Other World Bank researchers went back and followed the advice of Angelucci and De Giorgi, performing a more holistic analysis and including the effects on non-participants.[27] The results were shocking: children in non-participant families saw a 34 per cent increase in stunting! So the positive effects (the 40 per cent increase) for the participant group was almost completely offset by the non-participant group. How did that happen? Stunting increased the most in villages off the beaten track and where many residents were receiving the cash benefits. The price of food had risen significantly: eggs, for instance, had increased by 25 per cent! Other foodstuffs such as rice had also become so expensive that non-participants had been forced to consume less. Apparently, there hadn't been a supply response (e.g. more people raising chickens) or the supply response took a long time to materialize. This is a clear example of an unintended price effect that was not picked up by the initial impact evaluation due to its narrow research design.

What conclusion should we draw here? Should we stop these cash transfer programmes? The World Bank argues that this would be throwing out the baby with the bathwater. After all, cash transfers have been driving poverty down.[28] What does need to happen is that policymakers need to take a more systematic approach when they design a programme. Some World Bank staffers suggest extending cash transfers to all residents of the most remote villages where many people are already benefiting. Another option would be to complement cash transfer programmes with interventions boosting productive capabilities, to enable a more swift supply response to the increased local demand. This would prevent cash transfers from penalizing non-recipients so much and would be a good way to mitigate the unintended effects.

6.3 Hypochondriacs in the aid system: inflated fears of the Dutch disease (currency appreciation)

After one of my presentations at the World Bank of an earlier version of the typology of unintended effects, I received the feedback that I had omitted the macroeconomic effects of aid, especially the so-called Dutch disease effect. The World Bank official quipped: 'How could you not deal with this effect as a Dutch man? You know how important we find these effects.' He continued to make his point: 'As foreign aid inflows sometimes constitute more than 20 per cent of a country's GDP, this creates all types of distortions, for instance with respect to the exchange rate. We can't really take your typology seriously if you don't take this on board.' I was taken quite aback by this feedback; did I overlook a side effect that trumped all others? I decided to dig into this potential side effect.

To research this claim I took three steps: (1) to understand the theory behind it, (2) to find cross-country statistical evidence for it, and (3) to look for actual occurrences in countries.

Step 1: understand the diagnosis and the symptoms of the Dutch disease. The Dutch disease refers to a situation where, due to an influx of foreign capital (normally a good thing), the local currency appreciates so much that the export sector of the economy becomes less competitive. Currency appreciation thus reduces the long-term capacity for economic growth (a bad thing). This happened in the Netherlands in the 1970s following the discovery of the largest gas field in Europe, which ended up dooming the prospects of the Dutch agricultural sector and economic growth in the Netherlands for decades: the Dutch disease. According to the World Bank official who was lecturing me, this doesn't only apply to resource booms, but also to aid booms.

Step 2: cross-country statistical evidence. The most prominent study on aid-induced Dutch disease finds that a rise in foreign aid inflows reduces manufacturing in recipient countries.[29] Manufacturing exports often act as a motor for economic growth and development in lower middle-income countries, so any adverse effects on exports are worrisome from a growth perspective. Through statistical regressions covering dozens of countries, they found that aid inflows have systematic adverse effects on a country's competitiveness, as reflected in the lower relative growth rate of potentially export-oriented industries. They claim that this is why it is hard to find robust evidence that foreign aid fosters growth. In development economics, statistical cross-country regressions, such as those by Rajan and Subramanian, are often king.[30] In my view, we always need to complement these econometric studies with country-specific case studies to really dig into the mechanisms at play. Therefore, I moved to step 3: concrete country evidence.

Step 3, the proof of the pudding: concrete country evidence. With over one hundred low-income countries, there must be ample evidence: so many countries are aid-dependent, and this must be easily detectable. Luckily, quite a few individual country case studies look at aid-induced Dutch disease at the country level, but they have a tough

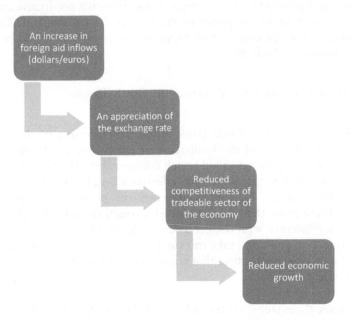

Figure 6.5 A simplified causal chain of aid-induced Dutch disease: this is how Dutch disease works, supposedly.

time demonstrating it, whether it is Bangladesh, Ethiopia, or Syria.[31] And the list goes on and on. Just no study finds it happening in practice recently. Strikingly, for Uganda, Morrissey finds that the aid shocks even contribute to a depreciation of the currency.[32] Of over one hundred countries, the only rigorous study after the 2000s that establishes aid-induced Dutch disease that I could find focusses on Ghana,[33] but even the case of Ghana is contested.[34]

Considering the evidence, Morrissey et al. conclude that 'generalizing statements according to which foreign aid systematically undermines recipient countries' competitiveness' is an exaggeration.[35] They conclude that aid-induced Dutch disease is becoming less problematic these days, as recipient countries have improved their performance of neutralizing foreign aid inflows by closing their money taps. In addition, aid flows as a percentage of income in recipient countries are falling (as countries grow more prosperous), further mitigating the problem.

Christopher Adam convinces me that there is hence little evidence that aid-induced Dutch disease effects are either large or widespread amongst low-income countries, at least against most plausible counterfactuals.[36] He wonders, like me: why does this narrative remain so pervasive then? He claims that those who have other problems with foreign aid (for instance, that it stimulates corruption) misuse Dutch disease label to address these other political-economy concerns. While my book is a plea to take unintended effects seriously, the hypochondria concerning the Dutch disease also shows that we shouldn't take (some of them) too seriously. In the introduction, I mentioned that not all unintended effects are downplayed, some are even exaggerated: the Dutch disease seems a case in point. Next time an official comes up to tell me that I have blind spot for the most important side effects, I will not be at a loss of words anymore.

How to tackle price effects and exchange rate effects

Policymakers

- **Improve targeting of in-kind contributions or reduce it altogether.** Unintended price depression effects of international interventions exist; however, aid agencies can avoid them. They can reduce those of in-kind food aid by smarter targeting or local purchasing. For in-kind food aid this means being more aware of the timing (sending food aid during the lean season), the amounts (not so much food aid that the market is distorted), and the type of food (not food that is produced at the local market).

Practitioners

- **Consider price effects when providing cash transfers.** Unintended price rise effects can also be dealt with. Smarter targeting of cash transfers implies that in more remote areas with small markets and a high number of participants, all households should receive a transfer to avoid non-participants being inadvertently punished. Alternatively, local production capacities should be boosted to support a supply response.
- **Do not simplify aid impact stories.** Do not communicate simplistic stories about in-kind aid from the Global North to the Global South. Whether it concerns second-hand clothes, second-hand tools, or other in-kind goods, there is a risk that they distort local markets and production capacity, and do not reach those most in need.

Evaluators

- **Measure impact beyond the direct target group.** Don't only analyse the effects of an intervention by just looking at the target group, but also to potentially affected non-target groups, both the positive multiplier effects and the negative inflation effects.
- **Measure the impact of aid workers and their cash.** Measure the effects of the programmatic intervention itself, but also look at what the arrival of aid workers and their cash and currency does to the system they enter.

Notes

1 Karen Büscher and Koen Vlassenroot, 'The humanitarian industry and urban change in Goma,' *Open Democracy*, 21 March 2013, www.opendemocracy.net/en/opensecurity/humanitarian-industry-and-urban-change-in-goma/
2 Michael Carnahan, William Durch, and Scott Gilmore, *Economic Impact of Peacekeeping* (New York: United Nations, Peacekeeping Best Practices Unit, 2006), www.stimson.org/wp-content/files/file-attachments/EIP_FINAL_Report_March2006doc_1.pdf
3 Celia W. Dugger, 'Charity finds that U.S. food aid for Africa hurts instead of helps,' *New York Times*, 14 August 2007, www.nytimes.com/2007/08/14/world/americas/14iht-food.4.7116855.html
4 Gawain Kripke, *Food Aid or Hidden Dumping? Separating Wheat from Chaff* (Oxford: Oxfam, 2005), https://policy-practice.oxfam.org/resources/food-aid-or-hidden-dumping-separating-wheat-from-chaff-114492/
5 Ibid., 2.

6 Eric Muñoz, 'Never mind the waste… here are the benefits of food aid monetization,' *Oxfam*, 30 November 2012, https://politicsofpoverty.oxfamamerica.org/never-mind-the-waste/

7 Trylee Nyasha Matongera, Shenelle Lottering, Romano Lottering, and Thomas Marambanyika, 'The relief food aid and its implications on food production and consumption patterns: A case study of communal farmers in Chigodora Community, Zimbabwe,' *Review of Social Sciences* 2, no. 3 (2017): 24–38, https://doi.org/10.18533/rss.v2i3.73

8 Getaw Tadesse and Gerald Shively, 'Food aid, food prices, and producer disincentives in Ethiopia,' *American Journal of Agricultural Economics* 91, no. 4 (2009): 942–955, https://doi.org/10.1111/j.1467-8276.2009.01324.x

9 Awudu Abdulai, Christopher B. Barrett, and John Hoddinott, 'Does food aid really have disincentive effects? New evidence from sub-Saharan Africa,' *World Development* 33, no. 10 (2005): 1689–1704, https://doi.org/10.1016/j.worlddev.2005.04.014

10 Ryan Cardwell and Pascal L. Ghazalian, 'The Effects of Untying International Food Assistance: The Case of Canada,' *American Journal of Agricultural Economics* 102, no. 4 (2020): 1056–1078, https://doi.org/10.1002/ajae.12084

11 She also did an excellent TED talk with over one million views: Josette Sheeran, 'Ending hunger now,' *TEDx Talks*, 29 July 2011, video, 19:10, /www.youtube.com/watch?v=CdxVbUja_pY

12 David Tschirley, Robert Myers, and Helder Zavale, *MSU/FSG Study of the Impact of WFP Local and Regional Food Aid Procurement on Markets, Households, and Food Value Chains. MSU International Development Working Paper No. 134* (East Lansing, MI: Michigan State University, 2014), www.canr.msu.edu/fsg/publications/idwp-documents/idwp134.pdf

13 Cynthia Donovan, Megan McGlinchy, John Staatz, and David Tschirley, *Emergency needs assessments and the impact of food aid on local markets. MSU International Development Working Paper No. 87* (East Lansing, MI: Michigan State University, 2006), www.canr.msu.edu/fsg/publications/idwp-documents/idwp87.pdf

14 U.S. Government Accountability Office, *International Food Assistance: Funding Development Projects through the Purchase, Shipment, and Sale of U.S. Commodities Is Inefficient and Can Cause Adverse Market Impacts* (Washington, DC, 2011), www.gao.gov/products/gao-11-636

15 Karen Tranberg Hansen, 'Helping or hindering? Controversies around the international secondhand clothing trade,' *Anthropology Today* 20, no. 4 (2004): 3–9, https://doi.org/10.1111/j.0268-540X.2004.00280.x

16 Steven Haggblade, 'The flip side of fashion: Used clothing exports to the third world,' *The Journal of Development Studies* 26, no. 3 (1990): 505–521, https://doi.org/10.1080/00220389008422167

17 Garth Frazer, 'Used-clothing donations and apparel production in Africa,' *The Economic Journal* 118, no. 532 (2008): 1764–1784, https://doi.org/10.1111/j.1468-0297.2008.02190.x

18 Rudolf Traub-Merz and Herbert Jauch, 'The African Textile and Clothing Industry: From Import Substitution to Export Orientation,' in *The Future of the Clothing Industry in Sub-Saharan Africa*, edited by Herbert Jauch and Rudolf Traub-Merz (Bonn: Friedrich-Ebert-Stiftung, 2006).

19 Esther Katende-Magezi, *The Impact of Second Hand Clothes and Shoes in East Africa* (Geneva: CUTS International 2017), http://repository.eac.int/handle/11671/1848

20 Emily Anne Wolff, 'The global politics of African industrial policy: The case of the used clothing ban in Kenya, Uganda and Rwanda,' *Review of International Political Economy* 28, no. 5 (2021): 1308–1331, https://doi.org/10.1080/09692290.2020.1751240

21 Linda Calabrese, Neil Balchin, and Maximiliano Mendez-Parra, 'The phase-out of secondhand clothing imports: what impact for Tanzania?,' *Overseas Development Institute*, 23 October 2017, https://odi.org/en/publications/the-phase-out-of-second-hand-clothing-imports-what-impact-for-tanzania/

22 European Parliament, *Cash for development? The use of microcredits and cash transfers as development tools* (Brussels, 2020), https://www.europarl.europa.eu/thinktank/en/document/EXPO_STU(2020)653624.

23 Council of the European Union, *Council Conclusions on Common Principles for Multi-Purpose Cash-Based Assistance to Respond to Humanitarian Needs* (Brussels: Council of the EU, 2015), https://data.consilium.europa.eu/doc/document/ST-10184-2015-INIT/en/pdf

24 Susan W. Parker and Tom Vogl, *Do Conditional Cash Transfers Improve Economic Outcomes in the Next Generation? Evidence from Mexico. Working Paper 24303* (Cambridge, MA: National Bureau of Economic Research, 2018), www.nber.org/papers/w24303

25 Manuela Angelucci and Giacomo De Giorgi, 'Indirect effects of an aid program: How do cash transfers affect ineligibles' consumption?,' *American Economic Review* 99, no. 1 (2009): 486–508, https://doi.org/10.1257/aer.99.1.486

26 World Bank, *Philippines Conditional Cash Transfer Program Impact Evaluation 2012* (Washington, DC, 2014), http://hdl.handle.net/10986/13244

27 Deon P. Filmer, Jed Friedman, Eeshani Kandpal, and Junko Onishi, *Cash Transfers, Food Prices, and Nutrition Impacts on Nonbeneficiary Children. World Bank Policy Research Working Paper 8377* (Washington, DC: World Bank, 2018), https://documents.worldbank.org/en/publication/documents-reports/documentdetail/989031522077749796/cash-transfers-food-prices-and-nutrition-impacts-on-nonbeneficiary-children

28 World Bank, 'In fighting poverty, cash transfer programmes should be wary of negative spillovers,' 27 December 2019, www.worldbank.org/en/news/feature/2019/12/27/cash-transfer-programs-should-be-wary-of-negative-spillovers

29 Raghuram G. Rajan and Arvind Subramanian, 'Aid, Dutch disease, and manufacturing growth,' *Journal of Development Economics* 94, no. 1 (2011): 106–118, https://doi.org/10.1016/j.jdeveco.2009.12.004

30 I performed quite a few of these myself. Actually, my most popular articles have made use of these regressions (please take note: if you want to get cited in development studies, use cross-country regressions). However, I have become increasingly wary of these regressions as stand-alone evidence tools.

31 Respectively for Bangladesh, Ethiopia, and Syria: Sakib Bin Amin and Muntasir Murshed, 'An empirical investigation of foreign aid and Dutch disease in Bangladesh,' *The Journal of Developing Areas* 52, no. 2 (2018): 169–182, http://dx.doi.org/10.1353/jda.2018.0029; Pedro M. G. Martins, 'Do large capital inflows hinder competitiveness? The Dutch disease in Ethiopia,' *Applied Economics* 45, no. 8 (2013): 1075–1088, https://doi.org/10.1080/00036846.2011.613794: 1075–1088.; Haitham Issa and Bazoumana Ouattara, 'Foreign aid flows and real exchange rate: Evidence from Syria,' *Journal of Economic Development* 33, no. 1 (2008): 133–146, http://dx.doi.org/10.35866/caujed.2008.33.1.007

32 Oliver Morrissey, Lionel Roger, and Lars Spreng, *Aid and Exchange Rates in Sub-Saharan Africa: No More Dutch Disease? CREDIT Research Paper No. 19/7* (Nottingham: University of Nottingham, 2019), www.nottingham.ac.uk/credit/documents/papers/2019/19-07.pdf

33 Derick Taylor Adu and Elisha Kwaku Denkyirah, 'Foreign aid-real exchange rate Nexus: Empirical evidence from Ghana,' *Cogent Economics & Finance* 6, no. 1 (2018): 1499184, https://doi.org/10.1080/23322039.2018.1499184

34 Peter Arhenful, 'The effect of foreign aid on real exchange rate in Ghana,' *Advances in Management and Applied Economics* 3, no. 5 (2013): 151, www.scienpress.com/Upload/AMAE%2fVol%203_5_11.pdf

35 Morrissey et al., *Aid and Exchange Rates.*

36 Christopher Adam, 'Dutch Disease and foreign aid,' in *The New Palgrave Dictionary of Economics*, online edition (London: Palgrave Macmillan, 2013), https://EconPapers.repec.org/RePEc:pal:dofeco:v:7:year:2013:doi:3909

Further reading

Abdulai, Awudu, Christopher B. Barrett, and John Hoddinott. 'Does food aid really have disincentive effects? New evidence from sub-Saharan Africa.' *World Development* 33, no. 10 (2005): 1689–1704. https://doi.org/10.1016/j.worlddev.2005.04.014

Adam, Christopher. 'Dutch Disease and foreign aid.' In *The New Palgrave Dictionary of Economics*. Online edition. London: Palgrave Macmillan, 2013. https://EconPapers.repec.org/RePEc:pal:dof eco:v:7:year:2013:doi:3909

Adu, Derick Taylor, and Elisha Kwaku Denkyirah. 'Foreign aid-real exchange rate Nexus: Empirical evidence from Ghana.' *Cogent Economics & Finance* 6, no. 1 (2018): 1499184. https://doi.org/10.1080/23322039.2018.1499184

Amin, Sakib Bin, and Muntasir Murshed. 'An empirical investigation of foreign aid and Dutch disease in Bangladesh.' *The Journal of Developing Areas* 52, no. 2 (2018): 169–182. http://dx.doi.org/10.1353/jda.2018.0029

Angelucci, Manuela, and Giacomo De Giorgi. 'Indirect effects of an aid program: How do cash transfers affect ineligibles' consumption?' *American Economic Review* 99, no. 1 (2009): 486–508. https://doi.org/10.1257/aer.99.1.486

Arhenful, Peter. 'The effect of foreign aid on real exchange rate in Ghana.' *Advances in Management and Applied Economics* 3, no. 5 (2013): 151–169. www.scienpress.com/Upload/AMAE%2fVol%203_5_11.pdf

Büscher, Karen, and Koen Vlassenroot. 'The Humanitarian Industry and Urban Change in Goma.' *Open Democracy*, 21 March 2013. www.opendemocracy.net/en/opensecurity/humanitarian-industry-and-urban-change-in-goma/

Calabrese, Linda, Neil Balchin, and Maximiliano Mendez-Parra. 'The phase-out of second-hand clothing imports: What impact for Tanzania?' *Overseas Development Institute*, 23 October 2017. https://odi.org/en/publications/the-phase-out-of-second-hand-clothing-imports-what-impact-for-tanzania/

Cardwell, Ryan, and Pascal L. Ghazalian. 'The effects of untying international food assistance: The case of Canada.' *American Journal of Agricultural Economics* 102, no. 4 (2020): 1056–1078. https://doi.org/10.1002/ajae.12084

Carnahan, Michael, William Durch, and Scott Gilmore. *Economic Impact of Peacekeeping.* New York, NY: United Nations, Peacekeeping Best Practices Unit, 2006. /www.stimson.org/wp-content/files/file-attachments/EIP_FINAL_Report_March2006doc_1.pdf

Council of the European Union. *Council Conclusions on Common Principles for Multi-Purpose Cash-Based Assistance to Respond to Humanitarian Needs.* Brussels: Council of the EU, 2015. https://data.consilium.europa.eu/doc/document/ST-10184-2015-INIT/en/pdf

Donovan, Cynthia, Megan McGlinchy, John Staatz, and David Tschirley. *Emergency Needs Assessments and the Impact of Food aid on Local Markets.* MSU International Development Working Paper No. 87. East Lansing, MI: Michigan State University, 2006. www.canr.msu.edu/fsg/publications/idwp-documents/idwp87.pdf

Dugger, Celia W. 'Charity finds that U.S. food aid for Africa hurts instead of helps.' *New York Times*, 14 August 2007, www.nytimes.com/2007/08/14/world/americas/14iht-food.4.7116855.html

European Parliament. *Cash for Development? The Use of Microcredits and Cash Transfers as Development Tools.* Brussels: European Parliament, 2020. www.europarl.europa.eu/thinktank/en/document/EXPO_STU(2020)653624

Filmer, Deon P., Jed Friedman, Eeshani Kandpal, and Junko Onishi. *Cash Transfers, Food Prices, and Nutrition Impacts on Nonbeneficiary Children.* World Bank Policy Research Working Paper 8377. Washington, DC: World Bank, 2018. https://documents.worldbank.org/en/publication/documents-reports/documentdetail/989031522077749796/cash-transfers-food-prices-and-nutrition-impacts-on-nonbeneficiary-children

Frazer, Garth. 'Used-clothing donations and apparel production in Africa.' *The Economic Journal* 118, no. 532 (2008): 1764–1784. https://doi.org/10.1111/j.1468-0297.2008.02190.x.

Haggblade, Steven. 'The flip side of fashion: Used clothing exports to the third world.' *The Journal of Development Studies* 26, no. 3 (1990): 505–521. https://doi.org/10.1080/00220389008422167

Hansen, Karen Tranberg. 'Helping or hindering? Controversies around the international second-hand clothing trade.' *Anthropology Today* 20, no. 4 (2004): 3–9. https://doi.org/10.1111/j.0268-540X.2004.00280.x

Issa, Haitham, and Bazoumana Ouattara. 'Foreign aid flows and real exchange rate: Evidence from Syria.' *Journal of Economic Development* 33, no. 1 (2008): 133–146. http://dx.doi.org/10.35866/caujed.2008.33.1.007

Katende-Magezi, Esther. *The Impact of Second Hand Clothes and Shoes in East Africa.* Geneva: CUTS International 2017. http://repository.eac.int/handle/11671/1848

Kripke, Gawain. *Food Aid or Hidden Dumping? Separating Wheat from Chaff.* Oxford: Oxfam, 2005. https://policy-practice.oxfam.org/resources/food-aid-or-hidden-dumping-separating-wheat-from-chaff-114492/

Martins, Pedro M. G. 'Do large capital inflows hinder competitiveness? The Dutch disease in Ethiopia.' *Applied Economics* 45, no. 8 (2013): 1075–1088. https://doi.org/10.1080/00036846.2011.613794

Matongera, Trylee Nyasha, Shenelle Lottering, Romano Lottering, and Thomas Marambanyika. 'The relief food aid and its implications on food production and consumption patterns: A case study of communal farmers in Chigodora Community, Zimbabwe.' *Review of Social Sciences* 2, no. 3 (2017): 24–38. https://doi.org/10.18533/rss.v2i3.73

Morrissey, Oliver, Lionel Roger, and Lars Spreng. *Aid and Exchange Rates in Sub-Saharan Africa: No More Dutch Disease? CREDIT Research Paper No. 19/7.* Nottingham: University of Nottingham, 2019. www.nottingham.ac.uk/credit/documents/papers/2019/19-07.pdf

Muñoz, Eric. 'Never mind the waste… here are the benefits of food aid monetization.' *Oxfam*, 30 November 2012. https://politicsofpoverty.oxfamamerica.org/never-mind-the-waste/

Traub-Merz, Rudolf, and Herbert Jauch. 'The African textile and clothing industry: From import substitution to export orientation.' In *The Future of the Clothing Industry in Sub-Saharan Africa*, edited by Herbert Jauch and Rudolf Traub-Merz. Bonn: Friedrich-Ebert-Stiftung, 2006.

Parker, Susan W., and Tom Vogl. *Do Conditional Cash Transfers Improve Economic Outcomes in the next generation? Evidence from Mexico. Working Paper 24303.* Cambridge, MA: National Bureau of Economic Research, 2018. www.nber.org/papers/w24303

Rajan, Raghuram G., and Arvind Subramanian. 'Aid, Dutch disease, and manufacturing growth.' *Journal of Development Economics* 94, no. 1 (2011): 106–118. https://doi.org/10.1016/j.jdeveco.2009.12.004

Sheeran, Josette. 'Ending hunger now.' *TEDx Talks*, 29 July 2011. Video, 19:10. www.youtube.com/watch?v=CdxVbUja_pY

Tadesse, Getaw, and Gerald Shively. 'Food aid, food prices, and producer disincentives in Ethiopia.' *American Journal of Agricultural Economics* 91, no. 4 (2009): 942–955. https://doi.org/10.1111/j.1467-8276.2009.01324.x

Tschirley, David, Robert Myers, and Helder Zavale. *MSU/FSG Study of the Impact of WFP Local and Regional Food Aid Procurement on Markets, Households, and Food Value Chains. MSU International Development Working Paper No. 134.* East Lansing, MI: Michigan State University, 2014. www.canr.msu.edu/fsg/publications/idwp-documents/idwp134.pdf

World Bank. 'In fighting poverty, cash transfer programmes should be wary of negative spillovers.' 27 December 2019. www.worldbank.org/en/news/feature/2019/12/27/cash-transfer-programs-should-be-wary-of-negative-spillovers

World Bank. *Philippines Conditional Cash Transfer Program Impact Evaluation 2012.* Washington, DC, 2014. http://hdl.handle.net/10986/13244

U.S. Government Accountability Office. *International Food Assistance: Funding Development Projects through the Purchase, Shipment, and Sale of U.S. Commodities Is Inefficient and Can Cause Adverse Market Impacts*. Washington, DC, 2011. www.gao.gov/products/gao-11-636

Wolff, Emily Anne. 'The global politics of African industrial policy: The case of the used clothing ban in Kenya, Uganda and Rwanda.' *Review of International Political Economy* 28, no. 5 (2021): 1308–1331. https://doi.org/10.1080/09692290.2020.1751240

7 Marginalization effects

Can aid unintentionally increase inequality?

Unintended marginalization effects occur when an external intervention contributes to an increase in inequality by weakening or leaving behind already vulnerable groups, in either a relative or an absolute sense.

What flavours do we see?

1 **Elite capture effects.** An external intervention increases the divide between the relatively well-off and the impoverished because the upper class siphons off the aid.
2 **Regressive targeting effects.** The external intervention is provided in such a way that certain barriers make it more difficult for the already marginalized to benefit from the aid.
3 **Charitable consumerism effects.** The external intervention is driven more by the individual needs of the donor than the needs of the beneficiaries, and the resulting intervention weakens the intended beneficiary.

In which instances have unintended marginalization effects been observed? Three examples:

1 Elite capture effects: the leaders of the ethnic group in power benefit directly from the aid either directly by redirecting a part of the aid to offshore tax havens, or indirectly by channelling their aid to their (ethnic) constituents as happened in Sierra Leone.
2 Regressive targeting effects: the fair trade movement has been focussing more on volumes of sales, leading to work on plantations instead of with smallholders, and with little attention for the landless workers on smallholder plots. This can tilt the power in certain exporting areas towards the relatively well off.
3 Charitable consumerism effects: Western youngsters are going on a holiday in a low-income country, but also decide to volunteer at an 'orphanage' during their stay, but are creating a new sense of dependency.

Key concepts from complexity thinking that help in understanding marginalization effects:

1 **Interconnectivity.** There is an interconnectivity between the beneficiaries/ participants of the aid and fair trade system and those who aren't part of this

DOI: 10.4324/9781003356851-7

This Chapter has been made available under a CC-BY-NC-ND license.

system. For instance, while the fair trade intervention focusses on strengthening the small holders (and they often succeed in that), this intervention can also affect these landless peasants negatively. It is hence important to employ a systems-based approach, instead of just an actor-oriented approach.

2 **Alternative impact pathways.** While international volunteer activities are often aiming to reduce marginalization, they might end of doing the reverse because alternative impact pathways dominate. This was, for instance, visible in the orphanage tourism sector, where the activities created more dependence: the output ('rescuing' 'orphans') ended up undermining the outcome (a society where children are taken care of in the best way possible). Community members disliked the work volunteers were doing, but valued the money they injected in the community as tourists.

Figure 7.1 Marginalization effects in action.
Source: Maarten Wolterink.

Marginalization as a result of international development efforts can take many different shapes and forms. The spread of Western-based medical treatment in health programmes has been one of the promoters of a marginalization of (effective) traditional medicines.[1] The donor-funded promotion of language curricula (often colonial languages) has been one of the chief contributors to the marginalization of minority languages, which has especially hurt indigenous populations.[2] Some authors go as far as to say that entire local knowledge systems have been undermined by international development programmes, not unlike the marginalization of indigenous knowledge systems (epistemologies) under colonialism.[3] In the context of this 'epistemic' marginalization, I decided to focus on three rather material marginalization effects: regressive targeting, elite capture, and charitable consumerism effects. I wish I could objectively substantiate this choice, but I have to confess that my personal experiences have predominantly dictated it, as the following story on the fair trade movement illustrates.

7.1 Regressive targeting: how about the 'fair' in 'fair trade'?

I spent the first seventeen years of my life in the small agricultural village of Achterveld, in the centre of the Netherlands. My mother had a practice as an exercise therapist, and my father was the general physician of the village. It might seem that this background may not put me on the international development path that I have chosen, but my parents were early adopters of the fair trade movement. They started a Fair Trade shop in the parish of the village church in the 1980s, back when fair trade was still an outlandish phenomenon (forty years before Starbucks would sell about 8 million cups of fair trade cups of coffee per day!). The shop was open on Saturday morning. They would sell coffee, honey, and chocolate, and I have to admit of mediocre quality. As a kid I would hang around in the 'shop' and discuss with my parents, who claimed that 'trade' was much better than 'aid,' as this was a more dignifying solution for poverty, on the condition that this trade was fair.

The importance of 'fair trade' was spoon-fed to me and I have been a big supporter of it ever since. I even went on a summer camp when I was 17 with the 'Youth for Alternative Trade,' the Youth Wing of the Fair Trade movement in the Netherlands (yes, these camps existed in the Netherlands). When I was a special envoy for natural resources in the Netherlands two decades later, I gave a TED talk on the need for more fair trade gold.[4] Was I procrastinating my research on the side effects of fair trade, because I was unconsciously afraid that it might affect my deep-held belief that fair trade works? Of all the research I have done for this book, the research on the unintended effects of fair trade has been the most sobering to me.

The fair trade movement engages in the exporting countries with two key actors: smallholder farmers and their cooperatives (at least that is how it all started before Starbucks needed enough coffee for 8 million cups of coffee per day). Fair trade offers four types of advantages: capacity building, market interventions (e.g. longer contracts, better pre-financing), premium payments, and better labour standards. A systematic review of over a hundred studies and evaluations of impact certification initiatives such as fair trade found many positive effects.[5] For instance, the price the farmers received for their products was significantly higher. In addition, school attendance by smallholder producers increased significantly. So why do I start to talk about fair trade initiatives in the chapter on marginalization?

The main problem is that these idealized smallholders often don't produce your fair trade tea, coffee, or bananas.[6] Landless peasants and seasonal labourers are often working on these 'fair trade' plots for these smallholders. These landless peasants are poorer than the fair trade smallholders, but they fall outside the scope of fair trade regulations. This means that while the price that the smallholder farmers receive per unit increases and they can send their kids to school, the day labourers don't necessarily benefit. The daily workers are also regularly excluded from fair trade services, such as access to health care, since they are not members of the cooperative.[7]

Since these day labourers work on fair trade plots and are already marginalized, you might think that studies looking into the effects of fair trade look at those workers. Alas, this is only the case for less than one quarter of the studies.[8] The certification literature typically analyses the smallholders who supposedly only use family labour, although also these farmers often employ landless peasants. As we will often see throughout this book, many of the studies and evaluations in the development sector are donor-driven, also in the fair trade sector. They tend to invest relatively little in research, and if they do, they often employ a tunnel vision: they focus their research on those actors where they expect to find most impact. Programme evaluation watchdog 3ie criticized this myopic view of fair trade and their evaluations: 'many fair trade organizations ... establish a minimum price for producers but do not deal with the conditions of workers that the producers may employ.'[9]

Of the over 100 studies and evaluations that Schaefer et al. studied,[10] only eight looked systematically at the effects on the (day) wage earners on the fair trade plots. Five out of the eight studies found a significant and negative effect of fair trade certification on wages.[11] They found that if employers of these workers were selling fair trade-certified products, then workers usually had to accept inferior wages (30 per cent less) and working conditions.[12]

We need more research on why these workers on fair trade plots earn less: we just don't know! Hence, to ascertain that nobody is left behind, we need to find out who the excluded populations are from impact studies.[13] Excluded populations tend not to be missing at random: minorities, immigrant groups, or unhoused people are more often excluded. It is upon us to trace them and talk to them, to understand how (our) external interventions affect them, instead of just assuming that effects on them were the same as for others. Fair trade studies often refrain from doing so, and this is where it went wrong.

> My parents thought in the 1990s that they would gain more impact with their fair trade work if they would mainstream fair trade with the local supermarket and the local gift shop, since people would not have to go to the parish on Saturday morning if they wanted to buy fair trade. My parents talked to the owners of the two shops in the village and these shops started to sell fair trade products at their request. By the end of the 1990s, the Saturday-morning shop in the parish could close down: the mainstreaming mission was accomplished, in Achterveld at least.

Because of mainstreaming, fair trade currently also certifies mainstream producer firms that are global leaders in their sector.[14] That's why Renard, a long-time observer – and supporter – of fair trade argues that there is an increasing gap between the philosophy and the practice of fair trade.[15] In their quest to go to scale, more and more fair trade products are actually produced on plantations instead of on smallholder farms. Some authors say it is not the fair trade movement that succeeded in winning over the big brands, but the big brands that have successfully 'fairwashed' themselves. Large brands such as Nestlé can argue that they are engaged in 'fair trade' and have no clear minimum volume requirements, sometimes sourcing even less than 1 per cent of their products in this way.[16] Because of mainstreaming, organizations prefer to work with more formally prepared cooperative organizations as to be able to purchase bulk

Figure 7.2 There are clear advantages to fair trade (not talking only about the taste!), but are there trade-offs for the poorest when scaling?

Source: Wikimedia Commons.

produce of good quality, organizations that frequently employ large numbers of landless peasants.

Since its start in the 1950s with Arthur Lewis and Simon Kuznets, a big question in development economics has been whether a rise in inequality is a prerequisite for further growth.[17] The hypothesis is that local capital accumulation is needed in economies that need to take off so that local investments can materialize. In other words, isn't it smart for the fair trade movement to focus on the smallholders, instead of the landless peasants? Isn't it smart to stimulate plantations so that smallholders can learn from these efficient practices? Small might be beautiful, but also not scalable.

This discussion on (relative) marginalization as a consequence of development intervention is much broader than just fair trade. It is also a major dilemma in general private sector development (e.g. supporting micro-enterprises or larger firms) and financial sector development (e.g. financing micro-finance institutions or banks). The key question is how much (relative) marginalization we are willing to accept as a side effect of aid. This is a moral question, which I will not answer in this book.

To find a way out of this distributional dilemma when scaling, the following questions can guide actors. Can upscaling take place without marginalization? Is there a tipping point? Is it possible to move to scale and offset increasing levels of inequality? Does the scaling lead to mission drift, neglecting the ultimate objectives?

Let's look back at my parents and their fair trade shop in the parish with these guiding questions in hand. Should we turn back time and should they start selling badly tasting chocolate again that is produced by the poorest of the poor? The answer to the last guiding question ('has the scaling led to mission drift?') is positive. The original objective of fair trade was to change the market structure, which is not happening anymore. A rebalancing appears warranted: without withdrawing fair trade products from the local supermarket, re-opening a more radical shop in the parish appears warranted.

Actors often have difficulty learning if the lesson that needs to be learnt challenges deep-held beliefs (see Chapter 2). Well, I am no different from the other actors when it comes this obstacle to learning, as the time it took me to look objectively at the fair trade movement indicates. My learning was definitely bounded.

7.2 Elite capture effects: it's our turn to eat

In her compelling book *It's Our Turn to Eat*, Michaela Wrong describes how elite capture, also of aid, is a fact of life in Kenya.[18] Since the Kenyan case has been so well-researched over the last decades, let me use the case of Kenya to show how this works in practice. In the 1980s and 1990s, donors provided most of their aid to Kenya as programme aid. Programme aid has a broader scope than project aid and provides more flexibility to the implementer. A programme often consists of multiple projects. The donors had serious concerns about the governance situation in Kenya and the corruption it facilitated. To address this unintended effect, they decided to shift to project funding. With this type of funding it is more difficult for elites to take a slice of for themselves, as the intended outcomes (or lack thereof) are more readily observable.

But the project aid also wasn't immune to corruption. As it was no longer possible 'to eat' it, leaders started to redirect it subtly to its constituencies, as Briggs shows. Most project aid in Kenya was directed to those regions that shared the president's ethnicity (or were aligned with the president).[19] Even though health indicators were worse for the people of the Migori region, for example, they never had a Migori president to ensure that money would come their way. The leaders' constituencies were not in the poor region of Migori, but in the better-off regions such as the Rift Valley and Mount Kenya regions of the country, contributing to further marginalization of the peripheral regions such as Migori.

I love the quantitative research by Axel Dreher and his teams because they make measurable what others consider immeasurable. Now they have shown that this channelling of aid towards the preferred region of the president is not just happening in Kenya, but across the African continent. They composed a data set of the birthplaces of more than hundred African presidents and geo-tagged over thousand Chinese aid projects.[20] They found that Chinese projects were often redirected to the birthplace of African presidents. This was especially happening in countries with competitive elections and in the year before the presidents had to get re-elected. Dreher et al. call attention to a fancy school in the village of Yoni, in Sierra Leone, financed by Chinese development aid: 'Why would anyone want to build a wonderful school in the middle of nowhere?' He explains, 'Yoni is the home village of Sierra Leone's president, Ernest Bai Koroma.'[21]

The Chinese aid comes in very handy to generate extra support for the incumbent. It bolsters the ethnic group of the presidents, and leaves other ethnic groups at a disadvantage. Interestingly, this channelling of aid funding to birthplace regions could not be detected for World Bank funding; these projects and programmes are so regulated that this is not possible at this level. But then again, elite capture can occur at all levels, from the president to a village mayor and anywhere between.

Sometimes it takes effort to comprehend how elite capture works in practice. Luckily, the senior officials of the prime minister of Uganda behaved in 2012 so brazenly that it became clear. In accordance with a joke common in my development studies classes in the DRC: during an international conference in Italy, the Italian hosting minister invites the international guests to his enormous villa. The Italian minister is smoking a cigarette at his balcony and is talking to the Ugandan minister. The Italian minister points at the nice road, which is visible at some distance. The Italian minister asks the Ugandan if he can see the road, which the latter confirms. The Italian minister boasts: 'Do you know how I paid for this villa? I took 10 per cent.' The next year, the Uganda minister is hosting an international conference in Uganda, and invites the Italian minister to the small palace where he lives. Again, they smoke a cigarette on the balcony. The Ugandan minister asks: 'Do you see the road?' The Italian minister sees some shacks, but he can't see a road. The Ugandan minister asks: 'How do you think I paid for this small palace? I took 100 per cent.' This is exactly what the senior Ugandan officials did with EUR 4 million of Irish aid money in 2012. The money was destined for displaced people in northern Uganda through a Peace Recovery and Development Programme, and managed by a trust fund in the prime minister's office.[22] When after months of waiting not a single shilling of the funding arrived in Northern Uganda, donors woke up and started an investigation together with Ugandan investigators. They found out that the money had been sent to a dormant secret account from which all the money had been withdrawn (they clumsily did not send the money to one of the tax secrecy jurisdictions, where the money would have been irretrievable). The donors threatened to stop all aid, and the Ugandan government returned the disappeared money. They overplayed their hand: it could have remained off the radar if they had enriched themselves with 10 per cent like the Italian minister.

7.2.1 *Complicity of Western tax havens to hide aid money captured by elites*

It is easy to point fingers at the elite capture of aid in developing countries. Still, the story is only complete with the international financial accomplices that make this possible, such as banks and tax havens. The Economist journal had the scoop on why yet another chief economist left the World Bank in 2020: it was directly related to a paper on the elite capture of foreign aid.[23] Whereas the World Bank projects do not allow for a geographic redirection within the country (see above), unfortunately, local elites are quite apt at redirecting part of the World Bank funding to offshore tax jurisdictions. It was not some activist NGO that claims this, but a research paper by bank staffers themselves. The paper was held back by senior officials at the bank, which contributed to Chief Economist Goldberg leaving already after 15 months in office. What did the paper find exactly that made it so controversial?

Andersen et al. found that disbursement of World Bank aid (in a sample comprising the 22 most aid-dependent countries in the world) coincides with increases in the value of bank deposits in tax havens in the same quarter.[24] In short, the finding is that about 7.5 per cent of World Bank aid leaks back to tax havens. By contrast, there is no increase in deposits held in non-havens. While other interpretations are possible, these findings indicate elite capture. With the rich getting richer, the sense of relative deprivation of the rest of the population is increasing.

7.3 Charitable consumerism effects

7.3.1 #Stoporphanagetourism

'Urgent action needed to halt trafficking of children in world's orphanages–report' was the headline by *The Guardian*.[25] In one fell swoop, my mind was in Arusha, back in 2007. I was conducting research together with a colleague, near the adjacent touristic Serengeti Park. In the city, NGOs were herding together just like the wildebeest in the park. We organized several sessions with Dutch NGOs. During a break with instant coffee, we heard one participant ask the other: 'But how did you get your orphans?' Sometimes a casual question, at an unexpected moment, says more than dozens of questionnaires filled in a socially desirable way: this region is characterized by more 'demand' for 'orphans' than 'supply' – and that was a problem for the white helpers. There had to be an orphanage. Naturally, there had to be many orphans.

This is not only the case in touristy Serengeti: from the coasts of Thailand to the mountainous attractions of Nepal, the number of orphanages has grown enormously in recent decades, especially in areas with many holiday goers. Out of Nepal's 75 districts, the five tourist districts hold over 90 per cent of all the orphanages in Nepal.[26] The so-called 'voluntourism' – combining tourism with volunteering – is becoming an increasingly common way for young Western tourists to enjoy their holiday while having the feeling that they give something back to the country they visit. But is that feeling justified?

The Guardian confirmed the findings of a research on 'voluntourism' on which I had worked with colleagues.[27] This research showed that volunteer orphanages can actually lead to further marginalization of underprivileged children and their families. The study revealed several major problems. For example, it regularly happens that children from underprivileged families are taken away to live in orphanages. Moreover, the ever short-lived, varying contacts for children with volunteers can lead to attachment problems. In addition, there is a risk of child abuse since the background of volunteers is rarely checked. There is also an opportunity cost: support that could go to more family-oriented support for vulnerable children ends up with institutions that encourage separation.

A final criticism centres on the so-called 'white saviour syndrome' of international volunteering, as a privileged group from the West donating time and money to vulnerable groups in low- and middle-income countries risks reproducing neo-colonial and racist stereotypes. In short, voluntourism engenders a host of unintended marginalization effects, from the very immediate effects on children and their families to the problematic narratives it perpetuates.[28]

Groups of concerned individuals address the side effects of this orphanage tourism (as is the case for many of the side effects researched for this book). For instance, campaigns such as #StopOrphanageTourism of the Better Care Network have had an

Figure 7.3 A campaign by Norwegian students ridiculing the white saviour syndrome.

Source: iKind for SAIH.

effect. Our research shows that several commercial providers have stopped or adjusted their volunteering offers. There are also associations like Volunteer Correct, which have sound quality criteria for their member organizations and do not allow volunteer trips to orphanages. Has orphanage tourism completely disappeared, then? No: our research actually shows that there is a further 'informalization' of volunteer tourism going on. Small-scale development organizations, or private development initiatives (PDIs), account for a growing voluntourism market.[29] Many PDIs, especially Christian ones, continue to offer 'orphanage tourism' to young people, for example in Bulgaria and Ghana.

We tried to find out why this disempowering practice continues. One of the reasons we found in our surveys is that PDI members emphasize the enjoyment of their voluntary work as an important determining factor in deciding where (not) to spend their money. We refer to this as the fun factor. They explain that the degree of enjoyment largely depends on the extent to which interventions could yield results with a clearly visible and immediate effect on the population. This explains why so many PDIs build orphanages instead of setting up and sustaining regional family-based care programmes.[30]

7.3.2 *International child adoption*

My PhD student Shila de Vries researches whether international child adoption can also be seen as charitable consumerism, and whether it marginalizes 'first families.' Shila was herself adopted from Bangladesh, and her testimony (together with her fellow adoptee Monoara – see textbox) illustrates how international child adoption can indeed have disempowering effects, for both first families and adoptees themselves.

Testimonies by Shila de Vries and Monoara: uprooted from Bangladesh

Figure 7.4 Drawing made by the son of Monoara (Hamida) about reunifying his mother and grandmother.

It is November 1977. An airplane lands at Schiphol. On board are young children from Bangladesh, amongst them Shila and Monoara. Their new Dutch adoptive parents are waiting for them. Between 1975 and 1980, the same thing happened each month: a flight arrived from Bangladesh with around 10 children on board who were getting 'new' parents in the Netherlands. The beginning of a fairy-tale for all involved? Not quite, as the story of Shila and Monoara points out.

'My mom's last look is burnt into my brain'

As Monoara was relatively old (six years old in reality, but four on paper) when she came to the Netherlands, she still vividly remembers her life in Bangladesh. Smells, colours, sounds. She remembers being dropped off by her mom at the shelter and her mom crying incessantly. Years later, she still has the last desperate look of her mom burnt into her brain. 'My mom was illiterate. She signed a paper with her thumb. She had no idea that the papers said that she agreed to me being adopted. The papers also said that my dad had passed away, which wasn't true.' Monoara's mother thought that she dropped off her child for a few months to gain some strength – the family was struggling to make ends meet – and then return home. Little did she know that it would be 41 years later when she would see her daughter again. And they were even lucky to be reunited. To this date, Shila doesn't know anything about her family.

The interests of 'wish parents'

Both Shila and Monoara have always felt a gap in their lives. The lack of recognition of where they came from, of their 'roots,' made them feel lost at times. Shila, now doing her PhD on international adoption, explains that learning about the existence of malpractice and abuse in international adoption added another layer of hurt to this feeling.

> Sure, many adoptive parents didn't knowingly contribute to malpractices, but they could have known that things could go wrong. By not looking into the situation seriously, by not checking papers for example, you allow these things to happen. To some extent you place your own interest in having a child over the interest of the child itself.

International adoption can hence often be seen as a form of 'charitable consumerism' (see Section 7.3).

Child protection system

Are they against international adoption altogether? Shila: 'No, not necessarily. But I don't think it can be done in a way to prevent negative effects from occurring. The international adoption system doesn't work. And why should a child be saved by breaching one of their fundamental human rights, the right to identity?' To her, all efforts ('and money!') should be invested into strengthening child protection services in the country itself, 'just like we have in the Netherlands.' She also adds: 'The adoption culture is intertwined with development thinking. A nice aspect of development is solidarity, but nasty aspects are colonialist and racist thinking. If we recognize this, we can make the change.' This has become a focus of Shila's PhD research.

7.3.3 *White saviour advertisements*

The 'white saviour syndrome' is also observable in fundraising campaigns by large international NGOs. To counter this trend, an initiative by Norwegian students called Radi-Aid developed parodies of these dehumanizing advertisements. In a smooth campaign video, mimicking videos by Western celebrities who raise funds to 'save Africa,' they show Africans collecting their radiators to donate to Norwegians who are freezing to death. By turning the tables, they convinced many aid agencies in Norway to change their advertisement practices. MSF Norway has even publicly apologized for perpetuating racist stereotypes through its advertisements.[31] However, international NGOs still find it often hard to resist the 'easy money' that this generates, as the Save the Children Netherlands example showed.

While the international NGO Save the Children has publicly expressed solidarity with the #BlackLivesMatter campaign, their Dutch fundraising campaigns have continued reproducing racial stereotypes. The 'Fly in the Eye' award, which is an award for the most degrading humanitarian communication, nominated them – and that is a record – five consecutive times for it.[32] While there is a code of conduct in the Netherlands on respectful communication drafted by the aid sector association, they don't enforce it amongst their members. Instead of communication that empowers citizens and organizations in the

Figure 7.5 The campaign Radi-Aid turns the tables and asks Africans to donate radiators to Norway.

Source: iKind for SAIH.

Global South, these types of fundraising campaigns contribute to their marginalization and need to be stopped.

How to tackle marginalization effects

Policymakers

- **Develop intervention methods that reduce possibilities for elite capture.** This can be done by including local checks and balances, but also by financing more research into how the Global North facilitates corruption in the development sector, for instance, how aid money ends up in tax havens.
- **Design interventions keeping inequality in mind.** Interventions can exacerbate regional or other inequities or dampen them. External interventions have to deal with a local context that necessarily has some marginalized groups, and can never make everyone an equal beneficiary; the challenge is to make sure that non-beneficiaries are not further marginalized by an intervention, but can also indirectly benefit.

- **Strengthen (enforceability of) communication codes of conduct for aid industry associations.** Many associations of development organizations have a code of conduct that promotes respectful advertising. However, when members of these associations opt for disempowering advertisements, no sanction follows. Development agencies should stick to the commitments to communication and be held accountable if they don't.

Practitioners

- **Verify before supporting an intervention whether it is about 'charitable consumerism' or sustainable development.** This can be done by analysing if it empowers people in the country where the intervention is carried out. Wherever possible, push aid actors to reduce dependency.
- **Scale up responsibly.** When scaling up, ensure that this isn't to the detriment of the initial target group of the intervention.
- **Avoid white saviour narratives.** When communicating about development interventions, avoid messaging that perpetuates the white saviour narrative and other stereotypes: this disempowers and marginalizes local responses. Stimulate communication that empowers citizens and activists from the Global South.

Evaluators

- **Perform pre- and post-checks on 'no one left behind' in programmes.** Are there any elements of the programme that prevent access for the most marginalized?
- **Perform (direct and indirect) elite-capture checks of interventions.** Pay in these checks particular attention to ethnical favouritism, often a blind spot for external actors.
- **Ensure the most vulnerable are included in the research design.** When financing and analysing impact evaluations, verify if the least powerful are also included in the research design.

Notes

1 WHO Programme on Traditional Medicine, WHO *Traditional Medicine Strategy 2002–2005* (Geneva: World Health Organization, 2002), https://apps.who.int/iris/handle/10665/67163
2 Helen Pinnock and Gowri Vijayakumar, *Language and Education: The Missing Link* (London: Save the Children, 2009), www.savethechildren.org.uk/content/dam/global/reports/education-and-child-protection/Language%20Education%20the%20Missing%20Link.pdf
3 Laurent Umans, 'Intervention, facilitation and self-development: Strategies and practices in forestry cooperation in Bolivia,' *Development and Change* 43, no. 3 (2012): 773–795, https://doi.org/10.1111/j.1467-7660.2012.01774.x
4 Dirk-Jan Koch, 'The uneasy truth about gold,' *TEDx Talks*, 25 July 2016, video, 16:05, www.youtube.com/watch?v=EX8Tt6iY6CU
5 Carlos Oya, Florian Schaefer, and Dafni Skalidou, 'The effectiveness of agricultural certification in developing countries: A systematic review,' *World Development* 112 (2018): 282–312, https://doi.org/10.1016/j.worlddev.2018.08.001
6 Christopher Cramer, Deborah Johnston, Carlos Oya, and John Sender, 'Fairtrade cooperatives in Ethiopia and Uganda: Uncensored,' *Review of African Political Economy* 41, sup1 (2014): S115–S127, https://doi.org/10.1080/03056244.2014.976192
7 Ibid., S121.
8 Oya et al., 'Effectiveness of agricultural certification,' 292.

9 International Initiative for Impact Evaluation, 'Fair and square: Better market share, more benefits through Fairtrade,' *3ie Enduring Questions Brief* no. 13 (2010): 2, www.3ieimpact. org/evidence-hub/publications/impact-evaluation/fair-and-square-better-market-share-more-benefits

10 Oya et al., 'Effectiveness of agricultural certification.'

11 Ibid., 292.

12 Cramer et al. 'Fairtrade cooperatives,' S116.

13 Christopher Cramer, Deborah Johnston, Bernd Mueller, Carlos Oya, and John Sender, 'How to do (and how not to do) fieldwork on fair trade and rural poverty,' *Canadian Journal of Development Studies/Revue canadienne d'études du développement* 35, no. 1 (2014): 170–185, https://doi.org/10.1080/02255189.2014.873022

14 Examples are Afriflora Sher, a Dutch company operating in Ethiopia (the largest rose producer in the world) and Mouton Citrus, one of South Africa's leading Citrus and Rooibos producers.

15 Marie-Christine Renard, 'Quality certification, regulation and power in fair trade,' *Journal of Rural Studies* 21, no. 4 (2005): 419–431, https://doi.org/10.1016/j.jrurstud.2005.09.002

16 Daniel Jaffee, 'Weak coffee: Certification and co-optation in the fair trade movement,' *Social Problems* 59, no. 1 (2012): 94–116, https://doi.org/10.1525/sp.2012.59.1.94

17 Timothy Patrick Moran, 'Kuznet's Inverted U-Curve Hypothesis: The Rise, Demise, and Continued Relevance of a Socioeconomic Law,' *Sociological Forum* 20, no. 2 (2005): 209–244, www.jstor.org/stable/4540893

18 Michela Wrong, *It's Our Turn to Eat: The Story of a Kenyan Whistle-blower* (London: Fourth Estate, 2009).

19 Ryan C. Briggs, 'Aiding and abetting: Project aid and ethnic politics in Kenya,' *World Development* 64 (2014): 194–205, www.sciencedirect.com/science/article/abs/pii/S0305750X14001570

20 Axel Dreher, Andreas Fuchs, Roland Hodler, Bradley C. Parks, Paul A. Raschky, and Michael J. Tierney, 'African leaders and the geography of China's foreign assistance,' *Journal of Development Economics* 140 (2019): 44–71, https://doi.org/10.1016/j.jdeveco.2019.04.003

21 Ibid., 44.

22 Muriel Visser, Zoe Driscoll, Stephen Lister, and Dan Opio, *Evaluation of Irish Aid's Uganda Country Strategy Programme 2010–2014* (Oxford: Mokoro, 2015), www.irishaid.ie/media/irishaid/allwebsitemedia/30whatwedo/IA_UgandaCSP_FinalReport_Final_05-05-2015.pdf

23 The Economist, 'The World Bank loses another Chief Economist,' 13 February 2020, www.economist.com/finance-and-economics/2020/02/13/the-world-bank-loses-another-chief-economist

24 Jørgen Juel Andersen, Niels Johannesen, and Bob Rijkers, 'Elite capture of foreign aid: Evidence from offshore bank accounts,' *Journal of Political Economy* 130, no. 2 (2022): 388–425, https://doi.org/10.1086/717455https://doi.org/10.1086/717455

25 Nicola Kelly, 'Urgent action needed to halt trafficking of children in world's orphanages–report,' *The Guardian*, 14 December 2021, www.theguardian.com/global-development/2021/dec/14/urgent-action-needed-to-halt-trafficking-of-children-in-worlds-orphanages-report

26 Martin Punaks and Katie Feit, 'Orphanage voluntourism in Nepal and its links to the displacement and unnecessary institutionalisation of children,' *Institutionalised Children Explorations and Beyond* 1, no. 2 (2014): 179–192, https://doi.org/10.1177/2349301120140206

27 Sara Kinsbergen, Esther Konijn, Simon Kuijpers-Heezemans, Gabriëlle op 't Hoog, Dirk-Jan Koch, and Mieke Molthof, 'Informalisation of international volunteering: A new analytical framework explaining differential impacts of the 'orphanage tourism' debate in the Netherlands,' *Journal of International Development* 33, no. 8 (2021): 1304–1320, https://doi.org/10.1002/jid.3577

28 Simon Kuijpers-Heezemans, *Volunteer touRism: The Epitome of Global Citizenship?*, doctoral thesis (Nijmegen: Radboud University 2022), http://hdl.handle.net/2066/283621

29 Kinsbergen et al., 'Informalisation of international volunteering.'

30 An alternative impact pathway is actually dominating the value created by these volunteers in the eyes of the communities. This surprising finding was the result of the PhD thesis (of one of my co-authors) that focusses exclusively on this topic. Kuijpers-Heezemans finds in his PhD that local community members judge the volunteer work by the volunteers as predominantly negative (37 per cent more negatives than positives). Many community members (rightfully) think that the work done by those volunteers (like painting walls of schools) could be done by the community members themselves. However, the community members think that these volunteers create a lot of value by being a tourist: they inject cash in the economy, by hiring taxis, eating out, etc. (63 per cent more positives than negatives).
31 Leger Uten Grenser, 'Anti-racism: When you picture Doctors without Borders, what do you see?,' 6 December 2022, video, 3:54, www.youtube.com/watch?v=8DFemg94ufU
32 Expertise Centre Humanitarian Communication, 'Humanitarian Communication Awards 2021,' n.d., accessed on 1 February 2023, https://humanitairecommunicatie.nl/awards-2021/

Further reading

Andersen, Jørgen Juel, Niels Johannesen, and Bob Rijkers. 'Elite capture of foreign aid: Evidence from offshore bank accounts.' *Journal of Political Economy* 130, no. 2 (2022): 388–425. https://doi.org/10.1086/717455
Briggs, Ryan C. 'Aiding and abetting: Project aid and ethnic politics in Kenya.' *World Development* 64 (2014): 194–205. /www.sciencedirect.com/science/article/abs/pii/S0305750X14001570
Cramer, Christopher, Deborah Johnston, Bernd Mueller, Carlos Oya, and John Sender. 'How to do (and how not to do) fieldwork on fair trade and rural poverty.' *Canadian Journal of Development Studies/Revue canadienne d'études du développement* 35, no. 1 (2014): 170–185. https://doi.org/10.1080/02255189.2014.873022
Cramer, Christopher, Deborah Johnston, Carlos Oya, and John Sender. 'Fairtrade cooperatives in Ethiopia and Uganda: uncensored.' *Review of African Political Economy* 41, sup1 (2014): S115–S127. https://doi.org/10.1080/03056244.2014.976192
Dreher, Axel, Andreas Fuchs, Roland Hodler, Bradley C. Parks, Paul A. Raschky, and Michael J. Tierney. 'African leaders and the geography of China's foreign assistance.' *Journal of Development Economics* 140 (2019): 44–71. https://doi.org/10.1016/j.jdeveco.2019.04.003
Expertise Centre Humanitarian Communication. 'Humanitarian Communication Awards 2021.' n.d., accessed on 1 February 2023. https://humanitairecommunicatie.nl/awards-2021/
International Initiative for Impact Evaluation. 'Fair and square: Better market share, more benefits through Fairtrade.' *3ie Enduring Questions Brief* no. 13 (2010). www.3ieimpact.org/evidence-hub/publications/impact-evaluation/fair-and-square-better-market-share-more-benefits
Jaffee, Daniel. 'Weak coffee: Certification and co-optation in the fair trade movement.' *Social Problems* 59, no. 1 (2012): 94–116. https://doi.org/10.1525/sp.2012.59.1.94
Kelly, Nicola. 'Urgent action needed to halt trafficking of children in world's orphanages–report.' *The Guardian*, 14 December 2021. www.theguardian.com/global-development/2021/dec/14/urgent-action-needed-to-halt-trafficking-of-children-in-worlds-orphanages-report
Kinsbergen, Sara, Esther Konijn, Simon Kuijpers-Heezemans, Gabriëlle op 't Hoog, Dirk-Jan Koch, and Mieke Molthof. 'Informalisation of international volunteering: A new analytical framework explaining differential impacts of the 'orphanage tourism' debate in the Netherlands.' *Journal of International Development* 33, no. 8 (2021): 1304–1320. https://doi.org/10.1002/jid.3577
Koch, Dirk-Jan. 'The uneasy truth about gold.' *TEDx Talks*, 25 July 2016. Video, 16:05. www.youtube.com/watch?v=EX8Tt6iY6CU
Kuijpers-Heezemans, Simon. *Volunteer Tourism: The Epitome of Global Citizenship?* Doctoral thesis. Nijmegen: Radboud University 2022. http://hdl.handle.net/2066/283621
Leger Uten Grenser. 'Anti-racism: When you picture Doctors without Borders, what do you see?' 6 December 2022. Video, 3:54. www.youtube.com/watch?v=8DFemg94ufU

Moran, Timothy Patrick. 'Kuznet's inverted U-curve hypothesis: The rise, demise, and continued relevance of a socioeconomic law.' *Sociological Forum* 20, no. 2 (2005): 209–244. www.jstor. org/stable/4540893

Oya, Carlos, Florian Schaefer, and Dafni Skalidou. 'The effectiveness of agricultural certification in developing countries: A systematic review.' *World Development* 112 (2018): 282–312. https:// doi.org/10.1016/j.worlddev.2018.08.001

Pinnock, Helen, and Gowri Vijayakumar. *Language and Education: The Missing Link*. London: Save the Children, 2009. www.savethechildren.org.uk/content/dam/global/reports/education-and-child-protection/Language%20Education%20the%20Missing%20Link.pdf

Punaks, Martin, and Katie Feit. 'Orphanage voluntourism in Nepal and its links to the displacement and unnecessary institutionalisation of children.' *Institutionalised Children Explorations and Beyond* 1, no. 2 (2014): 179–192. https://doi.org/10.1177/2349301120140206

Renard, Marie-Christine. 'Quality certification, regulation and power in fair trade.' *Journal of Rural Studies* 21, no. 4 (2005): 419–431. https://doi.org/10.1016/j.jrurstud.2005.09.002

The Economist. 'The World Bank loses another Chief Economist.' 13 February 2020. www.econom ist.com/finance-and-economics/2020/02/13/the-world-bank-loses-another-chief-economist

Umans, Laurent. 'Intervention, facilitation and self-development: Strategies and practices in forestry cooperation in Bolivia.' *Development and Change* 43, no. 3 (2012): 773–795. https://doi. org/10.1111/j.1467-7660.2012.01774.x

Visser, Muriel, Zoe Driscoll, Stephen Lister, and Dan Opio. *Evaluation of Irish Aid's Uganda Country Strategy Programme 2010–2014*. Oxford: Mokoro, 2015. www.irishaid.ie/media/irish aid/allwebsitemedia/30whatwedo/IA_UgandaCSP_FinalReport_Final_05-05-2015.pdf

WHO Programme on Traditional Medicine. *WHO Traditional Medicine Strategy 2002–2005*. Geneva: World Health Organization, 2002. https://apps.who.int/iris/handle/10665/67163

Wrong, Michela. *It's Our Turn to Eat: The Story of a Kenyan Whistle-blower*. London: Fourth Estate, 2009.

8   Behavioural effects

Expect the unexpected!

Unintended behavioural effects occur when recipients or affected persons respond to an external intervention in unintended ways due to psychological factors that were insufficiently taken into consideration when the intervention was designed.

What flavours do we see?

1 **Rebound effects.** The improvement made possible by an external intervention increases (instead of reduces) the undesired behaviour because of an unintended and often unexpected behavioural response.[1]
2 **Backfire effects.** Social progress of members of a marginalized group due to an international intervention leads to a counterreaction by members of the dominant group. This backfire effect plays out at the micro-level (individual), whereas the backlash effect (Chapter 3) intervenes at the macro-level (society).
3 **Motivational crowding-out effects.** An external intervention incentivizes certain behaviours but actually undermines the intrinsic motivation for engaging in those behaviours.

Which themes have these unintended behavioural effects been noted for? Three examples:

1 Rebound effects: clean cooking stoves are a technological innovation that aims to reduce deforestation by decreasing the need for firewood. However, in Nepal it contributed to more deforestation, since the price of firewood decreased and households suffered from less indoor smoke pollution, pushing up consumption.
2 Backfire effects: financial empowerment programmes for women contributed in some instances to an increase in domestic violence in Bangladesh because husbands found their wives' social progress hard to swallow.
3 Motivational crowding-out effects: internationally supported payment for environmental services schemes, such as forest protection, which actually led to reduced willingness to continue providing those services once the payments come to an end in Mexico.

DOI: 10.4324/9781003356851-8

This Chapter has been made available under a CC-BY-NC-ND license.

Key concepts from complexity thinking that help in understanding backlash effects:

1 **Feedback loops**. For many behavioural effects, a feedback loop is only visible after the outputs lead to certain outcomes. Subsequently, feedback loop starts to occur which prevents these outcomes from being sustained over time. For instance, this happens with respect to the forest protection by means of payment for environmental services. The income received from the environmental services (output) leads to better protection of forests in the beginning (outcome). Still, these same outputs exercise a negative influence on the intrinsic motivation to protect the forest, leading to less protection after the financial incentive is removed.

2 **Alternative impact pathways**. Alternative impact pathways occur when certain outputs lead to different outcomes than envisaged. The example of the technical and vocational training programmes, which were supposed to reduce migration pressures, demonstrates this. The trained youngsters were much more interested in migrating after the training programme than before participating. The youngsters thought – probably correctly – that with their newly acquired skills they had more opportunities in the foreign labour market.

Figure 8.1 Behavioural effects in action.

Source: Maarten Wolterink.

This chapter on behavioural effects is far from exhaustive, as the effects on human behaviour are practically endless. For instance, there are behavioural responses concerning targeting. By introducing a certain cut-off point (of wealth or health) to be eligible for assistance, individuals are strongly incentivized to 'cheat' the system (adverse selection). This can entail certain innocent 'gaming' practices, such as hiding some wealth to comply with a targeting benchmark, which has also been documented in the Global North.[2] Yet one of my students, who went on a food aid monitoring mission in northern Nigeria, came back in shock. I invited her to share one of the unintended effects she had observed in her mission. Rather reluctantly, she shared that she had observed that some mothers deliberately malnourished one of their children as to receive food aid for the entire family. A rational behavioural response of the mother, but one that is hurtful and unacceptable. This type of behaviour says more about the aid agency than about the beneficiary.[3]

Another well-known behavioural effect is moral hazard. It differs from adverse selection as moral hazard contributes to behavioural changes only after a programme starts, while adverse selection leads to behavioural changes prior to a social programme (e.g. hiding wealth to get access to a social assistance programme). Claims about moral hazard have been made with respect to debt cancellation programmes: because 'recipient' governments know that their debts will be cancelled as part of an ongoing debt relief initiative, they will incur more of it.[4] Since we define behavioural responses as individual (and not institutional) responses, we will deal with moral hazard in the chapter on governance effects (Chapter 10).

In this chapter, I focus on three prevalent behavioural effects with respect to international development efforts: rebound, backfire, and motivational crowding-out effects.

8.1 The rebound effect: behavioural boomerangs

The Nepali government and the Danish Development Agency were perplexed. They introduced very efficient cook stoves in Nepal, to reduce deforestation. As we often see in this book, the agencies achieve their intended outputs: more and more families were adopting the improved cook stoves. Yet, something strange happened: household surveys showed that families with improved cooking stoves were cutting down more trees![5] This is the rebound effect in practice: people start demonstrating more – instead of less – of the undesired behaviour. In this case, the improved efficiency didn't reduce, but increased, firewood collection. How did that happen? We don't know exactly what happened in Nepal, but since improved cooking stoves have been introduced across the globe with development funding, we have some ways to explain this rebound.

Well, the new cooking stoves were cleaner and their usage was cheaper, so people were using the new stoves much more than the old ones. Let me explain: while the old stoves led to serious indoor air pollution, the new stoves are much cleaner, leading families to keep the cooking stove on all night. In addition, because the usage of the cooking stove requires less wood, it is much cheaper; they actually start to cook more meals, sometimes using multiple stoves.[6] Luckily, in most studies outside Nepal, the increased usage by some households didn't offset the overall reduction in wood consumption. This means that the rebound effect reduces the effectiveness of a programme, but doesn't make it useless. You can think about the introduction of LED lights: while many people leave lights on longer since it is cheaper, their energy efficiency is so much higher than the light bulb that there is still a positive effect, just not as much as intended.

I was interested to find out whether this rebound effect could also be encountered beyond the traditional innovation-resource use boomerang. Fortunately, one day

I received an email – and, when I did not reply fast enough, a phone call – from a group of international relations students at the University of Groningen who were very keen to carry out some research for the Ministry of Foreign Affairs. With the consent of the staff member responsible, I proposed that they should look into the unintended effects of the world's largest migration management programme: the European Union's Emergency Trust Fund for Africa (EUTF). They found the rebound effect in the migration management programme, so let's have a look at what they found.[7]

8.1.1 The EU's Emergency Trust Fund for Africa

I love working with students! One of the reasons is that they often conduct much more effective interviews than professional evaluators or researchers. Why might that be? Well, they are less threatening, so interviewees are more willing to share their true thoughts and feelings. Typically, civil servants are reluctant to talk about the unintended effects of their policies because of institutional pressures. In Chapter 2, I identified institutional barriers as one of the reasons why our policy learning is limited. Well, the students overcame these boundaries. When the students were planning their interviews with the staff at the EUTF (they interviewed about a dozen people), I got a call from one of the potential interviewees: 'how open should I be with your students?' I explained that it was our duty to provide the students with the most realistic picture possible. After all, 'they are the policymakers of tomorrow, and they need to understand the types of dilemmas that we need to grapple with.' When I read the interview transcripts, I was pleased to see that the interviewees had spoken plainly. [8]

Let us start with a short recap: the central goal of the EUTF is to address irregular migration from Africa to Europe. The EUTF takes a 'root causes approach,' with the central premise that irregular migration is a symptom of underdevelopment and that the EU can reduce this by focussing on development cooperation with countries of origin. Since its inception in 2015, the fund has committed nearly EUR 5 billion to projects in 26 countries across three regions: the Sahel and Lake Chad, the Horn of Africa, and the north of Africa. The EUTF has provided financial support for projects ranging from equipping and training the controversial Libyan coastguard to providing new livelihoods for erstwhile people smugglers in Niger, job creation programmes in Sudan, and many other projects.

The number of African migrants trying to reach Europe by crossing the Mediterranean has fallen sharply since the EU set up the EUTF, and, as the Fund proclaims proudly on its website, it has created over 55,000 jobs and helped 277,000 people to engage in income-generating activities. However, the number of African migrants who would like to migrate to Europe remains enormous and if we are being honest, the activities of the EUTF are a mere drop in the ocean. Remember that the population of Nigeria is 210 million (and set to double within just over twenty years). Some 48 per cent of adults of Nigeria say that they would emigrate from Nigeria if they had the chance.[9] And in reality, the biggest factors helping to reduce the number of migrants arriving from Africa recently have been the COVID pandemic and restrictions on search and rescue missions in the Mediterranean, factors completely beyond the control of the EUTF. There is a major evidence gap when it comes to linking the results achieved by the EUTF (the creation of thousands of jobs) and their actual impact on migration (the reduction in the number of migrants entering the EU). Correlation is not the same as causation, as many secondary school pupils will tell you, but some people are apparently ready to forget this basic rule when it is politically expedient to do so.

8.1.2 *Receiving job training makes people more determined to emigrate than ever*

How strong is the evidence that development actually reduces migration? There is a large body of literature on this question.[10] The assumption was that potential migrants would prefer to stay put because of improved economic perspectives, and current migration management programmes have been designed around this principle. However, a new school of thought shows a completely different behavioural response: the famous 'migration hump,' meaning that when people in lower income countries start to earn some money (enough to move to another country, sometimes including fees paid to human smugglers), migration actually tends to increase. I also allude to this theory when I discuss the unintended migratory push effects in Chapter 5. The migration hump hypothesis falls within our definition of a rebound effect: the external intervention leads to an increase – instead of a decrease – of the undesired practice (in this case migration) because of unintended individual-level behavioural responses.

Luckily, the EUTF also has its own independent 'Research and Evidence Facility' to test this 'migration hump' hypothesis. The EUTF Research and Evidence Facility has done detailed research involving the people who have benefited from EUTF interventions and how they feel about emigrating now. For instance, were those who had participated in the vocational and technical training programmes run by the EUTF less likely to emigrate? Data on a question like this could provide evidence to bridge the gap between results and impact.

The researchers interviewed people who had benefited from the training programme in Ethiopia and Uganda. The results were unmistakable: an impressive 80 per cent of trainees and graduates in Uganda *had* changed their opinion about emigrating,[11] but not in the way that the EUTF had been hoping. Of the 80 per cent who had changed their minds, only 10 per cent wanted to migrate less, while 70 per cent were now *more* interested in emigrating. The intervention had a totally different impact pathway than intended. The researchers concluded that this was probably because the graduates now felt better equipped to succeed in a new country. They had a certificate showing that they had skills and wanted to make use of these qualifications. Who could blame them for that?

Since the EUTF focusses on irregular migration, the evaluators also asked the trainees about this. Alas, a rebound effect seems likely. While less than one quarter of potential trainees accepted that people should move even without the right papers, nearly half of graduates agreed that people should seize any opportunity to move.[12]

The students and I did not seek to discredit vocational training programmes or job creation programmes in Africa. They have unmistakably improved many lives. The only thing I hope to achieve by drawing attention to these findings is to demonstrate that simplistic linear assumptions – such as 'foreign aid will reduce migration' – can create large blind spots. When the students published their critical findings, the ministry woke up. I received a call from some of the superiors of those who were interviewed: 'can you please tell whom your students interviewed exactly? We need to know!' While many civil servants have doubts about the success of these migration management programmes, such qualms are supposed to remain internal. Because of the students' innocence, the civil servants had let down their guard. Their article 'Learning in migration management? Persistent side effects of the EUTF' was eventually published in a top journal, indicating that they were not as innocent as they seemed.[13]

In the Introduction of the book, I explained that unintended effects are neither *a priori* negative nor an objective phenomenon: this also becomes very clear from this example. Migration often means a quantum leap forward for families in terms of wealth and well-being.[14] So while the increased willingness to migrate as a result of the training programme may be negative for the EUTF, it is likely to be positive from the perspective of the migrant. Considering the constant human drive to look for better opportunities, it appears even quite preposterous to think that some migration management programme can convince people to renege on this central tenet of human nature.

What we need is more independent and open-access research, such as the research done by the Research and Evidence Facility of the EUTF. Because only through this type of research, we can explore the unintended effects of development programmes: close enough to programming to speak to the beneficiaries but independent enough to ask the right questions. We need to break out of our tunnel vision and evaluate all the outcomes – whether intended or unintended – by funding critical and constructive research.

The debate on the effects of international aid on migration is one of the most heated debates currently in international development because international migration and xenophobia are at the forefront of so many political debates in the Global North. The more heated a debate is, and the more ideological it becomes, the more 'bounded' the learning is.[15] The students found that the EUTF policymakers turned a blind eye to many side effects, thwarting attempts to learn from them and prevent them in the future. Tellingly, the risk registrar of the EUTF focussed a lot on potential reputational risks to the EUTF. For instance, one of the identified risks is the 'Wrong perception that EUTF-funded actions support the agenda of countries violating human rights.'[16] Yet, nothing is said about potential rebound effects, let alone that it has been measured systematically.

A small side-step away from migration: rebound effects also hold for less controversial programmes, such as anti-corruption messaging. Donors have funded billboards and media campaigns explaining the evils of corruption to citizens in the Global South. A recent meta-evaluation called 'Message misunderstood: Why raising awareness of corruption can backfire' showed that the takeaway most often for those citizens was that it was apparently normal in their country to pay bribes.[17] There was a clear rebound effect as they showed an increased willingness to pay bribes.

8.2 The backfire effect: microfinance for women can lead to extra violence against them

Several studies have evaluated the use of microcredit or cash transfer programmes, especially those targeting women. They point to increasing conflict in women's relationships with their spouses, as documented by a thorough literature review by one of my co-workers, Maria van der Harst.[18] The effects are a result from shifting roles within the household as women become more economically independent. This can be perceived as a threat to the husband's breadwinner status. Female loan recipients experienced physical or verbal abuse from their husbands for various reasons, including disagreements over how to use the loan and who should have control over the money borrowed.[19] While many scholars have discussed a rise in conflict between intimate partners and domestic violence in some cases, other researchers have contested these findings. Some studies report improved relations within households, especially the more quantitative studies.[20] This shows the importance of triangulating statistical research.

Many academics have researched the effect of either microcredit or cash transfer programmes on household dynamics, but this problem can occur in a wide range of settings. For instance, women may face punishment if they participate in economic activities organized by aid organizations. Bamberger et al. discuss a project in Central America that was helping rural women to develop vegetable gardens.[21] Despite their husbands' positive attitude towards the project at public meetings, some women faced public repercussions and were 'seriously beaten for attending [project] meetings.'[22]

As noted before, there seems to be little consensus in the literature regarding the prevalence and direction of these behavioural effects involving spouses. Studies make contradictory claims or present inconclusive evidence regarding adverse effects on women. Applying an intersectional lens in which we add other individual characteristics (such as poverty levels) to the analysis can help us understand such contradictory conclusions. For instance, a study from Ghana shows that women who had to use the credit for subsistence (because they were already very poor) ended up suffering more harassment and abuse from their spouses.[23] To understand the differential behavioural responses of spouses, it is relevant to consider whether the women face other structural disadvantages (such as indebtedness). If multiple obstacles 'intersect' in the life of a woman, she is more likely to encounter a violent response from her husband.

Female economic empowerment practitioners are increasingly recognizing and addressing such feedback loops involving spouses. For instance, they are educating women about how to deal with potential backfire effects in safe space meetings, workshops on sexual and reproductive rights, and gender-equity seminars. This is being actively encouraged by agencies such as the World Health Organization and the United States Agency for International Development (USAID) in their programmes.[24] Here we see a clear example of organizations learning from potential unintended effects and trying to do something about them. We can see just how important this is when we look at the results of a female economic empowerment programme in Uganda, designed to measure the potential effects on male violence towards women who were participating in the programme.[25] They rolled out two versions: one with a financial component only and one with a financial component plus a women's training element. The results are shocking and demonstrate why it is important to think outside silos.

In the programme in Kampala, adolescent women were either given just a savings account or a savings account combined with a series of activities, such as a mentoring programme and reproductive health training. Both groups saw their economic assets improve. To those evaluating the programme from a narrow perspective, ignoring the behavioural responses of others, both interventions are a success. However, the girls who only had a savings account actually faced a much more serious response from others. They were more likely to have been sexually touched or harassed by men (the number was 9 –15 per cent higher amongst these girls) than the women who got the whole package. This suggests that just building economic assets without the protection afforded by strengthening social skills can leave vulnerable women at increased risk of sexual violence. It is heartening to see that so many organizations have taken these side effects on board in their economic empowerment programmes and are now including these gender components.

But I do feel that not all lessons have been learnt: it would be more effective to stop the problem at its source: the men who are beating their wives. Men need to understand, and can understand if they are taken along, that power isn't a zero sum game. Over the last decade or so the sector has been learning: programmes such as Promundo ('engaging men to prevent gender-based violence') show how important and effective it can be to include men. Their interventions (group-based discussions with men) showed a statistically significant change in attitudes correlated with opposition to violence against women and a statistically significant self-reported decrease in violence against female partners.[26] Also the quality of life of men who were together with those empowered women improved, and even their sex life improved according to some.[27]

8.3 The motivational crowding-out effect: undermining people's intrinsic motivation to protect local forests

The climate crisis and mass biodiversity loss are arguably the greatest global challenge of our time, and we need to address it first. One of the fastest-growing type of programme in this respect is the 'payment for environmental services' (PES) approach. The idea is to encourage landowners to move away from industrial land-use methods that deplete forests and exhaust their capacity to absorb carbon. They receive monetary and other incentives to make up for the loss of income and enable them to work towards more sustainable land use. You might know the saying, 'As long as we assign a value to dead trees and not to living trees, we have a big problem.' This approach suggests that we should assign value to living trees rather than dead ones: combatting deforestation (and other ecological problems) by rewarding people for conserving and protecting forests, rather than cutting them down.

We decided to take a closer look at the PES programmes because the world's largest donors and development agencies, such as the United Nations and the World Bank, are now embracing this approach. These programmes now involve billions of dollars, partly because companies and governments in the Global North want to offset their carbon emissions. Agencies give landowners and residents in the forests financial compensation if they leave the forest intact instead of cutting it down. Obviously, we did not measure whether the protected forests actually captured carbon – others can do a much better job of that – but we looked at the side effects of these programmes on the local population and the environment. Marloes Verholt, the researcher who worked on this component of the research, found about fifty studies that documented the side effects of these programmes.[28] So what did they find?

Seventeen studies looked at PES programmes involving forests. They identified one unintended effect more often than any other: the crowding-out (undermining) of the intrinsic motivation of local residents.[29] In this case, intrinsic motivation refers to local people's willingness to protect the forest *without* monetary compensation.

These findings have an obvious upside: regardless of how poor they are, people are generally willing to protect local forests even without being paid to do so. And the downside? People's intrinsic motivation is undermined as soon as they are given the opportunity to make money from the forest. If external parties turn the forest into a commodity through PES programmes, the local population often becomes more calculating. And if the payments stop, the forest is suddenly more vulnerable than ever because the intrinsic motivation of the local population has been undermined: there is hence a negative feedback loop.

A study of the beautiful Cambodian forest and a programme by Conservation International to protect this make it clear.[30] Conservation International signs Conservation Agreements with the villages in the forest. What is the deal? Local communities need to halt illegal logging, stop commercial poaching of protected species (e.g. Siamese crocodile, dragon fish, etc.), and stop the clearing of new plots in pristine forest for swidden agriculture. In exchange for this, Conservation International transfers a mix of collective in-kind payments (salary for contractual teachers in local schools), individual cash (salary for community patrollers), and in-kind productive incentives (community buffaloes). The economic value of these different forms of compensation was estimated to equal the opportunity costs of complying with conservation. The big question is: did it decrease the intrinsic motivation of the Cambodian villagers to protect the forest?

Researchers compared the values that villagers attached to the forest in villages that had entered into contracts with Conservation International with other villages, controlling for many factors. They found that for villages that had entered into a contract with Conversation International, the perceived monetary value of forest conservation had surpassed the value of shelter, food, and health the forest offered.[31] So, while in the past the subsistence value was highest (shelter, food, and health), now the money that could be extracted from it was the most important value. A similar study in Mexico found that deforestation rates rapidly went up after PES funding stopped, casting doubt on the permanence of the effects of PES programming.[32]

We interviewed the organizations behind these massive PES programmes (such as the World Bank), and asked them what they were doing about this dilemma: were they trying to develop a system that offers people enough (financial) incentive to protect the forests but does not undermine their intrinsic motivation to conserve valuable local habitats? While they had some ways of dealing with it (ensuring that the payments were not too high, and spreading it over a longer period), there was no overarching vision or strategy on this side effect. Apparently, the fact that providing a financial incentive might actually reduce people's motivation was beyond the imagination of those who had designed these programmes within a neoliberal paradigm, where human behaviour is dictated by monetary incentives. This is a clear example of an ideological limit to learning, bounding policymakers within an existing way of doing things: the programme community has not found a sustainable solution because such a solution would have to involve stepping outside of the neoliberal paradigm on which the intervention is based.

Let's look at other development programmes that have been scrutinized for their potential erosive effects on intrinsic motivation: performance-based financing programmes. I have been a vocal supporter of performance-based financing, as I have seen first-hand how it has energized so many professionals in the Global South. However, there have been convincing observations in Burkina Faso that performance-based health financing can lead to health professionals' gaming and a decrease in their intrinsic motivation.[33] Anne-Marie Turcotte-Tremblay wrote an exciting PhD on the unintended effects of performance-based financing in health (also looking at other effects than intrinsic motivation).[34] She found that health workers falsified medical registries to get extra payments. Staff members appeared fixated more on paperwork than care provision: one nurse was even busy falsifying a register while an unqualified staff member treated the child the nurse was supposed to take care of.

In summary, we need to be more cognizant on this potential side effect and experiment with it to understand under which conditions it materializes. We can experiment with the size of the payments, the duration, and the accompanying policies, and rigorously research how this impacts intrinsic motivation. Or perhaps it is even necessary to step outside of our neoliberal frameworks and rethink the way in which we monetize basic human values such as taking care of our community and our natural environment altogether.

It is high time to take behavioural side effects more seriously. If you haven't been convinced yet, read this testimony of Masamba. He was also a victim of behavioural responses to international development efforts. There was a massive push by the international community against sexual and gender-based violence (SGBV) in the DRC. Fighting impunity was a central tenet of this effort, and judges were stimulated to get more men convicted of SGBV. The projects worked, and more men were convicted. The generically overlooked behavioural response, however, was that judges would overreact to these incentives, even by convicting innocent men such as Masamba.

Testimony by Salomon Balangane: guilty or not, that's not the question

Figure 8.2 Masamba in prison.

Source: IF Productions.

Imagine spending ten years in prison for a rape you didn't commit, and then dying at age 47, only a few months after your release. This is what happened to Masamba in the DRC. How and why could this happen? Salomon, who was closely involved in Masamba's case and visited him every week in prison, tells his story.

Public court

My name is Salomon Balangane. Around 2010, I was working with IF Productions, who were making documentaries about sexual violence in DRC. At one point we filmed at a public court in South Kivu, where someone named Masamba was accused of raping the wife of his army chief, called 'the Captain.' Masamba was found guilty and sentenced to ten years in prison. But when I translated the footage from Swahili to English, I was surprised to discover that the doctor who was questioned and had examined the Captain's wife had actually testified that there were no signs of rape. So why did they sentence Masamba anyway?

Paying for 'justice'

We started investigating the case. Now I know that the NGOs supporting (mobile) courts in the eastern DRC incentivized judges to get people convicted for rape. It was to show that there is justice in Congo and that they're fighting sexual violence. But they took somebody that was just innocent in this situation and put him in jail for ten years! Years later, the Captain's wife even admitted to us that the story was made up. The team and I were so affected by this. We supported Masamba with legal counselling and I visited him every week in prison.

Prison life

Masamba's life in prison was very difficult, especially in the beginning. You cannot imagine what it was like. He was being tortured, he was sleeping on the floor, he had little food and his family couldn't visit him. He was so concerned for his children. He was such a good person. And Masamba kept saying that he believed that the truth would be revealed. We tried to get President Kabila to give a Presidential Grace, our last option, but to no avail.

Starting a new life

After ten years, Masamba was finally released from prison. With some money left in the IF Foundation, we helped him move to Kinshasa and bought him a motorbike. As his wife arrived in Kinshasa to be reunited, she received the news that he had just died – only a few months after leaving prison. He had started vomiting blood and we suspect it was an untreated hepatitis that caused his death. He was only 47 years old. I was heartbroken.

Follow-up

What I would like international organizations to do is that when they give funding, they follow up what happens with that money. I strongly believe that Masamba would still be alive today if he hadn't gone through what he went through.

Douma and Hilhorst found in their study on sexual violence in the eastern DRC that a growing number of people misuse the law to settle other types of (family) conflicts.[35] Framing somebody for rape has become an effective way to 'get somebody out of the way.' They found that '50 percent of the convictions lacked sufficient evidence,' but that judges convicted anyway because 'they faced a moral obligation' as NGOs provided both cases that needed to be taken up and the financial compensation during the mobile courts.

How to tackle unintended behavioural responses

Policymakers

- **Include the dominant group when empowering dominated groups.** For instance, when rolling out a programme focussing on strengthening the position of women, also include men.
- **Identify potential alternative impact pathways.** When designing, agencies need to identify potential alternative impact pathways, such as motivational crowding-out effects.

Practitioners

- **Adapt programmes to reduce potential motivational crowding-out effects.** Experiment with programmes to understand better potential motivational crowding-out effects. The duration of the programme (long) and the relative size of the payments (not too big) play a role, but other factors need more research.

Evaluators

- **Perform behavioural impact scan ex-ante.** More potential behavioural effects could be anticipated through scanning available rigorous research. Scanning available research can detect effects and the planning can be adapted accordingly.
- **Measure impact several years after the end of a programme.** Because behavioural effects are often the result of a feedback loop, it may take some time for these side effects to materialize, as the deforestation example shows.
- **Discount the total impact of the programme for rebound effects.** As we have seen with these cooking stoves, the impact of the intervention might be less, because participants of a programme start to consume more of the more efficient product.

Notes

1 The original definition of rebound effects is quite stringent and focusses only on rebound effects of technological innovations. These innovations can make resource use more efficient, but actually lead to an increase of resource use, because people started to consumer more. In this book, we look broader than just technological innovations and include all opposite behavioural responses.

2 Dealing with these side effects has led to draconian measures to 'hunt down' potential cheaters, including racial profiling. See, for example, Kaaryn S. Gustafson, *Cheating Welfare: Public Assistance and the Criminalization of Poverty* (New York, NY: New York University Press, 2011).

3 See, for example, *The Independent–Uganda,* 'Mothers in Kotido warned against starving children for food aid,' 25 September 2022, www.independent.co.ug/mothers-in-kotido-warned-against-starving-children-for-food-aid/; Emergency Nutrition Network, 'Ideas to prevent Mothers from starving their children in order to benefit from the nutritional treatment,' last updated 15 May 2012, www.en-net.org/question/717.aspx

4 William R. Easterly, *The Elusive Quest for Growth: Economists' Adventures and Misadventures in the Tropics* (Cambridge, MA: MIT Press, 2002).

5 Mani Nepal, Apsara Nepal, and Kristine Grimsrud, 'Unbelievable but improved cookstoves are not helpful in reducing firewood demand in Nepal,' *Environment and Development Economics* 16, no. 1: 1–23, https://doi.org/10.1017/S1355770X10000409

6 Nina R. Brooks, Vasundhara Bhojvaid, Marc A. Jeuland, Jessica J. Lewis, Omkar Patange, and Subhrendu K. Pattanyak, 'How much do alternative cookstoves reduce biomass fuel use? Evidence from North India,' *Resource and Energy Economics* 43 (2016): 153–171, https://doi.org/10.1016/j.reseneeco.2015.12.001

7 This section could also be part of the chapter of unintended migration and resettlement effects, but since the programmes explicitly focus on migration *and* because the behavioural aspect plays such an important role in explaining the unintended effect, it is located in this section of the book.

8 Their research didn't only find rebound effects, but also the risk that the programme would contribute to legitimizing authoritarian regimes and weaken the social contract in these states. Some of the effects they found will be dealt with in the chapter on governance effects. In this chapter we only focus on the rebound effect. The research by the students has been published here: Meindert Boersma, Louise Kroon, Dion McDougal, Gijs Verhoeff, Yue Wang, and Dirk-Jan Koch, 'Learning in migration management? Persistent side effects of the EUTF,' *International Migration* 60, no. 6 (2022): 81–94, https://doi.org/10.1111/imig.12965

9 Neli Esipova, Aita Pugliese, and Julie Ray, 'More than 750 million worldwide would migrate if they could,' *Gallup*, 10 December 2018, https://news.gallup.com/poll/245255/750-million-worldwide-migrate.aspx

10 de Haas, Hein, *Migration Transitions: A Theoretical and Empirical Inquiry into the Developmental Drivers of International Migration. Paper 24* (Oxford: International Migration Institute, 2010), www.migrationinstitute.org/publications/wp-24-10; Anna Triandafyllidou, *Routledge handbook of immigration and refugee studies* (London: Routledge, 2015).

11 Research and Evidence Facility, *The Impact of Youth Training and Employment on Migration Dynamics in the Horn of Africa* (London and Nairobi: EU Trust Fund for Africa (Horn of Africa Window) Research and Evidence Facility, 2019), https://data.unhcr.org/en/documents/details/85914

12 Ibid., 36.

13 Boersma et al., 'Learning in migration management?'

14 Paul Collier, *Exodus: How Migration Is Changing Our World* (Oxford: Oxford University Press, 2013).

15 Boersma et al., 'Learning in migration management?'

16 European Commission, 'EUTF for Africa Risk Register,' n.d., accessed on 1 February 2023: https://ec.europa.eu/trustfundforafrica/sites/default/files/risk_register_eutf_0.pdf

17 Caryn Peiffer and Nic Cheeseman, *Message Misunderstood: Why Raising Awareness of Corruption Can Backfire. U4 Brief 2023:1* (Oslo: Chr. Michelsen Institute, 2023), www.u4.no/r/BR2301

18 Maria van der Harst, Dirk-Jan Koch, and Marieke van den Brink, 'A review of unintended gender effects,' *Public Administration and Development*, forthcoming, 22 May 2023.

19 John Kuumuori Ganle, Kwadwo Afriyie, and Alexander Yao Segbefia, 'Microcredit: Empowerment and disempowerment of rural women in Ghana,' *World Development* 66 (2015): 335–345, https://doi.org/10.1016/j.worlddev.2014.08.027; Aminur Rahman, 'Micro-credit initiatives for equitable and sustainable development: who pays?,' *World Development* 27, no. 1 (1999): 67–82, https://doi.org/10.1016/S0305-750X(98)00105-3

20 Sidney Ruth Schuler, Syed M. Hashemi, and Shamsul Huda Badal, 'Men's violence against women in rural Bangladesh: undermined or exacerbated by microcredit programmes?,' *Development in Practice* 8, no. 2 (1998): 148–157, https://doi.org/10.1080/09614529853774

21 Michael Bamberger, Michele Tarsilla, and Sharlene Hesse-Biber, 'Why so many "rigorous" evaluations fail to identify unintended consequences of development programs: How mixed methods can contribute,' *Evaluation and Programme Planning* 55 (2016): 155–162, https://doi.org/10.1016/j.evalprogplan.2016.01.001

22 Ibid., 157.

23 Ganle et al. 'Microcredit.'

24 Amber Peterman, Tia M. Palermo, and Giulia Ferrari, 'Still a leap of faith: Microfinance initiatives for reduction of violence against women and children in low-income and middle-income countries,' *BMJ Global Health* 3, no. 6 (2018): e001143, https://doi.org/10.1136/bmjgh-2018-001143

25 Karen Austrian and Eunice Muthengi, 'Can economic assets increase girls' risk of sexual harassment? Evaluation results from a social, health and economic asset-building intervention for vulnerable adolescent girls in Uganda,' *Children and Youth Services Review* 47 (2014): 168–175, https://doi.org/10.1016/j.childyouth.2014.08.012

26 Instituto Promundo, *Engaging Men to Prevent Gender-Based Violence: A Multi-Country Intervention and Impact Evaluation Study* (Washington, DC: Promundo, 2014), https://promundo.org.br/wp-content/uploads/2014/12/Engaging-Men-to-Prevent-Gender-Based-Violence.pdf

27 Duncan Green, *How Change Happens* (Oxford: Oxford University Press, 2016), 37.

28 Koch and Verholt, 'Limits to learning.'

29 Ibid.

30 Colas Chervier, Gwenolé Le Velly, and Driss Ezzine-de-Blas, 'When the implementation of payments for biodiversity conservation leads to motivation crowding-out: A case study from the Cardamoms Forests, Cambodia,' *Ecological Economics* 156 (2019): 499–510, https://doi.org/10.1016/j.ecolecon.2017.03.018

31 Ibid., 504.

32 Gwenolé Le Velly, Alexandre Sauquet, and Sergio Cortina-Villar, 'PES impact and leakages over several cohorts: The case of the PSA-H in Yucatan, Mexico,' *Land Economics* 93, no. 2 (2017): 230–257, https://doi.org/10.3368/le.93.2.230

33 For the gaming effect, see Anne-Marie Turcotte-Tremblay, Idriss Ali Gali Gali, and Valéry Ridde, 'An exploration of the unintended consequences of performance-based financing in 6 primary healthcare facilities in Burkina Faso,' *International Journal of Health Policy and Management* 11, no. 2 (2020): 145–159, https://doi.org/10.34172/ijhpm.2020.83; for the decrease in intrinsic motivation effect, see Julia Lohmann, Adamson S. Muula, Nathalie Houlfort, and Manuela De Allegri, 'How does performance-based financing affect health workers' intrinsic motivation? A self-determination theory-based mixed-methods study in Malawi,' *Social Science & Medicine* 208 (2018): 1–8, https://doi.org/10.1016/j.socscimed.2018.04.053

34 Anne-Marie Turcotte-Tremblay, *The Unintended Consequences of a Complex Intervention Combining Performance-Based Financing with Health Equity Measures in Burkina Faso*, doctoral thesis (Montreal: Université de Montréal, 2020), https://papyrus.bib.umontreal.ca/xmlui/handle/1866/24272.

35 Nynke Douma and Dorothea Hilhorst, *Fond de commerce? Sexual violence assistance in the Democratic Republic of Congo. Research brief #4* (Wageningen: Wageningen University, 2012), https://edepot.wur.nl/348869

Further reading

Austrian, Karen, and Eunice Muthengi. 'Can economic assets increase girls' risk of sexual harassment? Evaluation results from a social, health and economic asset-building intervention for vulnerable adolescent girls in Uganda.' *Children and Youth Services Review* 47 (2014): 168–175. https://doi.org/10.1016/j.childyouth.2014.08.012

Bamberger, Michael, Michele Tarsilla, and Sharlene Hesse-Biber. 'Why so many "rigorous" evaluations fail to identify unintended consequences of development programs: How mixed methods can contribute.' *Evaluation and Programme Planning* 55 (2016): 155–162. https://doi.org/10.1016/j.evalprogplan.2016.01.001

Boersma, Meindert, Louise Kroon, Dion McDougal, Gijs Verhoeff, Yue Wang, and Dirk-Jan Koch. 'Learning in migration management? Persistent side effects of the EUTF.' *International Migration* 60, no. 6 (2022): 81–94. https://doi.org/10.1111/imig.12965

Brooks, Nina R., Vasundhara Bhojvaid, Marc A. Jeuland, Jessica J. Lewis, Omkar Patange, and Subhrendu K. Pattanyak. 'How much do alternative cookstoves reduce biomass fuel use? Evidence from North India.' *Resource and Energy Economics* 43 (2016): 153–171. https://doi.org/10.1016/j.reseneeco.2015.12.001

Chervier, Colas, Gwenolé Le Velly, and Driss Ezzine-de-Blas. 'When the implementation of payments for biodiversity conservation leads to motivation crowding-out: A case study from the Cardamoms Forests, Cambodia.' *Ecological Economics* 156 (2019): 499–510. https://doi.org/10.1016/j.ecolecon.2017.03.018

Collier, Paul. *Exodus: How Migration Is Changing Our World*. Oxford: Oxford University Press, 2013.

Douma, Nynke, and Dorothea Hilhorst. *Fond de commerce? Sexual violence assistance in the Democratic Republic of Congo. Research brief #4*. Wageningen: Wageningen University, 2012. https://edepot.wur.nl/348869

Easterly, William R. *The Elusive Quest for Growth: Economists' Adventures and Misadventures in the Tropics*. Cambridge, MA: MIT Press, 2002.

Emergency Nutrition Network. 'Ideas to prevent mothers from starving their children in order to benefit from the nutritional treatment.' Last updated 15 May 2012, www.en-net.org/question/717.aspx

Esipova, Neli, Aita Pugliese, and Julie Ray. 'More than 750 million worldwide would migrate if they could.' *Gallup*, 10 December 2018. https://news.gallup.com/poll/245255/750-million-worldwide-migrate.aspx

Ganle, John Kuumuori, Kwadwo Afriyie, and Alexander Yao Segbefia. 'Microcredit: Empowerment and disempowerment of rural women in Ghana.' *World Development* 66 (2015): 335–345. https://doi.org/10.1016/j.worlddev.2014.08.027

Gustafson, Kaaryn S. *Cheating Welfare: Public Assistance and the Criminalization of Poverty*. New York, NY: New York University Press, 2011.

van der Harst, Maria, Dirk-Jan Koch, and Marieke van den Brink, 'A review of unintended gender effects.' *Public Administration and Development*, forthcoming, 22 May 2023.

Green, Duncan. *How Change Happens*. Oxford: Oxford University Press, 2016.

de Haas, Hein. *Migration Transitions: A Theoretical and Empirical Inquiry into the Developmental Drivers of International Migration. Paper 24*. Oxford: International Migration Institute, 2010. www.migrationinstitute.org/publications/wp-24-10

Instituto Promundo. *Engaging Men to Prevent Gender-Based Violence: A Multi-Country Intervention and Impact Evaluation Study*. Washington, DC: Promundo, 2014. https://promundo.org.br/wp-content/uploads/2014/12/Engaging-Men-to-Prevent-Gender-Based-Violence.pdf

Koch, Dirk-Jan and Marloes Verholt. 'Limits to learning: The struggle to adapt to unintended effects of international payment for environmental services programmes.' *International Environmental Agreements: Politics, Law and Economics* 20, no. 3 (2020): 507–539. https://doi.org/10.1007/s10784-020-09496-2

Le Velly, Gwenolé, Alexandre Sauquet, and Sergio Cortina-Villar. 'PES impact and leakages over several cohorts: The case of the PSA-H in Yucatan, Mexico.' *Land Economics* 93, no. 2 (2017): 230–257. https://doi.org/10.3368/le.93.2.230

Lohmann, Julia, Adamson S. Muula, Nathalie Houlfort, and Manuela De Allegri. 'How does performance-based financing affect health workers' intrinsic motivation? A self-determination theory-based mixed-methods study in Malawi.' *Social Science & Medicine* 208 (2018): 1–8. https://doi.org/10.1016/j.socscimed.2018.04.053

Nepal, Mani, Apsara Nepal, and Kristine Grimsrud. 'Unbelievable but improved cookstoves are not helpful in reducing firewood demand in Nepal.' *Environment and Development Economics* 16, no. 1: 1–23. https://doi.org/10.1017/S1355770X10000409

Peiffer, Caryn, and Nic Cheeseman. *Message Misunderstood: Why Raising Awareness of Corruption Can Backfire. U4 Brief 2023:1*. Oslo: Chr. Michelsen Institute, 2023. www.u4.no/r/BR2301

Peterman, Amber, Tia M. Palermo, and Giulia Ferrari. 'Still a leap of faith: Microfinance initiatives for reduction of violence against women and children in low-income and middle-income countries.' *BMJ Global Health* 3, no. 6 (2018): e001143, https://doi.org/10.1136/bmjgh-2018-001143

Rahman, Aminur. 'Micro-credit initiatives for equitable and sustainable development: Who pays?' *World Development* 27, no. 1 (1999): 67–82. https://doi.org/10.1016/S0305-750X(98)00105-3

Research and Evidence Facility. *The Impact of Youth Training and Employment on Migration Dynamics in the Horn of Africa*. London and Nairobi: EU Trust Fund for Africa (Horn of Africa Window) Research and Evidence Facility, 2019. https://data.unhcr.org/en/documents/deta ils/85914

Schuler, Sidney Ruth, Syed M. Hashemi, and Shamsul Huda Badal. 'Men's violence against women in rural Bangladesh: Undermined or exacerbated by microcredit programmes?' *Development in Practice* 8, no. 2 (1998): 148–157. https://doi.org/10.1080/09614529853774

The Independent–Uganda. 'Mothers in Kotido warned against starving children for food aid.' 25 September 2022. www.independent.co.ug/mothers-in-kotido-warned-against-starving-child ren-for-food-aid/

Triandafyllidou, Anna. *Routledge Handbook of Immigration and Refugee Studies*. London: Routledge, 2015.

Turcotte-Tremblay, Anne-Marie. *The Unintended Consequences of a Complex Intervention Combining Performance-Based Financing with Health Equity Measures in Burkina Faso*. Doctoral thesis. Montreal: Université de Montréal, 2020. https://papyrus.bib.umontreal.ca/ xmlui/handle/1866/24272

Turcotte-Tremblay, Anne-Marie, Idriss Ali Gali Gali, and Valéry Ridde. 'An exploration of the unintended consequences of performance-based financing in 6 primary healthcare facilities in Burkina Faso.' *International Journal of Health Policy and Management* 11, no. 2 (2020): 145–159. https://doi.org/10.34172/ijhpm.2020.83

9 Negative spillover effects
Look beyond your own targets

Unintended negative spillover effects materialize when an external intervention negatively affects thematic or geographic areas or institutions outside of the intervention area.

What flavours do we see?

1 **Negative institutional spillover effects ('brain drain').** The capacities of more permanent local structures (e.g. a government agency) are weakened as international agencies hire the most talented staff without adequately compensating the local structure.
2 **Negative thematic spillover effects ('thematic crowding out').** An upsurge of international attention for a specific (sub) theme pushes out other thematic areas that also require attention.
3 **Negative geographic spillover effects ('leakage').** The international intervention solves a problem in one place, but this or another problem worsens elsewhere.
4 **Fungibility.** Aid resources do not pay for the item it is accounted for but for the marginal expenditure it makes possible.

In which instances have negative spillover effects been observed? Four examples:

1 Negative institutional spillover effects: in the Democratic Republic of Congo, the best students started to work for international agencies instead of strengthening local government structures.
2 Negative thematic spillover effects: while the fight against HIV-AIDS was successful, it drew resources away from other parts of the health sector, for instance, the basic vaccination programme.
3 Negative geographic spillover effects: in Brazil, the international forest protection programmes contributed to a decrease in logging in the Amazon, but contributed to a simultaneous increase in neighbouring Cerrado.
4 Fungibility: a recipient government reallocates its own funding away from the sector (or region) where the donor spends its aid resources. For instance, if the donor funds education, this frees up funding from the recipient government from the education sector and allocates this to the military, for instance. The donor funding makes marginal expenditure in the military possible.

DOI: 10.4324/9781003356851-9

This Chapter has been made available under a CC-BY-NC-ND license.

Key concepts from complexity thinking that help in detecting geographic spillover effects:

1 **Interconnectivity**. To determine the success of an intervention, it is relevant to find out where the inputs are coming from. For instance, where is the staff coming from? Where is the matching funding of the counterpart coming from; is it being detracted from other valuable initiatives? It is also important to determine whether the achieved outcomes interact with outcomes elsewhere. For example, are the jobs created by this programme replacing jobs elsewhere?

2 **Adaptive agents**. Sometimes the behaviour of agents appears to change in the programme area, but to determine if the programme really works as intended, it needs to become clear whether they also change their behaviour outside the intervention area. For instance, loggers might seize to log in the protected area, but aren't they just moving their activities elsewhere? The local population might no longer collect firewood from the protected area, but how do they get the energy for cooking now?

Figure 9.1 Leakage effects in action: donors all focussing on the same 'sexy' theme, drawing local resources towards this theme, leading to underfunding and understaffing of other themes.

Source: Maarten Wolterink.

If an external intervention leads to an increase in something somewhere, we need to check if it doesn't lead to its decrease somewhere else. I call this 'negative spillover effects,' because it resembles a bucket full of water that overflows if additional resources are poured in and you don't pay attention. If you just look at the bucket after a while, all might look fine. But if you look beyond the bucket, you see that water has been spilled everywhere.

While the ripple effects of Chapter 12 are positive, the negative spillover effects in this chapter are per definition negative. We will look at negative institutional spillovers, also known as brain drain effects (Section 9.1), thematic negative spillovers, also known a crowding out (Section 9.2), and negative geographical spillovers, also known as leakage (Section 9.3). We conclude this chapter with fungibility, which can be considered a kind of financial spillover effect.

9.1 Negative institutional spillover effects: brain drain

I spent the summer of 2007 in the Central African Republic (CAR) researching for my PhD. The topic of my PhD research was the geographical choices of aid agencies: I was trying to find out why the CAR was a so-called 'donor orphan,' a country with diffi-culty attracting international development donors (I will spare you the details of my findings). My main conclusion was that more agencies needed to engage in the CAR, and less in 'donor darlings' such as Tanzania. When in 2013, I was Africa director of an international NGO, I was glad that I could open an office there, even though the circumstances – an impending genocide – were dire.

When I was in Bangui (the capital of the CAR) setting up this office with my colleagues, we faced a major dilemma: how much should we pay the Central Africans in our employment? I wanted to follow two important moral considerations. My dilemma was that these two moral considerations led to totally opposing conclusions about the pay we should offer.

The first consideration is that we wanted to reduce the pay gap between local and expat staff. Not only does it demotivate local staff, it also smells of a hangover of colo-nialism, even racism. While I think that we should have as little international staff as possible (they are expensive and it is less sustainable), it was necessary to have at least one or two international staff in the CAR programme, who had the technical expertise of setting up radio-stations and develop anti-genocide programming, and understood how to perform the financial accounting for demanding donors such as US govern-ment. To attract those expatriates, we needed to pay a 'Western' salary: how could they otherwise support their families back home? If I wanted to reduce the pay gap between the expats and the local staff, I would need to offer high salaries to local staff (at least a net EUR 3,000 a month). They performed equally complicated tasks, such as managing offices in remote areas.

The second consideration, however, would propel me to offer lower salaries to the local staff. International actors had been contributing to a brain drain away from the local government and other public and private actors. In countries as diverse as Malawi, Sri Lanka, and Kosovo, international agencies had hired (some would say 'poached') highly valued civil servants from the administration to perform often support staff functions in their own programmes. In the case of Kosovo, a housekeeper for an international organization could earn three times as much as a minister. The effect may be that transitory organizations reduce the capacity of more permanent local institutions.[1] To prevent that from happening I needed to align the salaries I offered to the salary grid of the Central African government. In that case, we would have to offer them a maximum of net EUR 300 a month.

Therefore, a factor of 10 separated the minimum that I was supposed to offer according to the first paradigm and the maximum according to the second paradigm. Lemay-Hébert et al. argue that there is an equilibrium somewhere between these two extremes.[2] Low salaries for local staff of international NGOs reduce internal migration from government to NGOs because of a small wage differential, but increase the propensity to migrate internationally for these workers because of the wage gap with expatriates. Conversely, high salaries for local staff of international NGOs increase internal migration from government to NGOs because of a large wage differential, but reduce international migration because there is less need.

After a benchmarking exercise with other NGOs, we decide to offer the local staff about two times as much as their local counterparts in the administration, and five times as little as the expatriate staff. We did not recruit one government official, even though we really liked him, but we thought it would be better to keep him in the government. However, the next summer, when I came back, I found out that he was working for another international agency. The entire hiring and wage-setting exercise felt discomforting.[3] It highlights the dilemmas around one important side effect of the international development sector: the brain drain effect. The testimony of Ali Zafar (see textbox) expresses how this brain drain works out concretely.

Testimony by Ali Zafar on the 'brain drain' in Pakistan: 'time to move to the 21st century'

Figure 9.2 Ali Zafar.

My name is Ali Zafar (33). Originally from Pakistan, I'm currently an economics advisor for Save the Children, based in England. After finishing my studies, I worked for 2.5 years for the provincial and federal government on planning and development, before being 'poached' to work for the UN. First in Pakistan, and then abroad.

Running up and down the stairs

I do feel like I am part of the so-called brain drain. Working at public offices, it's an ungrateful job. The salary simply wasn't good enough and I was frustrated by the lack of professionalism, poor infrastructure and bureaucracy. When I was an intern, when you wanted to copy something, you needed to take 7 flights of stairs to go outside to a copy shop. And it's very hierarchical. The bosses are concerned with political games instead of what's best for the country. My boss once told me to change a number in a document. It is not evidence-based, or data-driven. It's hearsay, it's the way of the boss. You can easily get demotivated by this. The people who want to do something for their country and who have professionalism in their work, are the ones who are likely to leave.

From dentist to truck driver

The economic and political insecurity plays a role as well. I read the other day that in the last 12 months, a million young people have left Pakistan. Inflation is soaring, but salaries are not increasing, so they want to earn money outside of the country. I have a friend who is willing to leave his dental profession and move to Canada to drive trucks, all because of the economic situation. And with every political party, the civil government changes, and you don't know when you might not be needed anymore. It's a very volatile system.

Move into the 21st century

If the government would be able to retain human resources with better or at least matching privileges or compensation, then this sort of brain drain wouldn't be happening. They need to move into the 21st century by improving infrastructure, and getting out of the colonial way of working set up by the British. For example, recruitment of new staff is very outdated. Being able to communicate in English is often enough. If you're not hiring people for their intellectual capabilities, you're not going to get talent, especially if you're not going to pay them enough!

Three days at the Marriot

When I was still working for the UN in Pakistan, I gave training to former government colleagues. But it's not sustainable. Honestly, if donor agencies really want to make a difference in the country, it cannot be done by paying for a three-day decadent training at the Marriot Hotel. Invest that money in finetuning the skill set of those who are working in the civil government. Improve in computers, better internet, training on software use and data analysis. They are wasting money on indulging bureaucrats instead of investing in the country's people.

Maybe one day I'll go back as an economic advisor. Probably not to work for the government, but I'll be back to serve Pakistan. Definitely.

Because of the dilemmas I experienced, I decided to research this effect more in depth. The research made clear that I was not the only one facing this dilemma. Our first analysis shows that there were at least 537,648 local staffers of international aid agencies in 2016.[4] We analysed the wage differential between workers in the foreign-funded aid sector and the public sector. In the DRC, if a manager moved from a job in the public sector to a local NGO, she would almost quintuple her salary, from about USD 100 to USD 471. Moving to an American NGO, she would earn 10 times as much. If she worked for the bilateral donor agency, she would multiply her government salary by 27 times, or, if she worked for the United Nations – on a local contract – she would multiply her salary by 75 times. It is obvious that a cap on staff salaries for international agencies is necessary, both for local staff because of the brain effect and for international staff, for efficiency and equity reasons.

Jeanine Mkawu, one of my students in the DRC, researched the brain drain effect in the DRC by looking at the professional trajectories of the graduates of our university: who are their future employers? The question is particularly interesting because the university where I taught, the Catholic University of Congo, is considered the best university in the country. The university only admits the best students. She analysed the careers of 100 graduates from the faculty of economics and management. She came to the shocking conclusion that more than half of the alumni work for development

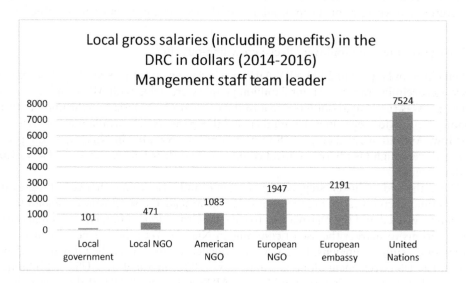

Figure 9.3 Wage differentials in the DRC, 2016.

Source: Koch and Schulpen, 'Individual-level wage effects.'

organizations, from Caritas to the World Bank (53 per cent), and that they are very satis-fied with their position. A small minority work for the government, but say that they are actively looking for another employer.

This 'negative spillover' of capacity is most often not just a short-term effect, but has long-term repercussions. Once national staff have worked in the environment of an inter-national organization, with its air-conditioned offices and steady electricity, it is hard for them to move back to the government. For instance, in Cambodia, the idea was that the national staff of the UN would move back to the public sector after the international intervention had ended. The reality was that local staff did not do that,[5] and that working for an international organization was the first step for emigration.[6]

While there does not seem to be an encompassing solution, there are interesting initiatives combatting the brain drain that need to be strengthened. For instance, in Zambia and Malawi, the Ministry of Health has promoted the retention of current per-sonnel by implementing a six-year emergency human resources programme.[7] Implemented in the early 2000s and supported by many international donors, the initiative seeked to improve incentives for local recruitment and retention of health workers. It has had a positive impact.[8] There has also been some movement on the side of the NGOs. The 2016 Charter4Change, signed by 35 international NGOs (as of February 2020), aims to 'address and prevent the negative impact of recruiting national NGO staff during an emergency.'[9]

But to solve these issues more far-reaching measures are needed. In 2005, major donors from the Global North made the Paris Declaration on Aid Effectiveness, where they pledged to focus on strengthening national systems instead of setting up parallel ones. Can we live up to this promise? Additionally, can we set up a staff compensation fund, in which international agencies hiring national staff members plough back money into the structures that have educated and prepared their new colleagues? Can we set up a circular system, in which international agencies take national staff members on loan from national structures, after which the national staff members have to return to their original structure? Can we agree on a cap of salaries of the expatriates to more reasonable levels?

9.2 Negative thematic spillover effects: crowding-out effects

When I lived in Nigeria in 2003, HIV-AIDS was ravaging and still expanding. Life expect-ancy was declining rapidly. About 7 million people were living with AIDS, and the preva-lence rate was rising to about 6 per cent of the population. Nigeria was the number three country worldwide regarding the number of AIDS patients. The availability of condoms was low. Antiretroviral therapy (ART) was even less available in Nigeria, as the prices were still very high (as pharmaceutical companies and their backers prevented a waiving of the patents).

Then, the aid industry stepped up its game and everything changed. Progressive donors funded civil society organizations that spearheaded a successful campaign to get the patens waived and big pharma had to cave in. Other donors funded social marketing organizations to market the use of condoms in Nigeria. Yet other agencies focussed on rolling out testing campaigns. By 2018, the prevalence rate was pushed down to 1.5 per cent.[10] The US government alone has until now (2022) invested over USD 90 billion in the so-called President's Emergency Plan for AIDS Relief (PEPFAR). If the international community sets its mind to something, and works well together with local partners, it can get impressive things done. Just like smallpox, which was eradicated by the international community in 1980, also HIV-AIDS can be combatted, even though we are not there yet.

Yet, this focus on one particular objective comes at a price. This section deals with this price: the thematic crowding-out effect. The international community used in its fight against HIV-AIDS the so-called 'vertical' approach. This means that, from the head-quarters of the international agencies in Geneva and New York to the smallest entity in Nigeria, a parallel structure was set up – a separate UN agency, separate implementation units in Ministries of Health worldwide, even separate clinics sometimes. Thematic crowding out occurs when external aid resources pull internal financial and human resources into the same subsector already receiving the external funding. These funds also need to be administered, drawing management resources away from other sectors. Hence, internal support for non-aid-supported sectors dwindles because of the external intervention. This happened with the HIV-AIDS response in Nigeria.

For example, in 2004, foreign aid earmarked for maternal, neonatal, and child health (MNCH) services constituted only 0.5 per cent of all health-specific foreign aid, while MNCH diseases still contributed to 45 per cent of the total disease burden in Nigeria (despite the rise in HIV-AIDS). In contrast, HIV contributed 6.3 per cent of Nigeria's total disease burden in 2004, yet 32 per cent of foreign aid was allocated to HIV programmes.[11] Doctors, nurses, and internal resources were disproportionally used to accommodate and accompany this funding and removed from the regular health care

Figure 9.4 Taking HIV-AIDS metrics as a yardstick, the vertical HIV-AIDS programming was a great success, but there are hidden costs to these vertical programmes.

Source: Isabel Corthier and MSF.

system. The consequence? A significant reduction in vaccinations in Nigeria. Statistical analysis by Chima and Franzini showed that a one-dollar increase in HIV aid per capita was associated with a decrease in the probability of receipt of vaccines by 8–31 per cent (depending on the disease). They suggest that donors rethink their funding strategies favouring more 'horizontal' approaches.[12] In these approaches the general health system is strengthened, not just for one but for all diseases, in a sustainable manner.

Findings from Mozambique in the health sector confirm the adverse effects of using a vertical (disease-specific) approach. Of the about 700 doctors that were trained in Mozambique since independence, over 25 per cent have stopped working in public health care, and are working for donors and NGOs and private initiatives.[13] This corresponds to the findings on 'brain drain' that I described in the first part of this chapter: capacity leaks away from the public sector to the private sector. Interventions in the parallel sector crowd out the response capacity of the state. Twenty-five per cent might not look like a lot and some argue that internal migration does not weaken health systems, as physicians largely leave to work for agencies that support the public sector. However, a detailed analysis by Sherr et al. shows that especially the senior-level physicians leave the public sector in Mozambique (for them the percentage is 47 per cent vs. 11 per cent for the younger doctors). This leaves junior managers with less training and experience in their place and weakens the health system.

I am not saying that the donors made a mistake by investing heavily in fighting the HIV-AIDS pandemic, but I am saying that more could have been done to avoid the thematic crowding-out effects. When I look at how the international community dealt with the next pandemic, that is, the COVID-19 pandemic, I have the impression that the aid sector is made of adaptive agents. In all the major COVID-19 policy initiatives, health systems strengthening is an integral part, at least on paper (which is a first step). How does that work in practice? As part of the COVID-19 vaccination response, the cold-chain storage of vaccines was improved in certain countries, such as Namibia. In these new cold chains, not just COVID-19 vaccines can be stored, but all vaccinations that need to be kept cold, such as the rabies vaccination, can be used.[14] In this way the COVID-19 response can strengthen the entire health system. Of course, there is often still a gap between theory and practice,[15] but at last the theory takes the crowding-out effect into consideration now.

9.3 Negative geographic spillover effects: leakage

I have always had a fascination with rainforests. While at primary school, my classmates and I made our own black and white 'magazine' dubbed *animal life*, which we sold to family and friends. We handwrote about 20 pages with pictures, puzzles, and hand-made infographics about endangered species. The second edition (after the first edition 'the seal') was called 'the monkey' and focussed on rainforests. We sent the proceeds, in my view the astronomical sum of 36 guilders (EUR 17), to Greenpeace, to support their programmes to combat deforestation. I remember vividly drawing an infographic comparing the length of Dutch trees to rainforest trees. I was dreaming at night about visiting these magnificent forests.

About a decade later, when I was 21, my dream came true. I could do an internship for an international NGO operating in the rainforest of eastern Cameroon. Our first stop was the sleepy capital Yaoundé. From the balcony of our hotel, I saw huge trucks with even larger trunks of tropical trees pass by every day. I was sad to see this happening. Something had to be done about this! While my internship was a failure,[16] I got a chance to visit a programme which appeared effective in the fight against deforestation: the community forest project in Lomié. I travelled with a ramshackle bus to the village. The bus got stuck in the middle of the forest three times, and we had to get out of it to push it. I did not mind at all: finally, I could smell the rainforest, hear the buzz of animal life and see the trees towering next to the side of the road: this is what I had been dreaming about! We arrived in the village in the middle of the night.

Over the coming days, the project staff showed me how the local Baka population (Pygmies) had turned the forest into a community forest. They had succeeded at keeping the industrial loggers at bay in part by engaging themselves in responsible tree cutting. The development organization had even provided a mobile seesaw to that effect (the project was hence called 'the mobile see-saw project'). It might sound contradictory, but they succeeded in maintaining the forest by monetizing a small part of it.[17] The forest that the project was supposed to protect was protected. In my view, the project was a big success. That was before I learned about geographic spillover effects, in the nature conservation literature called the leakage effect.

Leakage effects are the geographic spillover effects of a development intervention, such as climate mitigation. More specifically, leakage means more greenhouse gas emissions outside a project or programme boundary that is directly or indirectly attributable to the intervention implemented within those boundaries.[18]

Figure 9.5 Baka kids relaxing on a tree trunk close to Lomié.

Source: Henk Bothof.

There are primary and secondary leakages.[19] Primary leakage refers to direct leakage effects caused by the relocation of baseline activities or agents from one area to the next. You can also call it activity shifting: to produce the crops or obtain the fuel wood needed, already existing local deforestation agents are likely to move to surrounding areas to continue activities.

Secondary leakage occurs when forest conservation in one place indirectly creates incentives to deforest in other places. These indirect effects are usually caused by the reduction in the supply of commercial products (e.g. timber), which leads to higher prices for these products. Because of higher prices and to meet existing demand, production (e.g. logging) increases elsewhere. The difference from primary leakage is that the forest conservation activity causes incentives for others to start deforesting, rather than encourage deforestation agents to move to new places.[20]

In my positive appraisal of the programme's effectiveness in Lomié, I had not thought about that at all. It doesn't mean that the 'mobile see-saw' project wasn't effective, but we cannot say anything about its effectiveness until we measure the leakage effect. Unfortunately, I was in good company with my naïve positive appraisal, as many others when they measure the success of protected areas do not look beyond the projected area itself.

But detailed evidence from the Amazon region shows that we should. Greenpeace had started a successful campaign to push companies in Brazil to agree to a Soy Moratorium in the Amazon[21] (undoubtedly building on my earlier contribution of EUR 16). The moratorium entailed that actors such as the National Grain Exporters Association and commodity traders agreed to boycott farmers who grew soy on land cleared after 2006. The Banco do Brasil (a major Brazilian bank) further stimulated this accord by restricting credit to farmers who deforested after that date. By overlaying annual deforestation imagery from the Brazilian Space Agency on crop production after 2006, the monitoring system detected the noncompliant producers and creates a blocklist of them. The traders that signed the Soy Moratorium use the list to avoid noncompliant purchases.[22]

The Greenpeace-induced programme was a big success. A recent study by Heilmayr et al. showed that the Soy Moratorium contributed to 'one of the great conservation successes of the twenty-first century–an 84 per cent decrease in the rate of Brazilian Amazon deforestation.'[23]

Yet, if we look outside of the Amazon rainforest, this very optimistic story needs to be nuanced. We find evidence that the Soy Moratorium induced agricultural relocation into its less regulated ecosystem neighbour, the Cerrado. Within 100 km of the frontier with the Amazon, soy production increased by 31 per cent relative to the region farther away from the Amazon from 2007 until 2013. The deforestation leakage was estimated at 12.7 per cent (so for every 100 trees saved in the Amazon, 13 were cut in Cerrado), showing that the Amazon protection was having less carbon impact than proclaimed.[24] In this case we see that technological progress, such as satellite images, makes the monitoring of side effects easier. The technical barriers to learning are overcome, making policy learning a bit less bounded. Yet, if there is no political will to learn this lesson, deforestation will continue to increase as became clear during the Bolsanaro presidency in Brazil.

9.3.1 Offsetting your carbon footprint: think twice

Whether you buy a plane ticket for work or book a holiday, more and more often you can offset your carbon footprint. With a click on a small button at the end of your booking you can 'compensate your CO_2 emissions,' often by adding a couple of euros to your payment. I appreciate this opportunity and often tick the box, without really investigating how companies make it happen. Well, they do so by buying 'carbon credits,' meaning that the money is used to compensate people and companies who are saving carbon (for instance, by not cutting trees). The carbon credit market for avoided deforestation has become a serious business. Unfortunately, there is still a lot of haze on calculating and monitoring avoided deforestation, especially when it comes to leakage.[25] The flagship Forest Carbon Development Project (FCDP) of the World Bank, for instance, does not require monitoring leakage effects.[26] Measuring and monitoring international leakage was the weak spot for all the various carbon accounting mechanisms, whereas there is ample evidence that cross-border leakage occurs.[27] Some initiatives do monitor the primary leakage effects, but find it much harder to assess the secondary effects.[28]

Leakage is a common and real risk for anti-deforestation programmes, and a certain level of leakage will be unavoidable. However, leakage can be managed. For instance, leakage management at the project or programme level typically requires: (1) the identification of potential leakage effects associated with the mitigation activity; (2) a reduction of leakage through a smart project or programme design; (3) monitoring and accounting of leakage in a sufficiently large monitoring area; and, if the intervention is linked to carbon crediting, (4) discount of any leakage from greenhouse gasses benefits claimed.[29]

While – because of this research – I have been a bit more cautious about ticking this 'carbon compensation' box, I am not opposed to the idea of carbon credits per se. It is just important to verify that you actually get what you are paying for. Or, if you are more ambitious: play your part in developing an offsetting system that actually contributes to fighting climate change, instead of facilitating carbon-intensive luxury consumption by a small global minority.

9.4 Fungibility: adverse financial spillover effects not as bad as suggested

If there has been one potential side effect that has received ample attention in the aid debate, then it has been the issue of fungibility. Fungi-what? Fungibility is easiest to explain with an example. Imagine that you are a donor and decide to fund schools in a low-income country. Now that the government doesn't have to fund its schools anymore, it decides to spend the money allocated for schools on new gear for the military. The donor thinks it is funding a school, but in fact the donor is funding gear for the military. That's fungibility, and I classify it as negative spillover effect as the funding 'leaks' to other sectors.[30] In the literature on fungibility it is usually assumed that fungibility is bad. After all, it is thought, recipients are often corrupt and will not make the right choices on their own.

Because donors were not happy with fungibility, they all came up with ways to curb it. First, they started giving less and less money to governments, and set up their programmes separately. In addition, they forced recipient governments to match funding to the programme. For example, 'We give EUR 10 million to an AIDS programme in your country if you also give EUR 10 million to that AIDS programme.' Therefore, the assumption is that fungibility is bad, and we need to curb that because we fear negative spillover of our aid. If this sounds somewhat paternalistic, it does because it is, especially when you consider the problematic programming preferences of many donors.

Zunera Rana has developed a number of scenarios that show that fungibility does not have to be negative at all. In fact, according to her, it can even turn out to be positive, because donors often do not know any better, or at least do not act better than recipient governments.[31] Let me highlight two scenarios, one related to marginal added value and the other to inequality.

Donors often assume that they know what a recipient country needs. They believe they know where their money can make a difference. However, Zunera notices that donor preferences fluctuate very irrationally over time: for a few years, money flows in for social sectors and then donors stop; then the money flows in for employment, then it stops abruptly. These large fluctuations in aid funding say more about new hypes in the donor countries (e.g. migration management) than about shifting needs in developing countries. Therefore, it may be quite rational for recipient governments to cash in on a donor's hype, but divert their own resources elsewhere to cushion the donor shocks. For example: why put even more of their own money into the health sector, where the added value of their money is less, than, for example, in a sector where donors are not willing to help, such as infrastructure?

A second misconception is that donors would be good at tackling inequality. Donors often think they are good at ensuring that the poorest provinces and groups are included. After all, they have embraced the 'leave no one behind' slogan. According to Zunera, this is also a misconception. She studied donor behaviour in detail in Pakistan. There, she saw that donors steered clear of the most unsafe areas, where the population's needs were greatest. The local Ministries of Planning and Finance officials came up with a ruse: they decided to reallocate their own budget. For every rupee that donors invested in a popular and convenient province, the Pakistani government removed a rupee from there: 100 per cent fungibility. Donors were disappointed, since they wanted to show that health indicators in the popular provinces went up due to their aid funds. However, because the Pakistani government took its own money out of there, there would be no increase in health indicators at all in the provinces where donors had spent their money. However, donors should not mind: their money is indeed being spent usefully, just outside their field of view. So fungibility is not necessarily bad, but can lead to positive outcomes.

In the introduction of this book I tried to dismantle the myth that unintended effects are always downplayed: indeed, in the case of fungibility they might actually be overrated. After having accompanied Zunera in her PhD writing process, I can only concur: the concerns about fungibility are overdone. While fungibility is certainly happening, it is not necessarily bad.

9.4.1 Recap on negative spillover effects

While worries about fungibility have been largely overdrawn, other negative spillover effects are often underestimated, but have all the more negative impact. These negative spillovers can be institutional (brain drain), thematic (crowding out), or geographic (leakage). All three merit more of our attention.

How to tackle negative spillover effects

Policymakers

- **Promote horizontal instead of vertical programming.** Attempt to work with government structures and strengthen them, instead of creating parallel structures.
- **Assume that you don't know what is best.** The agency that you represent can display irrational behaviour. Hence, do not jump on the bandwagon to decry potential

fungibility, but aim to understand what actors in the recipient country are trying to achieve by redirecting funds.
- **Define common standards for leakage measurement and reporting.** This is currently still a weak element in many environmental programmes.
- **Coordinate amongst donors**: if the collective of donors starts harmonizing their funding decisions and communicating about them promptly, this will reduce the need for recipient governments to make last-minute (re)allocation decisions.

Practitioners

- **Consider that there are multiple interconnections between the intervention area and the non-target area.** Aim to detect these interlinkages. Maximize them if positive, and minimize them if negative.
- **Hire locally, but set up a compensation fund for organizations that you hire from.** Save money by hiring locally and investing funds in strengthening local human resource capacity. When hiring staff previously employed for local structures, compensate these structures.

Evaluators

- **Have a broad evaluation perspective.** Look at the impact on the target area and the non-target area, both in a geographic and a broader thematic sense.

Notes

1 Simon Harris, 'Disasters and dilemmas: Aid agency recruitment and HRD in post-tsunami Sri Lanka,' *Human Resource Development International* 9, no. 2 (2006): 291–298, https://doi.org/10.1080/13678860500522876
2 Nicolas Lemay-Hébert, Louis Herns Marcelin, Stéphane Pallage, and Toni Cela, 'The internal brain drain: Foreign aid, hiring practices, and international migration,' *Disasters* 44, no. 4 (2020): 621–640, https://doi.org/10.1111/disa.12382
3 There is another factor that adds to the dilemma: third-country nationals. They are not local, neither are they from the donor country, but they are from, for instance, a neighbouring country. This category is growing rapidly. This complicates issues, for them it costs much less to support their families back home than for a Swiss national, for example. Should they get the same salary?
4 Dirk-Jan Koch and Lau Schulpen, 'An exploration of individual-level wage effects of foreign aid in developing countries,' *Evaluation and Programme Planning* 68 (2018): 233–242, https://doi.org/10.1016/j.evalprogplan.2017.09.002
5 Carnahan et al., *Economic Impact of Peacekeeping*, 36.
6 Lemay-Hébert, 'Internal brain drain.'
7 For Zambia, see Melle Leenstra, *Beyond the façade: Instrumentalisation of the Zambian Health Sector*, doctoral thesis (Leiden: Leiden University, 2012), https://hdl.handle.net/1887/18587; for Malawi, see World Health Organization, *The World Health Report 2006: Working Together for Health* (Geneva: World Health Organization, 2006), www.who.int/publications/i/item/the-world-health-report---2006---working-together-for-health, 22.
8 Ibid.
9 Charter4Change, 'Commitment 4: Address and prevent the negative impact of recruiting national NGO staff during an emergency,' 19 August 2016, https://charter4change.org/2016/08/19/commitment-4-address-and-prevent-the-negative-impact-of-recruiting-national-ngo-staff-during-an-emergency/. Unfortunately, there are no clear indicators for monitoring this,

neither are signatories obliged to report, making it an interesting but not ground-breaking initiative. Nevertheless, we should strengthen these types of initiatives.

10 Nigeria Health Watch, 'Results of NAIIS–the largest HIV survey ever done are in: Nigeria not doing as badly as we thought!,' 14 March 2019, https://nigeriahealthwatch.com/results-of-naiis-the-largest-hiv-survey-ever-done-are-in-nigeria-not-doing-as-badly-as-we-thought/

11 Charles C. Chima and Luisa Franzini, 'Spillover effect of HIV-specific foreign aid on immunization services in Nigeria,' *International Health* 8, no. 2 (2016): 108, https://doi.org/10.1093/inthealth/ihv036

12 Ibid.

13 Kenneth Sherr, Antonio Mussa, Baltazar Chilundo, Sarah Gimbel, James Pfeiffer, Amy Hagopian, and Stephen Gloyd, 'Brain drain and health workforce distortions in Mozambique,' *PLoS One* 7, no. 4 (2012): e35840, https://pubmed.ncbi.nlm.nih.gov/22558237/

14 USAID, 'Building a specialized cold chain to deliver COVID-19 vaccinations in Namibia,' 3 January 2023, https://ghsupplychain.org/news/building-specialized-cold-chain-deliver-covid-19-vaccinations-namibia

15 Turcotte-Tremblay et al. 'unintended consequences of COVID-19.'

16 We were sent to eastern Cameroon to evaluate a microcredit programme of the NGO that we were interning with: I had never done an evaluation (let alone of a microcredit programme) but studied for two months to prepare. However, when we arrived in eastern Cameroon, there was no microcredit programme. Unsure what we should do, we decided to do a feasibility study for a microcredit programme, which consisted mainly of asking villagers if they would be interested in a credit. In terms of expectation management this was the worse we could have done: two white students asking very impoverished peasants if they wanted a loan (which never came).

17 Philippe Auzel, Willy Delvingt, R. Fetekè, and G. M. Nguenang, 'Small-scale logging in community forests in Cameroon. Towards ecologically more sustainable and socially more acceptable compromises,' *ODI Rural Development Forestry Network Paper* 25f (2001): 1–13, https://cdn.odi.org/media/documents/1224.pdf

18 Charlotte Streck, 'REDD+ and leakage: Debunking myths and promoting integrated solutions,' *Climate Policy* 21, no. 6 (2021): 843–852, https://doi.org/10.1080/14693062.2021.1920363

19 Sabine Henders and Madelene Ostwald, 'Forest carbon leakage quantification methods and their suitability for assessing leakage in REDD,' *Forests* 3, no. 1 (2012): 33–58, http://doi.org/10.3390/f3010033

20 Ibid., 37.

21 Fanny Moffette and Holly K. Gibbs, 'Agricultural displacement and deforestation leakage in the Brazilian Legal Amazon,' *Land Economics* 97, no. 1 (2021): 155–179, https://doi.org/10.3368/wple.97.1.040219-0045R

22 Ibid., 158.

23 Robert Heilmayr, Lisa L. Rausch, Jacob Munger, and Holly K. Gibbs, 'Brazil's Amazon Soy Moratorium reduced deforestation,' *Nature Food* 1, no. 12 (2020): 801–810, https://doi.org/10.1038/s43016-020-00194-5

24 Moffette and Gibbs, 'Agricultural displacement,' 156.

25 Thiago Chagas, Hilda Galt, Donna Lee, Till Neeff, and Charlotte Streck, *A Close Look at the Quality of REDD+ Carbon Credits* (Amsterdam: Climate Focus, 2020), https://climatefocus.com/publications/close-look-quality-redd-carbon-credits/

26 Ibid., 16.

27 Henders and Ostwald, 'Forest carbon leakage.'

28 Streck, 'REDD+ and leakage.'

29 Adapted from Streck, 'REDD+ and leakage.'

30 Please note that fungibility is not the same as corruption, as the money that leaks somewhere can still be put to productive use, as we shall see.

31 Zunera Rana and Dirk-Jan Koch, 'Is it time to "decolonise" the fungibility debate?,' *Third World Quarterly* 41, no. 1 (2020): 42–57, https://doi.org/10.1080/01436597.2019.1665012

Further reading

Auzel, Philippe, Willy Delvingt, R. Fetekè, and G. M. Nguenang. 'Small-scale logging in community forests in Cameroon. towards ecologically more sustainable and socially more acceptable compromises.' *ODI Rural Development Forestry Network Paper* 25f (2001): 1–13. https://cdn.odi.org/media/documents/1224.pdf

Carnahan, Michael, William Durch, and Scott Gilmore. *Economic Impact of Peacekeeping.* New York: United Nations, Peacekeeping Best Practices Unit, 2006. www.stimson.org/wp-content/files/file-attachments/EIP_FINAL_Report_March2006doc_1.pdf

Chagas, Thiago, Hilda Galt, Donna Lee, Till Neeff, and Charlotte Streck. *A Close Look at the Quality of REDD+ Carbon Credits.* Amsterdam: Climate Focus, 2020. https://climatefocus.com/publications/close-look-quality-redd-carbon-credits/

Charter4Change. 'Commitment 4: Address and prevent the negative impact of recruiting national NGO staff during an emergency.' 19 August 2016. https://charter4change.org/2016/08/19/commitment-4-address-and-prevent-the-negative-impact-of-recruiting-national-ngo-staff-during-an-emergency/

Chima, Charles C., and Luisa Franzini. 'Spillover effect of HIV-specific foreign aid on immunization services in Nigeria.' *International Health* 8, no. 2 (2016): 108–115. https://doi.org/10.1093/inthealth/ihv036

Harris, Simon. 'Disasters and dilemmas: Aid agency recruitment and HRD in post-tsunami Sri Lanka.' *Human Resource Development International* 9, no. 2 (2006): 291–298. https://doi.org/10.1080/13678860500522876

Heilmayr, Robert, Lisa L. Rausch, Jacob Munger, and Holly K. Gibbs. 'Brazil's Amazon Soy Moratorium reduced deforestation.' *Nature Food* 1, no. 12 (2020): 801–810. https://doi.org/10.1038/s43016-020-00194-5

Henders, Sabine, and Madelene Ostwald. 'Forest carbon leakage quantification methods and their suitability for assessing leakage in REDD.' *Forests* 3, no. 1 (2012): 33–58. http://doi.org/10.3390/f3010033

Koch, Dirk-Jan, and Lau Schulpen. 'An exploration of individual-level wage effects of foreign aid in developing countries.' *Evaluation and Programme Planning* 68 (2018): 233–242. https://doi.org/10.1016/j.evalprogplan.2017.09.002

Leenstra, Melle. *Beyond the façade: Instrumentalisation of the Zambian Health Sector.* Doctoral thesis. Leiden: Leiden University, 2012. https://hdl.handle.net/1887/18587

Lemay-Hébert, Nicolas, Louis Herns Marcelin, Stéphane Pallage, and Toni Cela. 'The internal brain drain: Foreign aid, hiring practices, and international migration.' *Disasters* 44, no. 4 (2020): 621–640. https://doi.org/10.1111/disa.12382

Moffette, Fanny, and Holly K. Gibbs. 'Agricultural displacement and deforestation leakage in the Brazilian Legal Amazon.' *Land Economics* 97, no. 1 (2021): 155–179. https://doi.org/10.3368/wple.97.1.040219-0045R

Nigeria Health Watch. 'Results of NAIIS–the largest HIV survey ever done are in: Nigeria not doing as badly as we thought!' 14 March 2019. https://nigeriahealthwatch.com/results-of-naiis-the-largest-hiv-survey-ever-done-are-in-nigeria-not-doing-as-badly-as-we-thought/

Rana, Zunera, and Dirk-Jan Koch. 'Is it time to "decolonise" the fungibility debate?' *Third World Quarterly* 41, no. 1 (2020): 42–57. https://doi.org/10.1080/01436597.2019.1665012

Sherr, Kenneth, Antonio Mussa, Baltazar Chilundo, Sarah Gimbel, James Pfeiffer, Amy Hagopian, and Stephen Gloyd. 'Brain drain and health workforce distortions in Mozambique.' *PLoS One* 7, no. 4 (2012): e35840. https://pubmed.ncbi.nlm.nih.gov/22558237/

Streck, Charlotte. 'REDD+ and leakage: Debunking myths and promoting integrated solutions.' *Climate Policy* 21, no. 6 (2021): 843–852. https://doi.org/10.1080/14693062.2021.1920363

Turcotte-Tremblay, Anne-Marie, Idriss Ali Gali Gali, and Valéry Ridde. 'The unintended consequences of COVID-19 mitigation measures matter: Practical guidance for investigating them.' BMC *Medical Research Methodology* 21, no. 1 (2021): 28. https://doi.org/10.1186/s12 874-020-01200-x

USAID, 'Building a specialized cold chain to deliver COVID-19 vaccinations in Namibia,' 3 January 2023, https://ghsupplychain.org/news/building-specialized-cold-chain-deliver-covid-19-vaccinations-namibia

World Health Organization. *The World Health Report 2006: Working Together for Health*. Geneva: World Health Organization, 2006. www.who.int/publications/i/item/the-world-health-report---2006---working-together-for-health

10 Governance effects

International development and the social contract, uneasy bedfellows

Unintended governance effects occur when external interventions unintentionally influence the quality and reach of institutions at any level in the recipient country.

What flavours do we see?

1 **Corruption effects.** The external intervention provides extra means for the elite for embezzlement and reduces possibilities for citizens to put a check on that.
2 **Democracy effects.** Leaders of a country use the foreign aid to bolster their grip on power and undermine democracy.
3 **Tax effects.** The arrival of foreign funds reduces (or increases) incentives for the recipient government to mobilize domestic resources.

In which instances have governance effects been observed? Three examples:

1 Corruption effects: aid can provide rents that can be distributed as spoils to political allies or appropriated by the ruling elites, from four-wheel drives to lucrative training missions abroad, as became clear in Iraq.
2 Democracy effects: strongmen can make use of foreign aid to reduce democracy. In Rwanda, the government claimed development results for international legitimacy, while strengthening its repression apparatus in the meantime.
3 Tax effects: Ethiopia was facing a rapid decline in donor funding in 2005 because of an electoral crackdown. The Ethiopian government hence developed plans to increase domestic resource mobilization, but donors started funding the Ethiopian government quite fast again, reducing the need for the government to introduce a better taxation system.

Key concepts from complexity thinking that help understand unintended governance effects:

1 **Non-linearity.** The relationship between aid and corruption is a complex one. There is a relationship, but it is non-linear: more aid does not inevitably lead to more corruption, nor to less corruption. The initial condition matters: if aid goes to a government with a strong pre-existing social contract, it can make use of the aid to strengthen its governance system. Yet, the reverse is also true: if aid goes

DOI: 10.4324/9781003356851-10

This Chapter has been made available under a CC-BY-NC-ND license.

to a government (or NGO) that is poorly organized or even already corrupt, aid can entrench poor governance practices.

2 **Alternative impact pathways.** Most international development efforts do not intend to have a governance effect. Still, these have governance ramifications in many instances: governance effects are often an unconsidered alternative impact pathway. An aid-induced alteration of the social contract can often explain the emergence of this unforeseen impact pathway.

Figure 10.1 Governance effects in action: foreign aid undermining the social contract by distorting government priorities.

Source: Maarten Wolterink.

To understand the potential governance effects of international aid, the term 'social contract' is essential. Social contract theory posits that there is an implicit agreement amongst the members of a society to cooperate for social benefits, for example, by sacrificing some individual freedom for state protection. The social contract contributes to an explanation of whether aid has positive or negative effects on governance in a recipient country, be it concerning corruption, democracy, or taxation. If aid strengthens the social contract, or if there is already a strong social contract, aid can further improve governance. Conversely, if the social contract is weak, or is weakened by international aid, it could worsen governance in a country. This might all sound a bit theoretical, so let me explain the differential governance outcomes of aid in two settings, which are similar in many ways but differ with respect to the social contract: Somaliland and Somalia.

The separation between Somaliland and Somalia in 1991 provides a rare opportunity for a natural comparison regarding the social contract in the context of international development. Although there are some differences, the two 'countries' (Somaliland is not internationally recognized) share characteristics such as geography and history, and were in a similar economic starting position in 1991. But whereas Somalia benefited from international support during the formative 1990s, Somaliland largely had to fend for itself in this crucial period. So you would expect that Somalia is performing much better on development indicators than its neighbour now, but the opposite is the case: paradoxically (at first glance), Somaliland now has much higher governance performance and political stability than its neighbour! I want to refrain from claiming a direct causal relation between the absence of foreign support and a strong social contract: we only have to look at countries that received little aid and don't have a strong social contract, such as the Central African Republic. Nevertheless, I think it is plausible that, in the absence of foreign support in the formative years of Somaliland, a stronger endogenous social contract could emerge. Whereas Somaliland has become a largely stable 'country' despite major shortcomings, this progress lacks in Somalia. Whereas the absence of aid appears to have forced local elites in Somaliland to reach a deal about domestic resource mobilization, the international presence (also driven in part by its continued instability) in Somalia allowed more extractive governance models to persist. Currently, differences

Table 10.1 Governance effects of international development and peacebuilding efforts: a comparison between Somalia and Somaliland

	Somalia	*Somaliland*
Malnutrition: wasting (too small children)	14.3 per cent (2009)[1]	13 per cent (2020)[2]
Democratic elections	Not free (7 out of 100)[3]	East Africa's strongest democracy[4]
Terrorism[5]	Continuous attacks from Al-Shabaab, who occupy certain parts	No terrorist attacks since 2008
Piracy[6]	Continuous off the coastline	Very little piracy
Peacekeeping missions[7]	Continuous peacekeeping missions	No blue helmets
Support for peace negotiations[8]	At least seventeen internationally sponsored sets of peace talks	No internationally supported peace talks
International development efforts[9]	The international community funded the majority of its annual budget.	Somaliland's government has had negligible access to external capital in its formative years
Impact of (absence of) aid on peace talks[10]	No pressure to come to peace agreements	No time to waste to finalize peace talks
Impact of (absence of) on taxation[11]	Port revenues didn't enter state coffers and continuous fighting between various armed groups for access to ports	A deal had to be struck for domestic resource mobilization, especially taxation of port revenues. Port revenues entered the coffers of the state.
Impact of (absence of) aid on accountability relations[12]	Continued competition to become preferred partners of the international community	Forced collaboration between elites
Impact of (absence of) aid on institutions[13]	A tendency towards more exclusive institutions	A trend towards more inclusive institutions

in aid levels have become less, with an increasing number of development agencies operating in Somaliland.

As the textbox shows, the literature indicates that international development efforts can be associated with weakening accountability relations.[14] However, the reverse can also be the case. Through the organization of elections and election monitoring missions, the international development cooperation system has contributed to improved democratic governance from the DRC to East Timor and many countries in between. In short, this is the puzzle we try to solve in this chapter: when and why do international development efforts have a negative effect on governance levels? We analyse this question by looking at corruption, democracy, and taxation respectively.

10.1 Corruption effects: feeding the beast?

I called the secretary of the Nigerian Ministry of Finance director another time. We were waiting for him to sign the Economic Management Capacity Programme (EMCAP) documents, and to my delight, she informed me I could pick them up. The European Commission contributed over EUR 10 million to the Ministry of Finance to combat corruption through this programme. I believed in it: if there was no more corruption in Nigeria, the country would most certainly take off. It was early 2003, and at 22 years, I was the youngest staff member of the Delegation of the European Commission in Abuja. So, it was my task to collect these papers. With the elevators in the Ministry being out of order, I climbed the stairs hastily while sweating like a dog. Arriving in the waiting area before the director's office, which was luckily air-conditioned, I was surprised to get just a few signed papers back. 'Oh yes, I forgot to tell you. We have lost some of the documents,' the secretary explained. They had signed the papers concerning the equipment: they could now purchase the project car and the computers. However, the papers that would enable a study to detect weaknesses in the financial management system of the Ministry were lost. I felt a true disappointment, and went back up the stairs to print the 'lost' documents again, realizing our programme was in trouble. What had I been thinking? Was I right to believe that the Nigerian Ministry of Finance officials would be our allies in the fight against corruption? They were the ones benefiting most from the cracks in the system. Had we been financing pyromaniacs to become firefighters? While EMCAP intended to improve governance, the reverse might have been happening instead.

For those of us in the development sector and who attend family reunions (I match both criteria), there often comes this irritating part in the conversation when you have to explain your work, and when your cousin starts mansplaining to you why aid does not work: 'It only breeds corruption. You need to stop wasting our money.' If you only read the headlines of conservative newspapers, such as the Daily Mail's 'Confirmed: Our foreign aid fuels corruption,' this seems indeed a logical argument to make during this family reunion.[15] Even though I am quite confident that I have studied the side effects of international development efforts probably more than my cousin, he wins the argument according to the rest of my family, as my answer is too long and boring. Since I have had the chance to practice my response to the claim that aid is fuelling corruption quite a few times (unfortunately also during welcome drinks with new neighbours), I hope it comes out convincingly this time around on paper.

Let me first provide a short definition of corruption, as there are wildly divergent views on corruption in the context of aid. A Western aid worker, who stays in a five-star hotel in the capital with a swimming pool, collecting USD 200 a day in per diems while the average annual income in the country is USD 200, is that corruption? An expat earning USD 10,000 a month tax-free, while a local colleague doing the same work making USD 1,000 a month, is that corruption? Corruption refers to obtaining private gains from public office through bribes, extortion, and embezzlement of public funds. So, while becoming rich while 'fighting' poverty is a sign of a sick system (and might induce corruption), it is not corruption as such.

According to Todd Moss, my former teacher at the London School of Economics (LSE), certain aid practices serve to reinforce the patrimonial element within recipient governments. Projects provide for the allocation of all sorts of discretionary goods to be politicized and patrimonialized, including expensive four-wheel drive cars, scholarships, decisions over where to place schools and roads, and so on. The common practice of paying cash 'sitting fees' for civil servants attending donor-funded workshops, where the daily rates can exceed regular monthly salaries, even turns training into rent to be distributed.[16] So my cousin and the Daily Mirror seem to have a point. However, whether aid really contributes to corruption depends on at least three factors, namely (1) the intent and resolve of donors, (2) the type of aid, and (3) the type of recipient.

First, the intent and resolve of donors matter. If donors are committed to reducing corruption, they may be able to use aid as leverage, making the continued flow of funds conditional on political and financial reform. These conditionalities can strengthen the social contract and the fight against corruption. There are often legitimate worries about conditionalities from donors, as often they have been misguided (we turn to that also in Section 10.3), detrimental to people with low incomes and reduce policy autonomy. However, they can also be beneficial for the population.

For example, Yanguas shows how the UK government used its aid in such a way to strengthen the possibilities for stronger domestic accountability relations in Sierra Leone by making payments contingent on for instance better government transparency.[17] For this to work, donors have to stick to the political conditions that they have imposed and coordinate with each other, which is often quite difficult for them, especially if geopolitics gets in the way.[18] If the recipient is for instance a geopolitically important country, there is more chance that the aid will lead to corruption. Why? These recipient governments know that donors are only bluffing about the conditionalities on aid. Even if they embezzle, they expect that the aid will keep on flowing: a typical case of moral hazard. Kersting and Kilby show that the leaders of these countries (for example, Iraq and Egypt) are correct. They can siphon off some of the aid without fear of serious repercussions. At this point, some of my family members started to lose interest in my argument.

Second, the type of aid determines if there are changed accountability relations and if these are negative. Actually, some of the aid can also reduce corruption when it funds institutional development within the government and civil society. The in-depth case study by Yanguas on the interaction between aid and corruption showed that when the British government provided targeted support to the Anti-Corruption Commission in the early 2000s in Sierra Leone, this contributed to a reduction in corruption. But, conversely, budget support can facilitate corruption, as the case of Uganda showed in Section 7.2 on elite capture. Donors can also unintentionally foster corruption if they provide aid that neither interests the recipient country's population nor the government, as misappropriated resources won't be missed (such as migration management programmes, see the cartoon).

A final factor that explains whether aid contributes to corruption relates to the initial level of governance. Governments tend to respond in the same way to increases in aid as they do to increases in resource rents (e.g., oil windfall gains): those with reasonable governance and a strong social contract against corruption generally tend to use the resources to strengthen their governance capacity. Those with weak levels of governance and a weak social contract see any aspirations for good governance go out of the window with this relatively easy funding. This also means that there is a non-linear relation between aid and corruption: it ultimately depends on the initial level of governance.[19]

By the time I had explained to my cousin that there were nuances to his claim, namely the intent and resolve of the donor, the type of aid, and the initial level of governance, all the family bystanders had already wandered off.

Let us return to the Daily Mirror and their 'it has been Confirmed: Our foreign aid fuels corruption' article. They base themselves on the report 'DFID's Approach to Anti-Corruption and its Impact on the Poor.' This report by the UK Independent Commission for Aid Impact indeed shows that in multiple instances DFID did not pay enough attention to these governance side effects. For instance, they financed the construction of extra police stations in Nigeria in order to bring the security provided by the police closer to the people. However, it also brought the disadvantages: mass extortions for minor infractions. By just focusing on the technical and visible aspects (construction), donors overlooked the invisible side effects (more extortion by state officials). The report showed that more can and should be done to deal with these type of effects, such as corruption perception surveys in and around intervention areas.

It is relatively easy, as the *Daily Mail* does, to find examples of how recipients have embezzled aid funding. However, also when it comes to corruption it takes two to tango, meaning that there should also be a critical regard towards how donor practices (from exorbitant salaries to geopolitical laxity and to making use of tax-havens[20] in export-financing) unintentionally contribute to corruption.

10.1.1 A zero-tolerance approach to corruption?

The *Daily Mail* would love to see a zero-tolerance policy against corruption in aid. But even though this book laments the inaction against side effects of aid, you would be mistaken to think that I would endorse such a zero-tolerance approach. Corruption research by Mushtaq Khan and others has taught us two things: (1) some degree of corruption can also contribute to development. For example, corruption can speed up bureaucratic processes. Many countries have progressed tremendously with some corruption in their system, and there is corruption in many of the wealthy countries today. (2) The wish for zero-corruption leads to aid going to projects where everything can be monitored and accounted for, but these often don't lead to the long-term structural changes needed for really uprooting corruption. Potentially more transformational programmes are shunned because of the perceived risk of corruption (we'll see the same in the following section on democracy programming). A zero-tolerance approach is hence neither feasible nor desirable. Khan proposes a different approach: sectoral anti-corruption strategies that target specific problems with a high developmental impact and that are also feasible to implement because at least some of the powerful engaged in these activities are likely to support their implementation in their own interest.[21]

10.2 Democracy effects: can aid inadvertently contribute to democratic backsliding?

The international community, if it plays it smartly, can stimulate democracy in countries in an effective way. For instance, the West-African country of Benin made a transition to democracy in 1990. Local activists demanded democratization (defined in this chapter as increased capacity by the population to influence the governance of a country). They were supported by the international community both diplomatically and financially. Foreign leaders such as French president François Mitterrand pushed verbally for a democratic opening, forgave debts when this opening occurred, and invested massive amounts of aid so that the population would experience a democratic dividend.[22] Statistical analysis indeed suggests a causal link between more donors and democratization.[23] But unfortunately, the international community doesn't always play it smartly.

What do countries such as Hungary, Ethiopia, Rwanda, Turkey, Sri Lanka, Russia, and Egypt have in common? They and many others have adopted anti-democratization measures over the past years, including anti-NGO legislation. It is getting increasingly difficult in these countries to register NGOs, receive funding from abroad, and play one of the key roles they are supposed to play: countervailing power to the state.

But these countries share something else.

These countries were all on the receiving end of international development efforts, and even democracy promotion programmes. Donors invested millions of dollars in these countries to promote democratization. International organizations and initiatives did more than just spend funds: they encouraged countries to participate in organizations such as the European Union (EU) and the Extractive Industries Transparency Initiatives to promote human rights and the rule of law. Despite all these carrots and sticks, there was democratic backsliding in these countries, as even academic freedom was increasingly curtailed. This section will try to understand the mechanisms behind this. The testimony of a Turkish professor, who was fired from his university in Ankara because of his critical research and positions gives a first hint on how aid can be associated with increased autocracy.

Testimony by a Turkish professor: 'I was fired on a Friday night as a university professor after signing a petition'

I am a former professor of political science at the University of Ankara, one of the most prestigious and progressive universities in Turkey. When I was dismissed in 2017, I was the head of the Department of International Relations.

Fired on a Friday night

It was on a Friday night in February when I, and about 35 others from my university, was fired by a governmental declaration. From one day to the next, I was cut off from everything. From my PhD students, my classes, everything. I was not allowed to enter the campus again, after 28 years of working there. It's all part of a trend of democratic backsliding since 2010. But the direct reason was a petition that I (and about a thousand others) had signed in 2015 to argue for peace in the bloody conflict between militants of the PKK (the Kurdistan Workers' Party,

Figure 10.2 Protest in Turkey after revising the national education curriculum.

Source: By Mark Lowen – Own work, CC BY-SA 4.0, https://commons.wikimedia.org/w/index.php?curid=82766779

a separatist group) and the military in the southeast of Turkey. This had angered president Erdogan.

After an attempted coup in 2016, the government declared a state of emergency, giving the president extra powers. Firing us, and many others in public positions, was an attack on free thinking, on academic life in Turkey. Even though we had nothing to do with the coup, it was a message that anybody who stands up against the government, against injustice, can be fired. It served to silence the opposition, which was partly successful.

3 billion euros for peace of mind

It was the Turkish government that decided to move from democracy to authoritarianism. But the EU played a key role. They became very transactional with Turkey. We had expected the EU to be an anchor for Turkey's rule of law. The process of Turkey's road towards EU membership should work to improve human rights and democracy, but it went backwards. The turning point? The so-called refugee deal in 2016. The EU, and Germany especially, were so eager to stop the refugee flow, that they began to tolerate Erdogan's authoritarian trajectory. Turkey would keep refugees in Turkey, and the EU would provide 3 billion euros in Official Development Assistance in return. And Turkish visa requirements would be eased. I find it unethical. You pay 3 billion euros and you have peace of mind. They allowed Erdogan to use refugees, human beings, as a foreign policy tool. He shouted in rallies: 'If you upset me, I will send the refugees to you!' He used it as blackmail. Both the EU and the Trump administration legitimized the democratic backslide. They didn't want to find the time and energy to find a better solution to ease the tension of the refugee flow.

The future

I still live in Ankara, and I am more in the media business now. I write for dailies and TV programmes and contribute to academic works. I can continue my work as long as I have internet connection and a computer. For me personally, the hardest part has been to sit for trial. Being in a courtroom, being accused of disseminating PKK propaganda. I have been on trial for three years, but I hope to be acquitted in June. And I am waiting for the elections, when everything can change again.

In addition to the testimony of the Turkish professor I performed a literature review to find out which mechanisms make international cooperation lead to a reduction in democracy, and I found the following three.

First, participation in international organizations can increase executive power through increased legitimacy and resources, even (or perhaps especially) if these international organizations aim to promote democracy, such as the EU. Government executives serve as the primary intermediaries between their states and the international organization. They are hence the gatekeepers and can siphon off resources and appoint representatives. The socio-economic support or security cooperation they receive prolongs their survival and shifts the domestic balance of power in favour of executives, as for instance the case of Victor Orbán in Hungary has shown. Geopolitics often determines whether these leaders can get away with it.[24]

Second, democracy promotion can provoke a counter-reaction by non-democratic actors. For instance, countries such as China and Russia have responded to the democracy promotion initiatives of the EU and the United States by stepping up their autocracy promotion in third countries, for instance, in Ukraine after the orange revolution.[25]

Third, international democracy promotion can make civil society and political actors more tame. In Morocco, the international support for political parties and civil society actors (and the focus on outputs such as workshops and learning sessions) reduced the willingness of local civil society organizations to confront high-level (including royal) corruption. The local actors took an increasingly a-political approach to corruption busting. It is easier to get funds for an innocent 'best practices seminar' than for a major sit-in in front of the royal palace. In sum, researchers conclude that democracy promotion made political parties in Morocco more professional while failing to make them more effective democratic actors.[26]

Let's look at Rwanda, where foreign support made pro-democracy actors less effective. In the book's introduction I shared the success of international development efforts in pushing up social indicators in Rwanda, but there is also a different story to be told. While Rwanda was one of those countries whose leaders were praised in the late 1990s for new leadership that heralded the renaissance of Africa, the country has become increasingly repressive over the last decades.

The international NGO I worked for operated in Rwanda when President Paul Kagame was further tightening his grip: opponents were jailed or assassinated, occasionally even abroad.[27] In this context, my organization aimed to contribute to 'participatory governance' with projects with laudable titles such as 'Advancing Civil Society Led Participatory Governance in Rwanda' (generously funded by the European Commission).[28] In order not to lose our license to operate (being shut down by the government) or to put our Rwandan staff in jeopardy, our projects became 'tame.'[29] We didn't take a stance when opposition leaders were jailed or executed. Maybe our projects were successful at the micro-level, but they had little or even adverse effects at the macro-level, by providing legitimacy and resources to the country's leaders. Looking outside of Rwanda, I realized that similar support patterns for democratization with ever-increasing levels of autocracy can be found in countries such as Cameroon. Also there, donors ultimately don't want to rock the boat too much, partially because of a fear of the unknown. Its leader Paul Biya has been ruling the country for over forty years, and this is neither because of his stellar development performance nor because of his democratic credentials, to put it mildly.

I started this section on the link between international development efforts and democracy positively with the example of Benin. It shows that aid can boost democracy, and we should continue trying. But let's not be naïve, as those opposing the democratization agenda have smart ways of turning good efforts around. How oblivious international donors can be to the mechanisms described above is exemplified by how they make the life of those democratic detractors extra easy by requiring that the donor's name is added to every small initiative. From the posters for 'get out to vote' campaigns to local election observation mission T-shirts: big logos make clear that external money is behind this. The branding of these election activities makes it appear as if democracy is a foreign idea. While the idea of donor support is to strengthen local accountability and democracy, the flag-planting makes it easier for those who oppose it to depict it as neocolonial interference. Donors ought to think more about strengthening the social contract instead of strengthening their visibility.

10.3 Tax effects: do the poor in rich countries subsidize the rich in poor countries?

Donors can play an important role in increasing government capacity if they make it an intended objective. For instance, the 'Tax Inspectors Without Borders' initiative has had great results. These tax officials from the Global North aim to support their colleagues from the Global South to increase domestic resource mobilization, with great effect. Capacity building programmes like these are true value for money: to date, Tax Inspectors Without Borders has generated additional revenues of more than USD 200 million, and has cost only a fraction of this.[30] But donors can also engender unintended tax effects, which we will focus on now.

When donors started to pull funding out of Kenya in the 1990s, this motivated the authorities to implement an ambitious tax reform programme that led to significant short-term revenue gains. But the opposite also happens! When in the mid-2000s the reverse happened and donors rapidly increased funding in Ethiopia, the government sharply reduced tax collection.[31] It could be the logical thing to do for a government in the short run: taxes are never popular, and if you have 'free' money, you can increase your popularity by lowering taxes. This will alter the social contract between the state and society, as the society will expect less and less of the state.

Luckily, I am not the only one who finds it important to know whether international development efforts lead to a reduction in taxes. Unfortunately, of all the riddles I have tried to solve, this is the one with the widest cacophony of answers. For instance, aid led to less domestic resource mobilization in Pakistan, Côte d'Ivoire, and Zambia.[32] Yet other studies show the opposite, for instance, in Indonesia and Ghana.[33] In these countries, an increase in aid allegedly led to increased taxation. These tax effects are not included in the result reports, leading to overestimating or underestimating results.

Also cross-country regressions (as opposed to the single country studies) show a very mixed image with respect to the effect of aid on tax efforts.[34] You know that I have some qualms about cross-country regressions, amongst others because of the data quality (see Section 6.2), but they contribute a highly relevant nuance to the discussion concerning the link between aid and taxation. These studies find that it depends on the aid composition, that is, grants vis-a-vis loans. The results indicate that concessional loans are generally associated with higher domestic revenue mobilization, while grants have the opposite effect, making governments less prudent about fiscal policy. The IMF hence suggests being careful in moving from loans to grants in international development.[35]

Regardless of the exact impact of aid on taxation, many developing countries need to raise more tax. Tax revenue collection as a share of GDP is only 15 to 20 per cent in lower and middle-income countries, but over 30 per cent in upper-income countries.[36] Earlier in this chapter, I wrote about how donors often get conditionalities wrong, and this has been particularly the case for taxation. As part of the 'Washington Consensus,' international donors demanded that recipient governments slash their taxes to attract foreign direct investment and stimulate business development. Alas, this reduction in taxes contributed to a high aid dependence: the budget of governments of Tajikistan, the West Bank and Gaza, Bhutan, and Ethiopia all consist for over 50 per cent foreign donor funding. Donors (and recipients) are increasingly aware that this is problematic, especially because of the volatility of aid flows and subsequent indebtedness. They therefore started jointly the Addis Tax Initiatives in 2015, which aims to ensure that more resources for development are mobilized in developing countries.

I conclude with one suggestion that would make for an obvious improvement in donors' internal consistency: even though donors now advise that more taxes everyone in developing countries must pay more taxes, strangely enough they find this does not concern themselves. They often negotiate tax exemptions for themselves, so that aid contractors can work tax-free in duty-free imported cars. This does not only smell of hypocrisy, but is also counterproductive, so let's stop it.[37]

How to tackle unintended governance effects

Policymakers (and politicians)

- **Adapt the aid modality to the initial governance level.** The better the governance, the more aid can be provided via the government. Conversely, if the governance level is poor, it is better to aid other actors (e.g., civil society) to increase the pressure for good governance and reduce negative side effects. This seems the obvious thing to do, but it is often not done.
- **Get conditionalities right and see them through.** Don't impose conditionalities that hamper democracy. When pro-democracy conditionalities are attached, it is relevant that donors show resolve to these conditionalities and see them through, even though it might hurt short-term geopolitical interests or funding ambitions. In the long run, geopolitical interests are best served if countries are democratic and well-governed.
- **Monitor and sanction worsening governance linked to participation in international bodies.** Accompany participation in international bodies by member states with clear monitoring (and sanctioning) mechanisms concerning governance. This enables civil society organizations, journalists, and others to hold these states accountable even as they seek to legitimize themselves through joining international organizations.
- **Reduce the branding of development interventions.** Realize that flag-planting can undermine the social contract. Use your messaging to strengthen the relationship between the government and the population rather than undermine it.

Practitioners

- **Don't depoliticize political actors.** Adapt pro-democracy programming in such a way that it does not depoliticize countervailing powers and doesn't legitimatize the powers that be.
- **Proactively support politicians and governors that are more favourable to democracy promptly.** For example, support a progressive minister, mayor, or provincial governor from the opposition. Be sharp on potential windows of opportunity. Once there is a democratic transition (e.g. when an autocrat has been overthrown), stand ready with quick support.
- **Plan in such a way that the social contract is strengthened.** If foreign funding is tailored well, it reinforces rather than weakens domestic resource mobilization efforts. Stop tax exemptions for aid agencies themselves.
- **Communicate so that stakeholders can access and understand it.** Communicate about international development efforts in a way that is available and accessible to citizens of recipient countries and provide them with the tools to track these efforts (and potential spills).

Evaluators

- **Perform joint political-economy analyses.** To better detect unintended effects more (preferably joint) political and economic analyses are needed, especially with an eye to governance performance: this will enable international development efforts to be more informed about potential side effects.

Notes

1 World Health Organization. *Nutrition Country Profile: Somalia* (Geneva: WHO, 2023), https://apps.who.int/iris/bitstream/handle/10665/367685/WHOEMNUT306E-eng.pdf?sequence=1

2 Central Statistics Department, Ministry of Planning and National Development, Somaliland Government, *The Somaliland Health and Demographic Survey 2020* (Hargeisa: Somaliland Government, 2021), www.somalimedicalarchives.org/media/attachments/2021/09/09/slhds2020_report_2020-1.pdf

3 Freedom House, *Freedom in the World 2022: The Global Expansion of Authoritarian Rule* (Washington, DC: Freedom House, 2022), https://freedomhouse.org/sites/default/files/2022-02/FIW_2022_PDF_Booklet_Digital_Final_Web.pdf

4 *The Economist*, 'Why Somaliland is east Africa's strongest democracy,' 13 November 2017, www.economist.com/the-economist-explains/2017/11/13/why-somaliland-is-east-africas-strongest-democracy

5 Joshua Keating, 'When is a nation not a nation? Somaliland's dream of independence,' *The Guardian*, 20 July 2018, www.theguardian.com/news/2018/jul/20/when-is-a-nation-not-a-nation-somalilands-dream-of-independence

6 Justin V. Hastings and Sarah G. Phillips, 'Order beyond the state: Explaining Somaliland's avoidance of maritime piracy,' *The Journal of Modern African Studies* 56, no. 1 (2018): 5–30, https://doi.org/10.1017/S0022278X17000519

7 Sarah G. Phillips, 'When less was more: External assistance and the political settlement in Somaliland,' *International Affairs* 92, no. 3 (2016): 629–645, https://doi.org/10.1111/1468-2346.12601

8 Ibid.

9 Keating, 'When is a nation.'

10 Sarah G. Phillips, *When There Was No Aid: War and Peace in Somaliland* (Ithaca: Cornell University Press, 2020).

11 Ibid.

12 Ibid.

13 Ibid.

14 This cannot just be observed in Somaliland, but also for instance in the Occupied Palestinian Territories. The international community has, with its enormous and decade-long financial support to the health and education sectors, eroded the link between the Palestinian authorities and its population, and also in some sense legitimized the Israeli occupation.

15 Daniel Martin, 'Confirmed: Our foreign aid fuels corruption – Official watchdog's verdict on aid spending that Cameron has defiantly ring-fenced,' *The Daily Mail*, 31 October 2014, www.dailymail.co.uk/news/article-2815115/Confirmed-foreign-aid-fuels-corruption-Official-watchdog-s-verdict-aid-spending-Cameron-defiantly-ring-fenced.html

16 Todd Moss, Gunilla Pettersson, and Nicolas van der Walle, *An Aid-Institutions Paradox? A Review Essay on Aid Dependency and State Building in Sub-Saharan Africa. Working Paper 74* (Washington, DC: Center for Global Development, 2006), www.cgdev.org/publication/aid-institutions-paradox-review-essay-aid-dependency-and-state-building-sub-saharan

17 Pablo Yanguas, *Why We Lie About Aid: Development and the Messy Politics of Change* (London: Bloomsbury, 2019). The sustainability of these improvements turned out to be limited. In addition to conditionalities, and arguably even more important, were technical partnership with a local champion and a new agency.

18 Haley J. Swedlund, *The Development Dance: How Donors and Recipients Negotiate the Delivery of Foreign Aid* (Ithaca: Cornell University Press, 2018).

19 Terry Lynn Karl, 'The perils of the petro-state: Reflections on the paradox of plenty,' *Journal of International Affairs* 53, no. 1 (1999): 31–48, www.jstor.org/stable/24357783

20 My research into export credit agencies shows that these agencies often make use of so-called tax-havens in their deals. Paying bribes from these tax-havens is relatively easy, because of their

lack of transparency. See Dirk-Jan Koch, 'Do transactions to tax havens and corruption attract officially supported export credit? Evidence from three European export credit agencies,' *SN Business & Economics* 2, no. 6 (2022): 49, https://doi.org/10.1007/s43546-022-00223-4

21 Mushtaq Khan, Antonio Andreoni, and Pallavi Roy, 'Anti-corruption in adverse contexts: Strategies for improving implementation,' *Anti-Corruption Evidence SOAS Consortium* working paper 13 (2019), https://ace.soas.ac.uk/publication/anti-corruption-in-adverse-contexts-strategies-for-improving-implementation/

22 Mamoudou Gazibo, 'Foreign aid and democratization: Benin and Niger compared,' *African Studies Review* 48, no. 3 (2005): 67–87, www.jstor.org/stable/20065140

23 Sebastian Ziaja, 'More donors, more democracy,' *The Journal of Politics* 82, no. 2 (2020): 433–447, https://doi.org/10.1086/706111

24 Anna M. Meyerrose, 'The unintended consequences of democracy promotion: International organizations and democratic backsliding,' *Comparative Political Studies* 53, no. 10–11 (2020): 1547–1581, https://doi.org/10.1177/0010414019897689

25 Assem Dandashly and Gergana Noutcheva, 'Unintended consequences of EU democracy support in the European neighbourhood,' *The International Spectator* 54, no. 1: 105–120, https://doi.org/10.1080/03932729.2019.1554340

26 Anna Khakee, 'Democracy aid or autocracy aid? Unintended effects of democracy assistance in Morocco,' *The Journal of North African Studies* 22, no. 2 (2017): 238–258, https://doi.org/10.1080/13629387.2017.1279971

27 Michela Wrong, *Do Not Disturb: The Story of a Political Murder and an African Regime Gone Bad* (New York: Public Affairs, 2021).

28 On the website of the project of the organization, you could read congratulatory statements about Rwanda such as 'Rwanda has made impressive progress. Rwanda is often celebrated as a champion of good governance and economic development.' These statements deliberately omit the dictatorial nature of the country. If the organization would however be more open about the lack of freedom of the press, for instance, they would have to close their doors the next day, and put their staff in jeopardy.

29 Sarah Sunn Bush, *The Taming of Democracy Assistance: Why Democracy Promotion Does Not Confront Dictators* (Cambridge: Cambridge University Press, 2015).

30 OECD, *Enhancing the Effectiveness of External Support in Building Tax Capacity in Developing Countries* (Paris: OECD, 2016), www.oecd.org/tax/enhancing-the-effectiveness-of-external-support-in-building-tax-capacity-in-developing-countries.pdf

31 Wilson Prichard, *Taxation, Responsiveness and Accountability in Sub-Saharan Africa: The Dynamics of Tax Bargaining* (Cambridge: Cambridge University Press, 2015).

32 For Pakistan, see Susana Franco-Rodriguez, Oliver Morrissey, and Mark McGillivray, 'Aid and the public sector in Pakistan: Evidence with endogenous aid,' *World Development* 26, no. 7 (1998): 1241–1250, https://doi.org/10.1016/S0305-750X(98)00048-5; for Côte d'Ivoire, see Mark McGillivray and Bazoumana Ouattara, 'Aid, debt burden and government fiscal behaviour in Cote d'Ivoire,' *Journal of African Economies* 14, no. 2 (2005): 247–269, http://dx.doi.org/10.2139/ssrn.412249; for Zambia, see Sonja Fagernäs and John Roberts, *Fiscal Impact of Aid: A Survey of Issues and Synthesis of Country Studies of Malawi, Uganda and Zambia. ESAU Working Paper 11* (London: ODI Economics and Statistical Analysis Unit, 2004), https://cdn.odi.org/media/documents/2491.pdf

33 For Indonesia, see Howard Pack and Janet Rothenberg Pack, 'Is foreign aid fungible? The case of Indonesia,' *The Economic Journal* 100, no. 399 (1990): 188–194, https://doi.org/10.2307/2233602; for Ghana, see Robert Osei, Oliver Morrissey, and Tim Lloyd, *Modelling the Fiscal Effects of Aid: An Impulse Response Analysis for Ghana. CREDIT Research Paper No. 3/10* (Nottingham: University of Nottingham, 2003), https://dx.doi.org/10.2139/ssrn.456940

34 John Thornton, 'Does foreign aid reduce tax revenue? Further evidence,' *Applied Economics* 46, no. 4 (2014): 359–373, https://doi.org/10.1080/00036846.2013.829207

35 Alexander Pivovarsky, Benedict J. Clements, Sanjeev Gupta, and Erwin H. Tiongson, *Foreign Aid and Revenue Response: Does the Composition of Aid matter? IMF Working Paper no. 03/*

176 (Washington, DC: IMF, 2003), www.imf.org/en/Publications/WP/Issues/2016/12/30/Fore
ign-Aid-and-Revenue-Response-Does-the-Composition-of-Aid-Matter-16823

36 World Bank, 'Increasing tax revenue in developing countries,' *World Bank*, 1 February 2021,
https://blogs.worldbank.org/impactevaluations/increasing-tax-revenue-developing-countries

37 Émilie Caldeira, Anne-Marie Geourjon, and Grégoire Rota-Graziosi, 'Taxing aid: the end of a
paradox?,' *International Tax and Public Finance* 27 (2020): 240–255, https://doi.org/10.1007/
s10797-019-09573-6

Further reading

Bush, Sarah Sunn. *The Taming of Democracy Assistance: Why Democracy Promotion Does Not
Confront Dictators.* Cambridge: Cambridge University Press, 2015.

Caldeira, Émilie, Anne-Marie Geourjon, and Grégoire Rota-Graziosi. 'Taxing aid: the end of a
paradox?' *International Tax and Public Finance* 27 (2020): 240–255. https://doi.org/10.1007/
s10797-019-09573-6

Central Statistics Department, Ministry of Planning and National Development, Somaliland
Government. *The Somaliland Health and Demographic Survey 2020.* Hargeisa: Somaliland
Government, 2021. www.somalimedicalarchives.org/media/attachments/2021/09/09/slhds2
020_report_2020-1.pdf

Dandashly, Assem, and Gergana Noutcheva. 'Unintended consequences of EU democracy support
in the European neighbourhood.' *The International Spectator* 54, no. 1 (2019): 105–120. https://
doi.org/10.1080/03932729.2019.1554340

Fagernäs, Sonja, and John Roberts. *Fiscal Impact of Aid: A Survey of Issues and Synthesis of
Country Studies of Malawi, Uganda and Zambia. ESAU Working Paper 11.* London: ODI
Economics and Statistical Analysis Unit, 2004. https://cdn.odi.org/media/documents/2491.pdf

Franco-Rodriguez, Susana, Oliver Morrissey, and Mark McGillivray. 'Aid and the public sector
in Pakistan: Evidence with endogenous aid.' *World Development* 26, no. 7 (1998): 1241–1250.
https://doi.org/10.1016/S0305-750X(98)00048-5

Freedom House. *Freedom in the World 2022: The Global Expansion of Authoritarian Rule.*
Washington, DC: Freedom House, 2022. https://freedomhouse.org/sites/default/files/2022-02/
FIW_2022_PDF_Booklet_Digital_Final_Web.pdf

Gazibo, Mamoudou. 'Foreign aid and democratization: Benin and Niger compared.' *African
Studies Review* 48, no. 3 (2005): 67–87. www.jstor.org/stable/20065140

Hastings, Justin V., and Sarah G. Phillips. 'Order beyond the state: Explaining Somaliland's
avoidance of maritime piracy.' *The Journal of Modern African Studies* 56, no. 1 (2018): 5–30.
https://doi.org/10.1017/S0022278X17000519

Karl, Terry Lynn. 'The perils of the petro-state: Reflections on the paradox of plenty.' *Journal of
International Affairs* 53, no. 1 (1999): 31–48. www.jstor.org/stable/24357783

Keating, Joshua. 'When is a nation not a nation? Somaliland's dream of independence.' *The
Guardian*, 20 July 2018. www.theguardian.com/news/2018/jul/20/when-is-a-nation-not-a-nat
ion-somalilands-dream-of-independence

Khakee, Anna. 'Democracy aid or autocracy aid? Unintended effects of democracy assistance in
Morocco.' *The Journal of North African Studies* 22, no. 2 (2017): 238–258. https://doi.org/
10.1080/13629387.2017.1279971

Khan, Mushtaq, Antonio Andreoni, and Pallavi Roy. 'Anti-corruption in adverse contexts: Strategies
for improving implementation.' *Anti-Corruption Evidence SOAS Consortium* working paper
13 (2019). https://ace.soas.ac.uk/publication/anti-corruption-in-adverse-contexts-strategies-for-
improving-implementation/

Koch, Dirk-Jan. 'Do transactions to tax havens and corruption attract officially supported export
credit? Evidence from three European export credit agencies.' *SN Business & Economics* 2, no.
6 (2022): 49. https://doi.org/10.1007/s43546-022-00223-4

Martin, Daniel. 'Confirmed: Our foreign aid fuels corruption – Official watchdog's verdict on
aid spending that Cameron has defiantly ring-fenced.' *The Daily Mail*, 31 October 2014.

www.dailymail.co.uk/news/article-2815115/Confirmed-foreign-aid-fuels-corruption-Official-watchdog-s-verdict-aid-spending-Cameron-defiantly-ring-fenced.html

McGillivray, Mark, and Bazoumana Ouattara. 'Aid, debt burden and government fiscal behaviour in Cote d'Ivoire.' *Journal of African Economies* 14, no. 2 (2005): 247–269. http://dx.doi.org/10.2139/ssrn.412249

Meyerrose, Anna M. 'The unintended consequences of democracy promotion: International organizations and democratic backsliding.' *Comparative Political Studies* 53, no. 10–11 (2020): 1547–1581. https://doi.org/10.1177/0010414019897689

Moss, Todd, Gunilla Pettersson, and Nicolas van der Walle. *An Aid-Institutions Paradox? A Review Essay on Aid Dependency and State Building in Sub-Saharan Africa.* Working Paper 74. Washington, DC: Center for Global Development, 2006. www.cgdev.org/publication/aid-institutions-paradox-review-essay-aid-dependency-and-state-building-sub-saharan

OECD. *Enhancing the Effectiveness of External Support in Building Tax Capacity in Developing Countries.* Paris: OECD, 2016. www.oecd.org/tax/enhancing-the-effectiveness-of-external-support-in-building-tax-capacity-in-developing-countries.pdf

Osei, Robert, Oliver Morrissey, and Tim Lloyd. *Modelling the Fiscal Effects of Aid: An Impulse Response Analysis for Ghana.* CREDIT Research Paper No. 3/10. Nottingham: University of Nottingham, 2003. https://dx.doi.org/10.2139/ssrn.456940

Pack, Howard, and Janet Rothenberg Pack. 'Is foreign aid fungible? The case of Indonesia.' *The Economic Journal* 100, no. 399 (1990): 188–194. https://doi.org/10.2307/2233602

Phillips, Sarah G. 'When less was more: External assistance and the political settlement in Somaliland.' *International Affairs* 92, no. 3 (2016): 629–645. https://doi.org/10.1111/1468-2346.12601

Phillips, Sarah G. *When There Was No Aid: War and Peace in Somaliland.* Ithaca: Cornell University Press, 2020.

Pivovarsky, Alexander, Benedict J. Clements, Sanjeev Gupta, and Erwin H. Tiongson. *Foreign Aid and Revenue Response: Does the Composition of Aid matter?* IMF Working Paper no. 03/176. Washington, DC: IMF, 2003. www.imf.org/en/Publications/WP/Issues/2016/12/30/Foreign-Aid-and-Revenue-Response-Does-the-Composition-of-Aid-Matter-16823

Prichard, Wilson. *Taxation, Responsiveness and Accountability in Sub-Saharan Africa: The Dynamics of Tax Bargaining.* Cambridge: Cambridge University Press, 2015.

Swedlund, Haley J. *The Development Dance: How Donors and Recipients Negotiate the Delivery of Foreign Aid.* Ithaca: Cornell University Press, 2018.

The Economist. 'Why Somaliland is east Africa's strongest democracy.' 13 November 2017. www.economist.com/the-economist-explains/2017/11/13/why-somaliland-is-east-africas-strongest-democracy

Thornton, John. 'Does foreign aid reduce tax revenue? Further evidence.' *Applied Economics* 46, no. 4 (2014): 359–373. https://doi.org/10.1080/00036846.2013.829207

World Bank. 'Increasing tax revenue in developing countries.' *World Bank,* 1 February 2021. https://blogs.worldbank.org/impactevaluations/increasing-tax-revenue-developing-countries

World Health Organization. *Nutrition Country Profile: Somalia.* Geneva: WHO, 2023. https://apps.who.int/iris/bitstream/handle/10665/367685/WHOEMNUT306E-eng.pdf?sequence=1

Wrong, Michele. *Do Not Disturb: The Story of a Political Murder and an African Regime Gone Bad.* New York: Public Affairs, 2021.

Yanguas, Pablo. *Why We Lie About Aid: Development and the Messy Politics of Change.* London: Bloomsbury, 2019.

11 Environmental effects

Uneasy trade-offs between ecology and development

Environmental trade-off effects occur when social and economic progress unintentionally contributes to environmental degradation.

What flavours do we see?

1 **Carbon surge effects**. The external intervention creates social-economic development, but CO_2 emissions also rise fast.
2 **Biodiversity decline effects**. The external intervention leads to social-economic benefits but reduces biodiversity, often through the intensification of agricultural industries.
3 **Animal welfare reduction effects**. The international support stimulates social and economic development, but this reduces animal welfare, for instance, through the promotion of the bio industry and battery cages.

In which instances have environmental effects been observed? Three examples:

1 Carbon surge effects: international development banks such as the World Bank invest in carbon-intensive sectors, such as aviation and airports. While contributing to jobs and economic development, significant carbon costs are involved, as the example of an IFC-funded airport in Samoa showed.
2 Biodiversity decline effects: the building of dams can have serious repercussions for biodiversity in the area that is inundated and the surrounding areas. Biodiversity offset programmes can provide solace, but they come with their own risks, as the example of a gorilla offsetting program in Cameroon shows.
3 Animal welfare reduction effects: international development banks have loaned and provided developing funding to Ukraine, so that Ukrainian firms could set up poultry firms that were undercutting European firms by reducing animal welfare.

A key concept from complexity thinking that helps in understanding unintended environmental effects

1 **Interconnectivity**. There is a clear interconnectivity between various development outcomes, especially between the economic and the environmental realm.

DOI: 10.4324/9781003356851-11

This Chapter has been made available under a CC-BY-NC-ND license.

There is a clear trade-off where economic advancement can harm the environment, as the examples show: the poultry farms in Ukraine (jobs versus animal welfare), the sliced mangoes in the supermarket (jobs versus climate), and dam (access to electricity versus biodiversity). Since many of the development actors are thematically organized (either focusing on economic development or environmental issues), this interconnectivity is too often overlooked.

Figure 11.1 Environmental effects in action.

Source: Maarten Wolterink.

I am a supporter of the Sustainable Development Goals (SDGs): I am glad that there's finally a comprehensive international development agenda that encompasses the Global North and South. And not only that: it also integrates environmental issues into its vision of development, such as biodiversity and climate change. When the United Nations launched the agenda in 2015, they made it clear right from the start that the agenda was 'integrated and indivisible.' Alas, reality turned out a bit more complex than that.

New studies show what we could have seen coming: many trade-offs between the SDGs.[1] Of course, there are synergies between the various goals (more about those in Chapter 12 on catalytic spillover effects).[2] Yet, we focus on the trade-offs between various development objectives in this chapter. For instance, installing more marine protected areas to advance SDG 14 'life below water' might reduce access to income for fishermen, undermining SDG 1 'no poverty.' We have already encountered the potential adverse effects of conservancy efforts on livelihoods in Chapter 7 on marginalization.

This chapter focuses on the other side of that socio-economic versus environment trade-off: how the attainment of social-economic objectives can impede environmental objectives (also a dilemma facing the Global North). Advancing the objectives of 'no poverty' (SDG 1) and 'zero hunger' (SDG 2) normally leads to destruction of the habitats of 'life on land' (SDG 15) and extra carbon emissions, undermining 'climate action' (SDG 13). Calling the SDG agenda 'integrated and indivisible' does not make these trade-offs go away. As you must know by now, I prefer to be open about these interlinkages and unintended effects to see if and how we can turn them around. In this chapter we will primarily zoom in on trade-offs between the SDGs, since they are the official development agenda. While systematic studies into the trade-offs between SDGs have found many of them, I will focus on three particular ones in this section, since they are either often overlooked (animal welfare) or can contribute to existential risks in the long run (climate change and biodiversity).

11.1 Carbon surge effects: how much carbon space may development cost?

11.1.1 My sliced mango

I was surprised to see huge posters of a very happy and smiling pineapple and mango farmer from Ghana in my supermarket across the corner. The posters read 'double tasty,' because (and I loosely translate): 'Our fruit not only tastes great, it also makes you feel good. This is because our growers, together with the AH Foundation [name of the supermarket, red.], contribute to better living conditions for the local community.' We only used to have uncooled unsliced mangoes in my supermarket, but now, below the new posters, I see new refrigerators with plastic packages with sliced and diced mangoes. With advice from a development NGO, the supermarket had contributed to employment schemes in Ghana, with apparent success.

As you probably know by now, I am always a bit suspicious when I read these grandiose feel-good claims, so I researched the supermarket's claims. Initially, it turned out my suspicions were unfounded: the evaluations showed that the schemes did create many jobs in Ghana.[3] Especially the jobs in the processing of the fruit in Ghana were new and created extra value. In small factories, new labourers now cut and package the mango in the plastic packages of my supermarket. These jobs did not exist before in Ghana: more value is added locally. They actually contribute to the transformation of the economic system by helping Ghana to move from a country that exports raw products (mangoes) to semi-transformed goods (mangoes that have been cut and packaged).

But what is the CO_2 impact of this added value? Mangoes used to be transported from Ghana to the Netherlands (and the UK, and other countries that are too cold for growing mangoes) by freight ship. The mangoes did not need to be cooled, as their skin would protect them to the temperatures. However, with their skin taken off, the mangoes need to be transported swiftly and in a cooled way: they are now transported as refrigerated air fright. Calculations show that the CO_2 footprint of these mangoes is as much as six times higher than those of old-school mangoes.[4] Don't get me wrong: I am not saying that we shouldn't process mangoes in Ghana (I don't mind at all that I don't have to cut the mango myself); I am saying that but rather that, to measure the true development impact, we shouldn't only look at the number of jobs created, but also at the side effects.[5]

Figure 11.2 'Dubbel lekker' (Double tasty). The advertisement that caught my attention.

Source: Olivier van Beemen.

The sliced mangos are just one small example of the massive impact of international development efforts on carbon emissions. Development banks invest millions in blueberries in the Global South, which are then flown into Europe and North America so that people in the Global North can enjoy an iced blueberry smoothie also when it's freezing during the winter. But the trade-offs are also broader than just agriculture: whether it is the investments of the Asian Development Banks into roads or the International Finance Corporation (IFC, the private-sector arm of the World Bank Group) into airports, these investments have massive carbon emissions, while contributing to economic development at the same time.

Currently, extreme weather events are wreaking catastrophic global havoc, from the Horn of Africa in 2021 (drought, contributing to famine) to Pakistan in 2022 (floods, leading to massive displacement). The IPCC calculates that, if governments fulfil their existing pledges (which they don't have a good track record for), the earth will heat by about 2.5 degrees Celsius compared to pre-industrial levels by the end of this century.[6] This catastrophe would trigger various tipping points that will spiral our planet's climatic systems out of control for centuries to come. Since the Global South is hit hardest by climate change, this would undo a lot if not all of our international development progress over the past half a century. So we have a major development dilemma: many of the countries of the Global South have contributed nothing to the climate disaster in which we find ourselves now. So isn't it unfair to prevent these countries from acquiring infrastructure such as roads and airports because of climate concerns? Let's flesh out this dilemma by looking at a particular case: the IFC investments in airports in the Global South.

11.1.2 How much carbon may development cost?

There are roughly two schools of thought on carbon and development trade-offs, which can be seen as a continuum. One school of thought focuses on a 'just transition' and one is purely environmentalist. Let me explain the deep ideological differences between the two schools of thought, and please consider in the meantime your position in this debate.

From a 'just transition' perspective, the Global South is the victim of historical and current overconsumption in the Global North. Roughly speaking, what needs to happen according to this school of thought is (a) to slash overconsumption of the rich; (b) use this carbon space to get everybody on the grid in the Global South and allow them to travel and explore their horizons; (c) tax the Global North and the rich for their historic contribution to climate disasters through a loss and damages fund and compensate the vulnerable, who suffer most from climate change. To make this concrete, they support the construction of airports (with development funding) in the Global South if necessary for local development. The carbon side effects are acceptable to them.

From an environmentalist perspective, the top priority is reducing carbon emission, and everybody should contribute. Regardless of past and current inequalities, fossil fuels need to be phased out (even if there is no alternative available) and carbon-intensive ways of transport such as air travel should not be supported under any circumstance: in short, no development funding for airports. Let's look at an investment by the IFC into an airport in Samoa to make the dilemma clearer.

The website of IFC proudly mentions how – with Official Development Assistance (ODA) from, amongst others, the United Kingdom and Sweden – it boosted the national airline carrier and airport of Samoa. Tourism is Samoa's largest industry, but expensive airfares and difficulties in reaching this small, isolated country in the Pacific have kept tourism growing at a rate below that of neighbouring islands, according to the IFC.[7] Because Polynesian Airlines (the Samoan national airline) faced severe financial and operational constraints, the government turned to the IFC. With IFC as the lead advisor, the government implemented an innovative public–private partnership and established a new national airline. The IFC explains that

> *Within two years, the new airline had turned an annual $6.6 million profit ... Improved airline services sparked an annual 15 percent increase in tourism, and tourist revenues reached $113 million in 2007. Polynesian Blue cut airfares by one-third and 2,000 jobs were created due to the expansion of the travel and tourism industries.*[8]

From a just transition perspective, it can be argued that Samoa still has the carbon space to make this investment since its historical emissions are a fraction of the Global North's.

However, from a purely environmentalist perspective, the project should not see the day of light. The IFC and the Samoa government obtained great economic and financial results, but the CO_2 impact of the otherwise successful project was not calculated.

Yet, if I had to develop the most unsustainable tourist destination on earth, I would come up with Samoa. First, tourists will have to fly to New Zealand (which is for many tourists already on the other side of the world), and then they will have to fly at least another 3 hours to Samoa. It's hard to find a place where the CO_2 footprint per additional tourist would be higher! And Samoa, as a Small Island Development State, is particularly vulnerable to climate change. Nowhere in the documentation was it mentioned that greenhouse gases might be a problem or that they were offset in one way or another. The IFC neither made clear how its contribution would make the investment cleaner than it would have been without them, so the environmental added value was unclear.[9]

I am not taking sides in this development dilemma. The only thing I argue for is that all the costs (hence also all the carbon effects) are disclosed and form a part of the decision-making process, which is currently not happening sufficiently. If there are high carbon costs, let's look for alternatives. Unfortunately, programmes are prepared in thematic silos, which limits learning. Institutional barriers make policy learning bounded, also in this domain. Let us make the trade-off explicit. And let's ensure that if development banks invest, they create environmental additionality, meaning that the project becomes greener than it would have been without their investments.

11.2 Biodiversity decline effects: the price of human progress?

Humanity has wiped out 60 per cent of mammals, birds, fish, and reptiles since 1970, leading the world's foremost experts to warn that the annihilation of wildlife is now an emergency threatening civilization. Many scientists believe that a sixth mass extinction is unfolding, the first caused by a single species: *Homo sapiens*.[10] Domesticated livestock, mostly cows and pigs, account for 60 per cent of the world mass of mammals and wild mammals for only 4 per cent.[11] So 'Houston, we have a problem.'

This problem is only aggravating with the rising number of humans and associated consumption levels: while we were with 3.6 billion people in 1970, we are now with over 8 billion. And the rising living standards – with all the roads, railways, tourism, etc. that come with them – leave increasingly little space for wild animals. Development agencies and banks realize that their investments have an unintended impact on biodiversity, so they have developed safeguards to address this unintended effect: biodiversity safeguards.

11.2.1 Scooping up colonies of ants

When I was the natural resources envoy of the Dutch government, I had the chance to visit and study mining sites from Colombia to Kazakhstan and from Germany to South Africa. How the Germans and the South Africans dealt with the side effects of mining were worlds apart. I had witnessed, as explained in section 5.1 on forced resettlement, the anomalies of coal mining-induced resettlement in South Africa: the resettled citizens were displaced from the graves of their ancestors. During my trips to South Africa, I also saw how coal-mining companies left biodiversity in tatters after mine closure. Many mining companies simply sold off their assets to unscrupulous investment firms just before closure and left the mining pits as sinkholes. In Germany, on the other hand, the German energy giant and coal mine operator (RWE) makes two products: cheap electricity and 'pretty new landscapes.'[12] These 'pretty new landscapes' are biodiversity offsets (and sometimes restorations) to compensate for amongst others the destruction of the ancient Hambacher Forest for the world's largest opencast lignite coal mine in the German Rhineland.

With the Dutch Ministry of Foreign Affairs, we organized a visit for the South African government and companies to these 'pretty new landscapes' in Germany. We started the trip in the huge open-pit mines where larger-than-life machines were scraping the earth's surface, just as we had seen in South Africa. Until then, we did not see much difference between the South African and German coal mines.

However, after the mine, we were driving and walking through beautiful nature. What surprised me, and the guests even more, was that we were now walking on top of a mining area that had been closed a couple of decades ago. What the guide told us flabbergasted our guests: they planted tree corridors to enable animals to find their way to other suitable forest areas, installed bat boxes and even scooped up entire colonies of ants and relocated them to the replanted forest area.[13] I never saw a delegation ask so many questions and take so many notes! The South African delegation was used to mining companies reneging on their biodiversity promises, and while also in this case much could be improved, it was biodiversity restoration and offsetting in practice.[14]

I am aware that a large body of academic literature opposes biodiversity (and carbon) offsetting categorically on ideological grounds.[15] They see it as a commodification of nature, leading to even more wealth accumulation for companies who can simply buy off the destruction they cause. In their view, biodiversity offsets provide a new mode of accumulation that takes the negative environmental effects of contemporary capitalism as its departure for a 'sustainable' model of accumulation for the future. Indeed, there is a long list of failed offset projects across the globe. While I hence understand the qualms people have about this, biodiversity offsetting is part of international development finance and will remain so in the near future, so we need to understand it, and see how we can strengthen it.

11.2.2 Biodiversity offsets 101

The World Bank has developed minimum guidelines for biodiversity offsetting. Biodiversity offsets differ from other kinds of conservation activities in two main ways: (1) unlike 'free-standing' conservation projects, biodiversity offsets are explicitly linked to one or more development projects that are causing some loss of biodiversity; (2) biodiversity offsets are normally expected to *fully* compensate for specified adverse impacts in a way that is measurable long-term, and additional to any other (ongoing or planned) conservation measures.[16]

Biodiversity offsets are meant to be a measure of last resort. There is a 'biodiversity loss mitigation hierarchy' (sorry for the many nouns). This means that developers must first deploy other strategies for addressing biodiversity effects. The mitigation hierarchy states that development project planners should (1) first seek to *avoid* damaging any biodiversity; (2) then seek to *minimize* any such damage; (3) then consider how to *restore* sites or species populations damaged by the project; (4) then – if adverse biodiversity impacts still remain – compensate or *offset* through specific actions (not merely cash), comprising a biodiversity offset.[17]

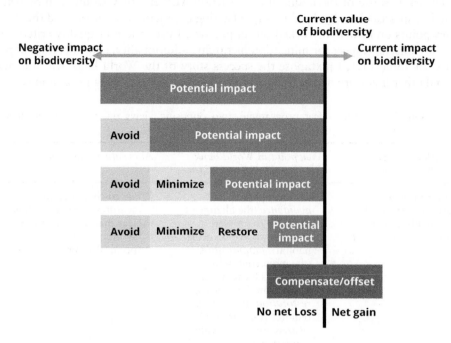

Figure 11.3 Biodiversity loss mitigation hierarchy: offsetting is a means of last resort.

Source: Adapted from BBOP, Biodiversity Offset Design Handbook.

11.2.3 Humans versus gorillas

The low-land gorillas (called silverback gorillas because of their silver-coloured back) that I saw in the eastern DRC struck me by both their size and their human expressions: the gorilla kids were playing while their mom was keeping a relaxed eye on them. Unfortunately, the numbers are down from about 17,000 in the mid-1990s to about 3,400 these days. The major reason: humans.

I always pay extra attention when there are human development projects that might endanger gorillas. I want to know whether the gorilla offsets are done properly: there are too few left to make any mistakes. But there is often little consensus over the success of these offsets: take for instance the offsetting programme linked to the Lom Pangar dam in Cameroon. This programme was included as a 'Case Study' in the World Bank User Guide for effective biodiversity offsetting,[18] but also as a case study in a report by Rivers International to showcase the negative impact of development programmes on this critically endangered species.[19]

With the aid of the World Bank, the government of Cameroon wanted to build the hydropower dam because it would finally provide energy to villages in the neglected eastern part of Cameroon. However, 300 gorillas were living next to the proposed dam in the middle of the forest, and the influx of workers would mean the gorillas would be at higher risk of being killed. Therefore, before the World Bank invested USD 130 million in 2010, they negotiated that a next-door forest would be extra protected by making it a national park: the Deng Deng National Park. So, while the gorillas would be at increased risk because of the influx of construction workers, they would also be better protected in an area close-by: biodiversity offsetting in practice. To understand the diverging viewpoints on how that worked out in practice, I used the four quality criteria for biodiversity offsets: respect for mitigation hierarchy, additionality, equivalence, and permanence. In Table 11.1, I juxtapose the success story of the World Bank with the academic and other literature on the impact of this biodiversity offsetting programme.

Table 11.1 One biodiversity offset programme, two opposing views on its effects: gorillas in the mist

Principles for correct biodiversity offsetting	Viewpoint in World bank Biodiversity Offset Guide[a]	Alternative viewpoints
Respect for mitigation hierarchy. First avoid, then minimize, then restore, and lastly offset.	Clear examples of *avoidance* (the alignment of access roads were reviewed to avoid gorilla habitat), *minimization* (the main contractor camp was located well away from the Park), and *restoration* (the Project requires restoration of cleared areas following construction).	While costly mitigation measures were taken, it is clear that the mitigation hierarchy was not specifically applied.[b]
Additionality. Biodiversity offsets must deliver conservation gains beyond those achieved by ongoing or planned activities that are not part of the offset.	While the Deng Deng area used to be a regular forest with high deforestation rates, it was gazetted as a National Park in March 2010 as an offset.	Even now that Deng Deng has become a national park, poaching is still a serious issue: 'In 2015 the ministry reported that 1,270 kg of wild meat was seized, including 20 kg of chimpanzee, and 290 kg of monkey and gorilla.'[c]
Equivalence. Biodiversity offsets should conserve the same biodiversity values (species, habitats, ecosystems, or ecological functions) as those lost to the original project, following a principle known as like-for-like.	The habitat quality was (and remains) distinctly higher within the offset area than in the inundated and cleared Project areas. The inundated area was 58,000 hectares, as was the new National Park.	The offset project was not operational and delivering the required biodiversity compensation before impacts from the development project occurred.[d]
Permanence. Biodiversity offsets should persist for at least as long as adverse biodiversity impacts from the original project persist; in practical terms, this often means in perpetuity.	The government has committed sixty game guards to focus on preventing poaching, illegal logging, and agricultural or housing encroachment within the Park. Financial flows are ensured because of income from the dam.	It remains 'dependent on Company compliance with financing commitments (thirty-year annual payments) and securing longer-term financing whether Deng Deng will be protected in perpetuity.'[e]

Table 11.1 (Continued)

Principles for correct biodiversity offsetting	Viewpoint in World bank Biodiversity Offset Guide[a]	Alternative viewpoints
Final result of the offset	As a result of the Lom Pangar Hydropower Project, this Park is now a 'key stronghold' for Gorillas. This offset appears to have achieved a substantial Net Gain.	Specific calculations on losses and gains of individual gorillas were not made.[f] 'The great ape population remains at risk of further degradation once the project concludes.'[g]

Notes:
[a] World Bank Group, *Biodiversity Offsets*.
[b] Rebecca Kormos, Cyril F. Kormos, Tatyana Humle, et al., 'Great apes and biodiversity offset projects in Africa: The case for national offset strategies,' *PLoS ONE* 9, no. 11 (2014): e111671, https://doi.org/10.1371/journal.pone.0111671.
[c] Rivers International, Advancing Ecological Civilization?, 73.
[d] Kormos et al., 'Great apes.'
[e] Rivers International, Advancing Ecological Civilization?, 73.
[f] Kormos et al., 'Great apes.'
[g] Arcus Foundation, *State of the Apes: Infrastructure Development and Ape Conservation* (Cambridge: Cambridge University Press, 2018), 181.

What lessons to learn concerning biodiversity offsets? Before I respond to that question, the divergent interpretations demonstrate once again the importance of independent research. To answer the question, it becomes clear from this example, the tricky element is that first the development programme starts, and that the offsetting follows later. This makes the current form of biodiversity offsetting a risky business: there is no certainty that the offsetting will materialize and be maintained. Therefore, I join the call to ensure that the developers materialize the offset and start a financial endowment before the development programme starts. Once vegetation loss is beyond a tipping point, the loss of biodiversity is irreversible and non-linear.[20] Once a species is extinct, it is extinct forever. The precautionary principle should hence apply: first the offset, then the project.

Back to the case study: I understand this is a tough development dilemma. The Cameroonians are craving for energy (which will save lives in hospitals), while measuring biodiversity for a proper baseline and measuring whether a biodiversity offset works takes money and time. Seeing this entire process through would delay projects and could even make them unaffordable (see the testimony by Ibrahim Zakaria on crippling safeguards related to clean energy in Chad). This is why we need to speak of development dilemmas.

To conclude on a positive note, there are not just trade-offs between development finance and biodiversity offsets: development finance can just as well stimulate biodiversity, for instance, by promoting agroforestry and regenerative agriculture. If finance institutions play it smartly, they can sway large-scale monoculture farms into these more biodiversity-friendly alternatives. Let's try to turn the biodiversity trade-offs into synergies!

Figure 11.4 One of the three hundred lowland gorillas left in Cameroon; at increased risk or saved
    because of dam construction?

Source: Wikimedia commons.

Testimony by Ibrahim Zakaria*

An avalanche of well-meant standards

*ZIZ SA is an energy company in Chad. One of their main projects is electrifying
cities of 20,000 people or more with solar-powered grids. Ibrahim Zakaria, the
CEO of ZIZ SA, speaks about the environmental, social, and governance (ESG)
standards of development financial institutions (DFIs).*

The big picture

Our view on the ESG 'safeguards'? Well, first of all, we don't see an issue with
ESG criteria as such. Of course we need to ensure a safe environment for our

Figure 11.5 Ibrahim Zakaria.

workers, with access to protective equipment and training, etc. And we don't want to expropriate anyone from their land. But we do get frustrated sometimes. Chad has an electricity rate of 6 per cent. As much as we understand the DFIs' focus on certain themes that are dear to them today (gender policy for example), we sometimes feel that they forget the bigger picture. We want to remind them that our countries face a dire situation: lack of development and high vulnerability to the climate crisis. As such, we need to focus on our primary mission: electrifying and decarbonizing.

The gap between Western worlds and frontier markets

The ESG criteria crystallize the gap between Western worlds and frontier markets. Investors want to reduce the infrastructural gap in Africa. Still, they decided to make it more difficult by having very stringent rules and requirements regarding environmental and social aspects that they have invented just for us. We feel hindered in our effort to accelerate socio-economic change in our countries by an avalanche of well-meant standards that were never applied in Western countries when they went through their own industrialization and electrification. That's where the frustration of local entrepreneurs and sometimes governments comes from.

The thorny issue of land

For example, we received (and paid for) a piece of land from the State in a document signed by all the local and regional authorities. Our responsibility under national law ended here and we could start work. But we had to take into account international standards. In some cases, it turned out that the same land had been sold by the municipality to private individuals. We had to identify all these affected people and compensate them. Because of this imbroglio, we spent three times the cost of the land on this project.

When ESG principles stop where it suits

These additional ESG costs are explained to you as normal and necessary to receive DFI's money, so some of the funds raised are spent on ESG implementation rather than on power equipment. Most of the ESG principles disappear when it comes to commercial negotiations though. All the talks about stakeholders' engagement and making sure the project does not let people worse-off no longer apply and certainly do not extend to the company's existing shareholders or founders. And although we are trying to electrify some of the poorest areas in the world, the risk premium and interest rates charged can be exorbitant. Our only ray of hope is that some DFIs (like FMO) are open to dialogue on these issues and are willing to make efforts.

* This testimony is based on presentations by ZIZ, an interview, and written input provided by ZIZ.

Let us finish with one of the trade-offs we would overlook if we only looked at the SDGs. Despite 17 goals, 169 SDG targets, and 232 unique indicators, we humans did not find it necessary to pay any attention to animal welfare. Animals were not at the SDG negotiation table, so they are on the menu. If we would like to come to a truly integrated agenda, animal welfare should also be included. This is something I discovered when I was growing up next to the 'chicken capital' of the Netherlands, and of Europe: Barneveld.

11.3 Animal welfare effects: animals were not at the SDG negotiation table, so they are on the menu

Barneveld has just about 30,000 residents, but houses more than 3 million chickens at any point of the year. It has a restaurant with just chicken products (called: 'The Egg'), a chicken museum (called 'Het Pluimvee Museum,' in case you would like to visit), and even a race of highly productive chicken named after it ('the Barnevelder'). With my father being the general physician of the region, I earned some extra pocket money by delivering his bills to his patients. I went with my bike from farm to farm at ten years old, and many of those farms were chicken farms. When I peeked into the stalls, I was depressed by what I saw: thousands and thousands of chicken living in eight-storey high cages, devoid of anything that would be natural to them, with no branches to sleep on, no natural products on the floor, just metal cages. Every chicken had less space than one A4 paper to live on. This bio-industry made the Netherlands one of the world's agricultural powerhouses: the Netherlands was exporting its chicken breasts to rich countries and chicken legs to low-income countries all over the world. It also made the farmers well-off: they didn't have trouble paying the bills. The images of that bio-industry also made me a vegetarian when I turned twelve, and I have been so ever since.

Animal rights activists have been very active and successful in Europe, including the Netherlands, over the last decades: the European Union banned the cages that I saw when I was delivering my father's bills. The chickens are now also required to have more space (now a maximum of nine chickens per square meter) and are increasingly allowed to go outside. When I go back to Barneveld, I now see many chickens scavenging outside, filling me with the feeling that progress is possible. Strangely enough, this progress is under threat, and even stranger: international development money plays a substantial role. Many chicken farms are closing their doors in Barneveld and the influx of cheap Ukrainian poultry plays a large role.

After this tour to the chicken farms of my youth, let me take you to MHP, a gigantic London stock exchange-listed poultry firm in Ukraine in 2018. This company, with little to no chicken exports only ten years ago, now owns the largest chicken farm in Europe with over 30 million chickens at any given time, and shows how adaptive agents can make use of discrepancies between standards.[21] Ukraine has taken over the role of the Netherlands in the global chicken market. How did this happen?

After the Russian invasion of Crimea, Ukraine secured a deal in 2015 with the European Union (EU), which allowed them to export more chicken to this market. EU imports of poultry meat from Ukraine subsequently tripled between 2015 and 2019. The competitiveness of Ukrainian poultry was partly made possible by undercutting Dutch and other firms by cutting down on animal rights. Whereas in Ukraine over 95 per cent of the chickens are still in (enriched) cages, this is less than 50 per cent in the EU.[22] This Ukrainian competitiveness made it attractive for international government-owned banks to invest in them. Not only were the banks supporting this bio-industry growth (with public funding), also chicken technology companies started exporting their expertise and equipment to them (as many Dutch companies did, often with exports guaranteed by the Dutch state bank Atradius).

With better access to the EU market and fewer rights for chicken came easy access to finance, even public finance such as a EUR 25 million loan from the European Bank for Reconstruction and Development (EBRD) in 2017.[23] After the Russian invasion of eastern Ukraine in 2022, the EBRD provided another loan to MHP of EUR 24 million, seemingly forgetting under geopolitical pressure its initial request that Ukraine bring its animal welfare practices in line with those of the EU.[24] This time, Japan paid the overhead costs with their ODA budget.

The EBRD substantiated the deals by explaining how the chicken farms would create jobs and enhance food security. However, the EBRD does not have any specific guidelines for chicken welfare, for instance, when it comes to overcrowding.[25] While this investment undoubtedly created jobs in Ukraine, hundreds of millions of chickens had to pay the price. Chicken that could live outside of cages in the Netherlands (where improvement in chicken welfare is also still needed) are now living in cages in Ukraine, partly thanks to development funding.[26]

This is just one example of how the voiceless often end up paying the ultimate price in international development programmes. Whereas some development banks now have animal welfare statements, many development banks still don't. Many support questionable farming technologies to countries with few animal welfare laws and even less reliable animal inspection services. I can only reach one conclusion: the development sector needs transparent animal impact assessments for high-risk projects.

In addition to animal impact assessments, animal protection could become part of international trade agreements. A promising first step has been the proposed text for the EU-Mercosur trade agreement. Mercosur is a trading block in South America and if they want to continue to export eggs to the EU (which they do a lot) they will need to have similar animal welfare standards for the laying hens as in Europe. This highlights how important it is, if we are interested in dealing with side effects of aid, sometimes it may be just as important to leverage trade instruments. Aid-related investments can then occur in contexts with stronger social-environmental regulations, making the standards to which aid investments need to live up to contingent on enforceable legislation rather than the whims of donors.

How to tackle unintended environmental effects

Policymakers

- **Plan in an integrated way.** Plan in a way that incorporates both environmental and economic objectives. If possible, turn trade-offs into synergies, by finding solutions that benefit both objectives. If not possible, calibrate carefully an optimum, considering (scientific advice on) non-linearities and feedback loops.
- **When raising environmental standards, be aware of the adaptive nature of market players.** Potential discrepancies across countries in regulations can lead to leakage (see Section 9.3 on leakage effects), simply relocating harmful practices. Always strive for a level regulatory playing field.

Practitioners

- **Respect the mitigation hierarchy when offsetting.** When working with offsets, respect the mitigation hierarchy and adhere to the core principles of additionality, equivalence, and permanence. Stick to the precautionary principle.
- **Develop and publish animal impact assessments.** In high-risk sectors such as animal farming, these are needed to enable researchers, journalists, and others to track mitigation measures.

Evaluators

- **Invest in measurement tools for biodiversity measurements.** It is costly to measure biodiversity, leading to projects being abandoned or delayed. Investing in them can drive overhead costs down and get more accurate insights on biodiversity effects.

Notes

1 For example, Alexis Rulisa, Luuk van Kempen, and Dirk-Jan Koch, 'When local trade-offs between SDGs turn out to be wealth-dependent: Interaction between expanding rice cultivation and eradicating malaria in Rwanda,' *Sustainability* 14, no. 4: 2100, https://doi.org/10.3390/su14042100

2 Francesco Fuso Nerini, Julia Tomei, Long Seng To, et al., 'Mapping synergies and trade-offs between energy and the Sustainable Development Goals,' *Nature Energy* 3, no. 1 (2018): 10–15, https://doi.org/10.1038/s41560-017-0036-5

3 Gertrude Dzifa Torvikey, Joseph Awetori Yao, and Joseph Kofi Teye, 'Farm to factory gendered employment: The case of blue skies outgrower scheme in Ghana,' *Agrarian South: Journal of Political Economy* 5, no. 1 (2016): 77–97, https://doi.org/10.1177/2277976016669188; Linda Kleemann, 'The relevance of certifications and business practices in linking smallholders and large agro-businesses in sub-Sahara Africa,' *International Food and Agribusiness Management Review* 19, no. 4 (2016): 65–78, https://doi.org/10.22434/IFAMR2015.0204

4 Loethe Olthuis, 'Hoe duurzaam zijn verse stukjes tropisch fruit?,' *De Volkskrant* 6 February 2016, www.volkskrant.nl/nieuws-achtergrond/hoe-duurzaam-zijn-verse-stukjes-tropisch-fruit~b3fa92f0/

5 Olivier van Beemen, 'Op zoek naar Kwabena, de Ghanese ananasboer van Albert Heijn,' *Follow the Money*, 3 September 2020, www.ftm.nl/artikelen/zoektocht-kwabena-ghanese-ananasboer-ah-lekker-gevoel. This research demonstrated the man on the posters was actually not aware that his face was on giant posters across the Netherlands, but starting a discussion on the use and abuse of images in international development is a whole debate in itself (which we treat in the chapter on marginalization). In the end, the supermarket settled with the man on the poster for an undisclosed amount.

6 Fiona Harvey, 'Current emissions pledges will lead to catastrophic climate breakdown, says UN,' *The Guardian*, 26 October 2022, www.theguardian.com/environment/2022/oct/26/current-emissions-pledges-will-lead-to-catastrophic-climate-breakdown-says-un

7 International Finance Corporation, *IFC Support to Transport* (Washington, DC: IFC, 2010), www.ifc.org/wps/wcm/connect/0cce4461-d2a5-45f5-9eea-e9bac02bcc53/IFC_Support2Infrastructure_Transport.pdf?MOD=AJPERES&CVID=lKbEx3x

8 International Finance Corporation, *Public-Private Partnership Impact Stories. Samoa: Virgin Samoa Airlines* (Washington, DC: IFC, 2013), www.ifc.org/wps/wcm/connect/991d2430-de89-42c9-a784-07b53c177933/PPPStories_Samoa_VirginSamoaAirlines.pdf?MOD=AJPERES&CVID=lHIp1QN

9 Ibid.

10 World Wildlife Fund, *Living Planet Report 2018: Aiming Higher* (Gland: WWF, 2018), www.worldwildlife.org/pages/living-planet-report-2018

11 Yinon M. Bar-On, Rob Phillips, and Ron Milo, 'The biomass distribution on Earth,' *Proceedings of the National Academy of Sciences* 115, no. 25 (2018): 6506–6511, https://doi.org/10.1073/pnas.1711842115

12 Andrea Brock, 'Securing accumulation by restoration – Exploring spectacular corporate conservation, coal mining and biodiversity compensation in the German Rhineland,' *Environment and Planning E: Nature and Space* 2020: https://doi.org/10.1177/2514848620924597

13 This is explained in more detail in National Geographic, 'Ancient forest home of squatter communities is doomed by coal,' 15 April 2018, www.nationalgeographic.co.uk/photography/2018/04/ancient-forest-home-of-squatter-communities-is-doomed-by-coal

14 The post-mine closure biodiversity programme at the site of the mine was a restoration programme, whereas the creation of new biodiversity hotspots in the vicinity was an offset.

15 Bram Büscher and Robert Fletcher, 'Accumulation by conservation,' *New Political Economy* 20, no. 2 (2015): 273–298, https://doi.org/10.1080/13563467.2014.923824

16 World Bank Group, *Biodiversity Offsets: A User Guide* (Washington, DC: World Bank Group, 2016), https://openknowledge.worldbank.org/handle/10986/25758

17 Ibid., also see Business and Biodiversity Offsets Programme, *Biodiversity Offset Design Handbook* (Washington, DC: BBOP, 2009), www.forest-trends.org/wp-content/uploads/imported/biodiversity-offset-design-handbook-pdf.pdf

18 World Bank Group, *Biodiversity Offsets*.

19 Rivers International, *Advancing Ecological Civilization? Chinese hydropower giants and their biodiversity footprints* (Oakland, CA: International Rivers, 2020), www.hydrobiodiversityimpact.org/

20 Tim Newbold, Derek P. Tittensor, Michael B. J. Harfoot, Jörn P. W. Scharlemann, and Drew W. Purves, 'Non-linear changes in modelled terrestrial ecosystems subjected to perturbations,' *Scientific Reports* 10, no. 1 (2020): 14051, https://doi.org/10.1038/s41598-020-70960-9

21 Oksana Grytsenko, 'Living next door to 17 million chickens: "We want a normal life",' *The Guardian*, 23 June 2018, www.theguardian.com/environment/2018/jun/23/living-next-door-to-17-million-chickens-we-want-a-normal-life

22 Eurogroup for Animals, *Animal Welfare in the Implementation of the EU-Ukraine DCFTA* (Brussels: Eurogroup for Animals, 2021), www.eurogroupforanimals.org/files/eurogroupforanimals/2020-07/Eurogroup percent20for percent20Animals percent20- percent20EU percent20Ukraine percent20trade percent20and percent20animal percent20welfare percent20May percent202019_0.pdf

23 This loan also included a gift of about USD 358,000 (counted as Official Development Assistance, from international donors such as the Global Environment Facility) for a biogas production facility next to the chicken stalls.

24 Vanora Bennett, 'EBRD lends €24 million to Ukraine's agribusiness company MHP,' *European Bank for Reconstruction and Development*, 17 June 2022, www.ebrd.com/news/2022/ebrd-lends-24-million-to-ukraines-agribusiness-company-mhp.html

25 European Bank for Reconstruction and Development, *Sub-sectoral Environmental and Social Guideline: Poultry Farming* (London: EBRD, 2016), www.ebrd.com/documents/environment/poultry-farming.pdf

26 Tim Steinweg, *Chicken Run: The Business Strategies and Impact of Poultry Producer MHP in Ukraine* (Amsterdam: SOMO, 2015), www.somo.nl/nl/chicken-run/

Further reading

Arcus Foundation. *State of the Apes: Infrastructure Development and Ape Conservation.* Cambridge: Cambridge University Press, 2018.

Bar-On, Yinon M., Rob Phillips, and Ron Milo. 'The biomass distribution on Earth.' *Proceedings of the National Academy of Sciences* 115, no. 25 (2018): 6506–6511. https://doi.org/10.1073/pnas.1711842115

van Beemen, Olivier. 'Op zoek naar Kwabena, de Ghanese ananasboer van Albert Heijn.' *Follow the Money*, 3 September 2020. www.ftm.nl/artikelen/zoektocht-kwabena-ghanese-ananasboer-ah-lekker-gevoel

Bennett, Vanora. 'EBRD lends €24 million to Ukraine's agribusiness company MHP.' *European Bank for Reconstruction and Development*, 17 June 2022. www.ebrd.com/news/2022/ebrd-lends-24-million-to-ukraines-agribusiness-company-mhp.html

Brock, Andrea. 'Securing accumulation by restoration – Exploring spectacular corporate conservation, coal mining and biodiversity compensation in the German Rhineland.' *Environment and Planning E: Nature and Space* 2020: https://doi.org/10.1177/2514848620924597

Büscher, Bram, and Robert Fletcher. 'Accumulation by conservation.' *New Political Economy* 20, no. 2 (2015): 273–298. https://doi.org/10.1080/13563467.2014.923824

Business and Biodiversity Offsets Programme. *Biodiversity Offset Design Handbook.* Washington, DC: BBOP, 2009. www.forest-trends.org/wp-content/uploads/imported/biodiversity-offset-design-handbook-pdf.pdf

Eurogroup for Animals. *Animal Welfare in the Implementation of the EU-Ukraine DCFTA.* Brussels: Eurogroup for Animals, 2021. www.eurogroupforanimals.org/files/eurogroupforanimals/2020-07/Eurogroup percent20for percent20Animals percent20- percent20EU percent20Ukraine percent20trade percent20and percent20animal percent20welfare percent20May percent202019_0.pdf

European Bank for Reconstruction and Development. *Sub-sectoral Environmental and Social Guideline: Poultry Farming*. London: EBRD, 2016. www.ebrd.com/documents/environment/poultry-farming.pdf

Fuso Nerini, Francesco, Julia Tomei, Long Seng To, Iwona Bisaga, Priti Parikh, Mairi Black, Aiduan Borrion, Catalina Sparature, Vanesa Castán Broto, Gabrial Anandarajah, Ben Milligan, and Yacob Mulugetta. 'Mapping synergies and trade-offs between energy and the Sustainable Development Goals.' *Nature Energy* 3, no. 1 (2018): 10–15. https://doi.org/10.1038/s41560-017-0036-5

Grytsenko, Oksana. 'Living next door to 17 million chickens: "We want a normal life".' *The Guardian*, 23 June 2018. www.theguardian.com/environment/2018/jun/23/living-next-door-to-17-million-chickens-we-want-a-normal-life

Harvey, Fiona. 'Current emissions pledges will lead to catastrophic climate breakdown, says UN.' *The Guardian*, 26 October 2022. www.theguardian.com/environment/2022/oct/26/current-emissions-pledges-will-lead-to-catastrophic-climate-breakdown-says-un

International Finance Corporation. *IFC Support to Transport*. Washington, DC: IFC, 2010. www.ifc.org/wps/wcm/connect/0cce4461-d2a5-45f5-9eea-e9bac02bcc53/IFC_Support2Infrastructure_Transport.pdf?MOD=AJPERES&CVID=lKbEx3x

International Finance Corporation. *Public-Private Partnership Impact Stories. Samoa: Virgin Samoa Airlines*. Washington, DC: IFC, 2013. www.ifc.org/wps/wcm/connect/991d2430-de89-42c9-a784-07b53c177933/PPPStories_Samoa_VirginSamoaAirlines.pdf?MOD=AJPERES&CVID=lHIp1QN

Kleemann, Linda. 'The relevance of certifications and business practices in linking smallholders and large agro-businesses in sub-Sahara Africa.' *International Food and Agribusiness Management Review* 19, no. 4 (2016): 65–78. https://doi.org/10.22434/IFAMR2015.0204

Kormos, Rebecca, Cyril F. Kormos, Tatyana Humle, Annette Lanjouw, Helga Rainer, Ray Victurine, Russell A. Mittermeier, Mamadou S. Diallo, Anthony B. Rylands, and Elizabeth A. Williamson. 'Great apes and biodiversity offset projects in Africa: The case for national offset strategies.' *PLoS ONE* 9, no. 11 (2014): e111671. https://doi.org/10.1371/journal.pone.0111671

National Geographic. 'Ancient forest home of squatter communities is doomed by coal.' 15 April 2018. www.nationalgeographic.co.uk/photography/2018/04/ancient-forest-home-of-squatter-communities-is-doomed-by-coal

Newbold, Tim, Derek P. Tittensor, Michael B. J. Harfoot, Jörn P. W. Scharlemann, and Drew W. Purves. 'Non-linear changes in modelled terrestrial ecosystems subjected to perturbations.' *Scientific Reports* 10, no. 1 (2020): 14051. https://doi.org/10.1038/s41598-020-70960-9

Olthuis, Loethe. 'Hoe duurzaam zijn verse stukjes tropisch fruit?' *De Volkskrant* 6 February 2016, www.volkskrant.nl/nieuws-achtergrond/hoe-duurzaam-zijn-verse-stukjes-tropisch-fruit~b3fa92f0/

Rivers International. *Advancing Ecological Civilization? Chinese hydropower giants and their biodiversity footprints*. Oakland, CA: International Rivers, 2020. www.hydrobiodiversityimpact.org/

Rulisa, Alexis, Luuk van Kempen, and Dirk-Jan Koch. 'When local trade-offs between SDGs turn out to be wealth-dependent: Interaction between expanding rice cultivation and eradicating malaria in Rwanda.' *Sustainability* 14, no. 4: 2100. https://doi.org/10.3390/su14042100

Steinweg, Tim. *Chicken Run: The Business Strategies and Impacts of Poultry Producer MHP in Ukraine*. Amsterdam: SOMO, 2015. www.somo.nl/nl/chicken-run/

Torvikey, Gertrude Dzifa, Joseph Awetori Yao, and Joseph Kofi Teye. 'Farm to factory gendered employment: The case of blue skies outgrower scheme in Ghana.' *Agrarian South: Journal of Political Economy* 5, no. 1 (2016): 77–97. https://doi.org/10.1177/2277976016669188

World Bank Group. *Biodiversity Offsets: A User Guide*. Washington, DC: World Bank Group, 2016. https://openknowledge.worldbank.org/handle/10986/25758

World Wildlife Fund. *Living Planet Report 2018: Aiming Higher*. Gland: WWF, 2018. www.worldwildlife.org/pages/living-planet-report-2018

12 Ripple effects

The underestimation of positive effects of international development efforts

Ripple effects occur when there are positive spillover effects beyond the beneficiary, intervention, area, or thematic focus. They can be considered unintended if the donor or implementing agency did not consider that these spillovers could happen in its formal evaluation parameters.

What flavours do we see?

1 **Thematically synergetic effects.** A positive effect of an external intervention in one thematic area crosses over to another thematic area.
2 **Catalytic effects.** The external intervention directly or indirectly contributes to additional development impacts in the same thematic area.
3 **Human interaction effects.** Because of the external intervention, new social ties are created between people.

In which instances have ripple effects been observed? Three examples:

1 Thematically synergetic effects: deworming initiatives and early childhood nutrition programmes positively affect test scores in schools.
2 Catalytic effects: in Bolivia, a development bank structured an innovative investment so that additional investors joined the deal and stimulated other investors to invest in similar innovations.
3 Human interaction effects: an external intervention often involves people moving around the globe or a country, and as these people move, new cross-cultural friendships and relationships are formed. These human interactions often lead to long-lasting ties, which can outlive a single aid intervention by years or even decades.

Key concepts from complexity thinking that help to understand ripple effects

1 **Interconnectivity.** International aid agencies are often thematically organized, and agencies are measuring their thematic effects. However, there are often synergies between various thematic development outcomes. For instance, girls who go to school longer generally also have healthier kids. Because many agencies fall short of measuring their outcomes beyond their thematic area of expertise, they underestimate their impact.

DOI: 10.4324/9781003356851-12

This Chapter has been made available under a CC-BY-NC-ND license.

2 **Adaptive agents.** We often assume that 'everything else remains equal' (ceteris paribus) in the development sector. When using control groups (groups that haven't received the treatment) we often assume that the external intervention does not affect their behaviour. This assumption often holds, but people are adaptive agents, and if they see that something is working out for a group of participants (e.g., a certain innovation), they will adapt their behaviour accordingly. This means that the true impact of development aid can often be higher than assumed.

Figure 12.1 Ripple effects in action: spreading of innovation beyond initial target group.

Source: Maarten Wolterink.

12.1 Thematically synergetic effects

I forgive you if after 11 chapters you think that my view is that the net effect of all these development interventions is negative, since negative side effects are often overlooked. But that's not the case: I believe that the positive effects of international development have been systematically underestimated as well, perhaps even more so. I first experienced that during a visit to Bangladesh at the beginning of my career. I was an account manager for various Dutch NGOs at the Ministry of Foreign Affairs, and I tried to visit as many programmes as possible. This brought me to the rice paddies of Bangladesh, where Cordaid (one of the NGOs I was responsible for) was working with, what they called, the hard-core poor.

I don't know what I tried to prove, but I failed miserably. I was sitting at the back of a rickshaw and the rider explained that he had been able to buy this vehicle because of NGO programmes. I ticked him on his shoulder while cycling on the sandy dikes between the paddies, and I said I would take over from him. While Bangladesh and the Netherlands are worlds apart, they share similar features, which gave me an erroneous sense of self-confidence: a lot of dykes, flat-areas, people everywhere and ... bikes. An avid biker, I think I tried showing off that I could also bike. But *mama mia*, it was so heavy and technical, with two people in the back seat, the unpaved narrow path ... I rode the rickshaw into a small ditch at an intersection of dykes. Luckily, nobody was hurt, the rickshaw didn't break down, and the bystanders had fun.

My mood remained upbeat. I was impressed by the vibrant associational life in the villages we visited and the progress I felt. In all of them, different organizations were active: sometimes it was BRAC, sometimes Grameen, or ASA, or sometimes multiple, and they were all testing – with the support of the international community – various new intervention methods. During a focus group, women who participated in a microfinance scheme explained to me – one after the other – how they progressed because of the microcredit. They raised more chicken and sold more eggs (economic output) and they used that money to ensure that their children completed secondary education: a thematic cross-over effect.[1]

12.1.1 Bangladesh: the aid lab for ripple effects

Naomi Hossain rightfully calls Bangladesh *the aid lab*: many aid interventions now commonplace in the development sector were developed (and tested) in Bangladesh, such as microcredit.[2] Hossain claims that when aid officials like me come to Bangladesh, we don't seek minerals or land or geopolitical advantage (or to show off our rickshaw riding skills), but to demonstrate that liberal democracy and a market economy with social protection works. I am unsure if that was the case for me, but I have to admit that I was relieved to see that aid was working, even better than intended.

Like Jeffrey Sachs, the tireless supporter of international development and solidarity, I am impressed by the many development indicators that have shown tremendous progress in Bangladesh.[3] I pick three (the three upward sloping lines in Figure 12.2). The percentage of children that went to secondary school rose from less than 20 per cent to over 70 per cent in about forty years. Equally impressive: life expectancy rose by more than twenty years in the same period. Also encouraging is that more women could better decide on their family size, as before the 1980s less than 1 in ten had access to birth control measures, and now that is over 60 per cent. Bangladesh has achieved significantly higher social progress compared to economies sharing similar income levels in terms of a wide range of social indicators.[4] Bangladesh reached lower-middle income status in 2015. It is on track to graduate from the UN's Least Developed Countries list in 2026.

International development efforts contributed to this: especially in the first two decades after independence (until the mid-1990s), the Bangladeshi education, health, and agricultural sector received tremendously important international aid transfers (over 30 per cent of capital formation). This declined to somewhere between 5 and 10 per cent as more means could be mobilized locally and social indicators increased. On average, all the support amounted to about USD 10 per capita per year since 1975.[5] Aid went not only to relatively 'innocent' social sectors as is sometimes mistakenly assumed, but

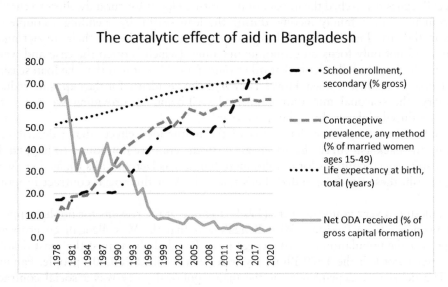

The catalytic effect of aid in Bangladesh

- • School enrollment, secondary (% gross)
- — Contraceptive prevalence, any method (% of married women ages 15-49)
- ••••• Life expectancy at birth, total (years)
- — Net ODA received (% of gross capital formation)

Figure 12.2 The success of Bangladesh as an 'aid lab.'

Source: World Development Indicators.

also to politically sensitive organizations such as trade unions. The NGO desk where I worked as a junior civil servant also funded the international department of Dutch trade unions to join the struggle of female garment worker associations in Bangladesh for safer working conditions. International aid permeated many parts of Bangladeshi society.

As you know by now, I am not naively optimistic about aid, and I am not using Bangladesh as a case to proof that aid is effective full-stop. But the Bangladeshi case does show that aid can have many ripple effects.

In Bangladesh, ripple effects took place among the educational, health, and sexual and reproductive rights themes, partially set in motion by foreign assistance. The increasing levels of women's education contributed to reduced birth rates (girls who stay in school start to have children later, and have less of them). This reduction contributed to healthier children and higher educational attainment of these children again, leading to more demands for contraceptives etcetera. The results that Bangladeshis achieved in one thematic sector spilled over to another.[6] The term 'interconnectivity' from complexity thinking (introduced in Chapter 2) describes the situation well. As Asadullah et al. explain, social and health indicators progressed at varying paces and intervals in Bangladesh, creating unintended synergies between different social indicators.[7]

Why do we know this so well for Bangladesh? The development community has been able to map the synergies between these interventions in Bangladesh in particular because of a learning culture.[8] The initial investment into good statistical information enabled an adaptive management style: 'From early on, aid was also used to support learning from doing, allowing the experimentation of course correction that needed to use resources well.'[9]

Another beautiful example of thematically synergetic effects in Bangladesh is between interest-free loans for seasonal migration and violence against women. Mushfiq Mubarak and his colleagues researched the impact of interest-free loans for rural dwellers to enable them to increase their family income during the lean season by spending a couple of months in the city. Luckily they did not employ a tunnel vision in their impact analysis: they did not only focus on economic outcomes (which is often the case and were positive by the way) but also looked at other outcomes. They found that the loan season reduced violence against women. How? They find clear evidence for the exposure reduction theory: the seasonal migration improved well-being by providing women with periods of reduced violence throughout the year.[10]

Bangladesh case taught me that many of the unintended effects that I describe in this book (the backlash effect, the governance effects, etc.) are not bound to happen. If there is a solid social contract (or development bargain as Dercon calls it), as there was in Bangladesh, these can be avoided. Let's take a look at this social contract in more detail.

Bangladesh is a very young country (1971) and one of the reasons for public support for independence from Pakistan (West Bengal) was that the West Bengali government didn't protect the population of East Bengal (now Bangladesh) against the most deadly cyclone ever recorded: the 1970 Bhola Cyclone, which killed 300,000 people. Famine raged. The ticket to independence for the major political party was a social contract between the elites, the population, and their aid donors that prioritized the protection of the population against crises of subsistence and survival.[11] Interestingly, donors were part of this 'development bargain,' and they were expected to contribute to it. Do you remember the social contract in Somaliland that I explained in Chapter 10? Their founding social contract explicitly excluded international support, which explains why as an NGO account manager, I was riding this rickshaw in 2005 in Bangladesh, and not a camel in Somaliland.

12.1.2 Synergies between the Sustainable Development Goals

I know, I know, I have made a big noise about trade-offs between the Sustainable Development Goals (SDGs), especially in Chapter 11 on the trade-offs between economic and environmental objectives. But so far I only told one half of that story, as systematic studies show that a majority of the relations between the SDGs are synergetic and positive.[12] Often, donors invest money in one sector and get additional results in another sector free of charge. Let me explain: aid programmes often aim to achieve specific results in one sub-theme (e.g., 'let's deworm kids'), and effects are measured at that level (e.g., 'how many kids are dewormed'), whereas these dewormed kids go on do great things (e.g., 'score much higher on educational test scores').[13]

Visual maps of SDGs show just how many different thematic synergies exist: below you will find the positive synergetic effects of SDG 6.1 'access to clean water.' Once people have access to clean water, many other SDGs come within reach, such as a reduction of illnesses amongst young kids (SDG 3.2), and better school results (as less time is spent on fetching water) (SDG 4.1).

Quite some agencies are successful in claiming unintended benefits as part of the programme ex-post. When they detect that a programme has a wider positive impact (e.g., the deworming program), they will present it to donors in the next iterations as a health intervention and a health *and* education intervention. In the book's introduction I explained that that is probably why we find less positive unintended effects, as they are gradually integrated into programming and become intended.

However, there are better ways to capitalize on synergies than just victory appropriation afterwards: strategic planning. Before starting interventions are developed, priority can be given to those interventions with maximum ripple-over effects. Therefore, organizational silos need to be discarded so that institutional boundaries to learning can be overcome. For instance, investment in Ethiopia's social safety net has had positive and deep interlinkages with many SDGs.[14] Donors would be smart to invest rather in these types of programmes, than for instance in programmes with lofty aims that hardly 'spill over' (e.g., increasing access to university education or supporting cultural activities).

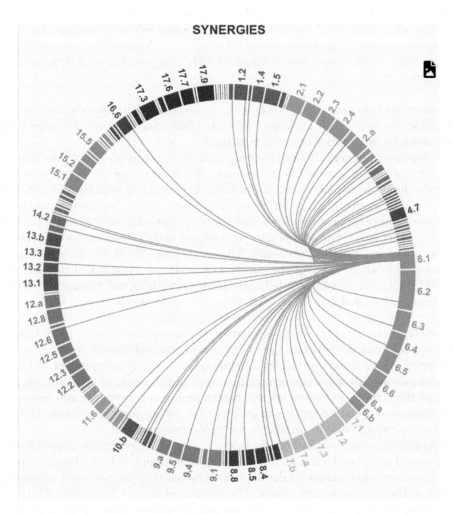

Figure 12.3 Positive interaction between the SDGs: the example of access to clean drinking water.

Source: Joint Research Council of the EU: Enabling SDGs.

12.2 Catalytic effects

12.2.1 *When a development bank underestimates its impact*

Spillovers do not only materialize thematically, but also because other actors who were not targeted join the development intervention. It is to these catalytic effects to which we now turn. Let me share the story of FMO, the national Dutch development bank (a portfolio of about EUR 13 billion), after the US development bank. They often commission independent evaluations, which they publish online. In an evaluation of a private sector development fund managed by FMO, evaluators criticize FMO for undervaluing their positive side effects:

> In the majority of case studies, the fund had catalytic effects in that it helped to mobilize other investors ex post, by reducing investees' perceived or actual risks … In 4 out of 20 case studies, the fund was successful in catalysing follow-up investments. FMO does not systematically analyse demonstration effects … however our case studies and some in-depth evaluations commissioned by FMO suggest that such demonstration effects often exist.[15]

Often evaluations rain on parade, but here the evaluations claim that the development bank is achieving *more* than it claims. So what effects are these development banks overlooking and how can they be better measured?

In development finance, the mobilization and demonstration effects are two key catalytic effects. Mobilization effects measure the leverage of an investment of a development bank: how much extra capital did they mobilize with their investment? These mobilization effects can be either ex-ante, when structuring an investment the development bank arranges for other financiers to come on board, or ex-post: by investing in a particular type of client, the investment makes the client more attractive for further financing by other investors. These catalytic effects are quite direct and easily measurable at the level of the client. The evaluators just asked the clients of FMO: 'Did the financing of FMO help you to attract additional finance?' 17 out of the 24 clients responded positively.[16] FMO never reported this ripple effect to their donors.

Conversely, demonstration effects are harder to measure as they are more indirect. Developing banks can demonstrate their early confidence and 'de-risk' transactions for other international financial institutions (IFIs) by taking an early commitment and sometimes additional risk. By serving as a 'stamp of approval' because of their size, age, and strong reputation, they can 'crowd in' commercial and impact investors into higher-risk markets. Because of the signals they send out, they can display to other investors (subtype 1) or clients (subtype 2) that the market is profitable and impactful.

Even though these demonstration effects are harder to measure, this does not mean that they should be ignored: the added value of these development banks largely depends on this. For quite some actors in development finance they are not even unintended effects but indirect or secondary effects. The evaluators do not blame just FMO, but also its donor, the Dutch government, for not including these demonstration effects in their metrics for success. Because of this lack of interest by the donor, demonstration effects are generally not an investment criterion for FMO and is therefore not included in

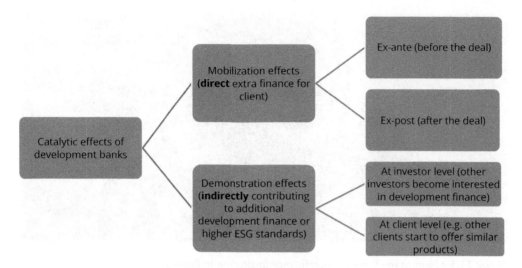

Figure 12.4 Catalytic effects of development banks.

Source: Adapted from Oomes et al., Evaluation of the FMO-MASSIF Fund.

investment decisions. Interestingly, other development banks, such as the European Bank for Reconstruction and Development, do consider demonstration effects, hence using more these potential ripple effects.[17]

12.2.2 Catalytic effects in Bolivia

Luckily, FMO takes the recommendation at heart and is increasingly measuring its potential catalytic effects. Luckily it is not rocket science: for example, they add it as a research question in their impact evaluations.

The investments of FMO to Sartawi, a microcredit organization in Bolivia's highlands, make the importance of integrating catalytic effects in our analysis clear. This innovative joint initiative coupled credit with capacity building for dairy farmers. In addition to measuring the direct impact of the loan and capacity building, the evaluators also tried to analyse mobilization and demonstration effects. They found both.[18] Their interviews with several stakeholders strongly suggested that FMO had acted as a mobilizing catalyst for Sartawi: the presence of FMO strengthened the trust of other funders in the microcredit organization. This allowed Sartawi to mobilize new funding sources and could increase existing investors' engagement.[19]

Furthermore, the Food and Agriculture Organization wrote a case about Sartawi in one of their books, highlighting the triangle business model of Sartawi as an innovation in the microfinance industry. Subsequently, other development finance institutions and Bolivian banks have started to implement similar programmes (combining credit with capacity building), indicating the catalytic effects employing demonstration.[20] This shows that mapping catalytic effects (both mobilization and demonstration) is possible, and if mapping them is possible, why not make it part of the investment decisions?

Figure 12.5 Client of the Sartawi microfinance institution in Bolivia.

We have now focused exclusively on the catalytic effects of development banks. Still, of course they are more widely detectable in the development sector, for instance, as a result of cash transfers.

Let me take you to the Dowa region of Malawi, where UNICEF and the government introduced a cash transfer programme to absorb yet another food shock in Malawi. The programme had multiplier effects for the region, as beneficiaries spent their money on a wide range of locally produced goods and services including education, health, and commerce.[21] The additional money circulating in the Dowa district ensured that local businesses also benefitted from the cash transfers. For each dollar transferred by the programme, an additional income of over USD 2 was generated as beneficiaries spend their transfers with local businesses, which spend a portion of that income in the local area.[22] Also in the case of Dowa, these ripple effects were not captured in regular and case studies evaluations, as they didn't look at multiplier effects.[23] Once again, the true positive impact of international aid was underestimated.[24]

I can go on and on, and move from development finance and cash transfers to improved labour rights beyond the target group because of fair trade or the adoption of new fruit trees beyond the initial target group of the NGO.[25] But it is also often the case that actors in development are too modest about catalytic effects, only discovering them later on an ad-hoc basis. To fully account for and capitalize on these effects, evaluators need to cast their results measurement wider and longer.

12.3 Human interaction effects: sex, love, friendship in aid

12.3.1 *Transactional sex as a means towards upward social mobility*

While working as the director of an NGO, I travelled across the DRC and Africa to visit our field offices (at one point, I was supervising about 30 offices in nine different countries), so I was often in the air and on the road. When I would visit the provincial field offices in countries like Nigeria, colleagues from the office of the national capital would usually accompany me. After a day at work, we would regularly go out for some fried fish and drinks, and after that the male staff would invite me to the local bar.

The first time I joined them, I was surprised by the number of well-dressed young women who were interested in striking up a conversation with us. As we got talking, it became clear that these were smart women and they invited us for a dance. Before I knew it, my colleagues and I were all dancing with them and this was when it started to dawn to me that actually, these women were sex workers trying to get picked up by potential clients – like us (I am quite slow in figuring these things out, I have to admit). Once the penny had dropped, I wanted to return to my hotel room as quickly as possible (alone!), but my colleagues – with whom I was sharing the car – clearly had different ideas. 'The fun is just getting started,' they shouted over loud music. They had no intention of leaving. So I was stuck: if I sat down by myself, the women would be over in a flash, and if I went onto the dancefloor, they would be right behind me as well. It was against the security guidelines to take a taxi by myself at night, but in the end, that was my only option.[26]

The next morning as I was walking down the hallway to an early breakfast, I saw one of last night's women coming out of the hotel room of one of my colleagues, and I greeted her shyly.

Murhega Mushanda and Dorothea Hilhorst have started researching sex work, humanitarian emergencies, and development agencies.[27] They and their team interviewed around 500 women engaged in transactional sex in the eastern DRC. Defining transactional sex can be tricky (as boundaries are blurred) but broadly speaking it refers to sexual relationships where exchanging gifts, money, or other services is an important factor. Transactional sex often makes the partners mutually dependent and emotionally vulnerable, but there is a clear power imbalance with one dominant person.[28] They conclude that there is an internationally ignored but real difference between 'survival sex' and 'transactional sex.' Survival sex is aimed at securing basic livelihoods (often in rural areas), while transactional sex (more often in urban areas) can also be an investment in a more solid future, such as education.[29]

The preferred clients of those engaged in transactional sex? NGO workers! Some 37 per cent of them said NGO workers were their favourite clients (even though they make up only 12 per cent of their clientele in the eastern DRC).[30] While sexual exploitation and abuse are clearly one of the unintended negative effects of aid that international agencies need to tackle head-on, assuming that all sexual relationships between aid workers and the population of the target country are exploitative and abusive does not do justice to the '50 shades of grey' of these often transactional relationships.[31]

That transactional effects are not a minor side effect, but a pervasive reality becomes clear in a systematic quantitative study of the association between a UN peacekeeping operation and transactional sex.[32] They find that more than 50 per cent of women in Monrovia (the capital of Liberia) have engaged in transactional sex, and more than 75 per cent of them have done so with UN personnel. An in-depth qualitative study by Kolbe into transactional sex in Haiti provides the stories behind the numbers.[33] The stories make clear that, even though there certainly is exploitation and abuse, voluntary transactional sex is not inherently exploitative: it is also a legitimate opportunity for women to engage in the aid and peacekeeping economy, enabling them to pursue their education, improve their housing conditions, etc.

While I realize that my proposal might not be politically feasible, I would like to share it with you: whereas I think that there should be a zero tolerance policy for inaction against sexual exploitation and abuse, I do not believe it is possible to apply zero tolerance to any sexual, let alone affectionate relationship, between aid workers or blue helmets and the local population. Human nature stands in the way, as the closing testimony by Georgette (end of chapter) also shows.

12.3.2 Friendship and relationships, both as a consequence and cause of international solidarity

In the last couple of years I tagged along with a colleague researcher who focusses on Private Development Initiatives and the role of friendship therein.[34] In about 50 per cent of the interviews, we heard about long friendships that have emerged because of the aid relationship and have nurtured their organizational partnership. These friendships sometimes last decades.

Let me develop the case of Andrew.[35] He was an aid worker in the 1980s in Burkina Faso, where he befriended the head of a local school, Vincent. Their families got to know each other, and on weekends they would go on family outings together. After Andrew returned to Europe he stayed in contact with this headmaster, and he started to sponsor disadvantaged children to enable them to attend school. Andrew would go back every four years and stay at Vincent's place. Over the years, their friendship strengthened, and Andrew even started a foundation in the Netherlands to support Vincent's school. When the school building needed refurbishment, Andrew started a fundraising campaign in the Netherlands, mobilizing enough funds for four new classrooms. Over the following decades, the friendship – and the collaboration – flourished, and Vincent even came to the Netherlands to visit the country and its schools, and meet the funders. The foundation is currently supporting twenty schools in the Sahel. Now both Andrew and Vincent are reaching retirement age: Vincent's daughter has already taken over as headmaster of the school, and Andrew is currently looking for a new chair of the foundation. His daughter-in-law appears interested. Regardless of whether the collaboration will continue, the friendship between Andrew and Vincent will persist. This friendship would not have existed without international development efforts, which in turn had a flywheel effect on education in the Sahel (a flywheel effect occurs when the process set in motion continues to exist after the initial stimulus has ceased).

What strikes me is that in my education and training we always treated international development work as formal, with clear rules and procedures. It comes back to this linear thinking in development, which negates the complexity of human interaction.[36] We often forget, however, that the human factor is all-pervasive in the development sector: both as a consequence of international aid and as a source of inspiration for international solidary. The closing testimony of Georgette shows both.

Testimony by Georgette Schutte: 'I am a product of opposites'

Georgette is a 42-year-old Mauritanian-Dutch woman. She works at the United Nations as a gender-based violence specialist. She lives with her two daughters in Mauritania, but travels the world for her work. She is speaking from Honiara, the Solomon Islands, where she is on a UN mission.

Figure 12.6 On the left Johannes Schutte and Awa Sarr in the 1970s, and on the right their 'aid baby' Georgette Schutte.

How it all started

My father, Johannes Schutte, is Dutch and was a development worker for the Lutheran World Federation (LWF). His first posting for this organization was Mauritania. When he met Awa Sarr, my mother, at an LWF event, it was love at first sight, but this was not the case for my mum in the beginning. Luckily, my father made a move and 42 years later, my parents are still very happy together. I was born exactly nine months after the wedding night!

Was there a clash of cultures?

Ooh yes! My parents' background was totally different. My father is a Christian. My mother is a devout Muslim, who had been forced into her first marriage at fifteen, with a man approximately the age of her father. She was his second wife and there was no love. She did something extraordinary: even before she met my father, she divorced her first husband, when divorce was prohibited. There was quite some resistance from my Mauritanian uncles to her marrying a Christian, but she went ahead anyway. While my uncles wanted my father to become a Muslim, my mum never pushed him. They respected each other and looked at their shared values, which was the desire to support people in need.

Building bridges

The love between my parents has been a great example for me and has allowed me to make friends with people across the globe. I am a product of opposites, and that has allowed me to act as a bridge between different cultures and religions. I can see that Western culture is getting dominant in many contexts. It pushes away important elements of other cultures. In my mother's culture, we have an excellent system for first-time mothers, who are supported by the extended family postpartum, for forty days. Many of our good traditions are being lost and replaced by

Western concepts. I started a podcast series in which I interview people about useful traditions that are being lost.

Financial spillover effects

I grew up in a very privileged way. My parents moved across Africa for my father's work and my parents sent me to an international school. I realize I am very fortunate compared to my extended family in Mauritania and Holland. My father has always helped out financially with his international NGO salary, and I do the same with my UN salary. We use our incomes to support those in need such as with school and medical fees or supporting family with rent/housing and other financial needs they may have.

What can international actors learn from the experiences of your parents and you?

Of course, my parents wouldn't have met without the aid sector, and I wouldn't exist. Because of all these aid workers there are so many mixed-ethnicity couples and friendships across the globe now. My suggestion to aid workers living in another country is to go out and meet locals, explore the culture and learn from it, and share their own culture. There is so much beauty in the world and interesting people, even in the international organizations they work for. Build personal bridges in this fragmented work. Beautiful things can grow from there!

How to maximize ripple effects

Policymakers

- **Avoid thematic silos.** If professionals are in siloed departments, with limited opportunities for joint interaction, learning, and decision-making, then it is virtually impossible to design and monitor programmes for catalytic effects.
- **Organize localized comprehensive research and learning.** The Bangladesh case showed the importance of investing in research programmes that cast a wide net, across disciplines and intervention areas.

Practitioners

- **Choose for programmes with thematic synergies.** When deciding which programme to start, try to start a programme with many potential synergies with other thematic areas.
- **Make catalytic potential explicit in investment decisions.** Some programmes and investments have more mobilization and demonstration effects than others. Make this potential an explicit part of the investment decision.
- **Consider the human factor when planning.** It cannot be assumed that people are robots without any sense of long-term loyalty and well thought-through economic aspirations. Stimulate aid workers to create personal linkages with their environment.

Evaluators

- **Measure the potential ripple effects of interventions.** This can be done by mapping the demonstration and mobilization effects.
- **Measure results beyond the initial target group and after the programme period.** Like with negative ones, we can only capture positive unintended effects if we broaden our temporal, geographic, and thematic scope. It is needed for evaluators to have this broader scope to get a complete view of the impact.

Notes

1 I have pointed out the negative behavioural responses to microcredit programmes in Chapter 8.

2 Naomi Hossain, *The Aid Lab: Understanding Bangladesh's Unexpected Success* (Oxford: Oxford University Press, 2017).

3 Jeffrey D. Sachs, *The End of Poverty: Economic Possibilities for Our Time* (New York: Penguin, 2006), 14.

4 M. Niaz Asadullah, Antonio Savoia, and Wahiduddin Mahmud, 'Paths to development: Is there a Bangladesh surprise?,' *World Development* 62 (2014): 138–154, https://doi.org/10.1016/j.worlddev.2014.05.013

5 Stefan Dercon, *Gambling on Development: Why Some Countries Win and Others Lose* (London: Hurst publishers, 2022), 227.

6 Asadullah et al., 'Paths to development.'

7 Spillover effects to non-beneficiaries have been documented in Bangladesh as well, see Oriana Bandiera, Robin Burgess, Selim Gulesci, and Imran Rasul, *Community Networks and Poverty Reduction Programmes: Evidence from Bangladesh. LSE STICERD Research Paper no. EOPP015* (London: LSE, 2010), https://ssrn.com/abstract=1717447

8 Dercon, *Gambling on Development*, 228.

9 While there is a willingness to learn and I use the Bangladesh case to showcase positive side effects, this doesn't mean that there aren't any negative side effects in Bangladesh. A joint Worldbank/UNICEF/Government of Bangladesh project provided about ten million shallow hand-pumped wells to provide pathogen-free groundwater for the prevention of waterborne diseases. However, the donors did not adhere to the 'do harm principle,' as the natural contamination of the groundwater with arsenic in these wells was not checked and was only discovered in the 1990s. As a consequence, an estimated 35–77 million people in Bangladesh have been chronically exposed to increased concentrations of arsenic through drinking water: Maria Argos, Tara Kalra, Paul J. Rathouz, et al., 'Arsenic exposure from drinking water, and all-cause and chronic-disease mortalities in Bangladesh (HEALS): A prospective cohort study,' *The Lancet* 376, no. 9737 (2010): 252–258, https://doi.org/10.1016/s0140-6736(10)60481-3

10 Ahmed Mushfiq Mobarak and Alejandra Ramos, 'The Effects of migration on intimate partner violence: Evidence for the exposure reduction theory in Bangladesh,' working paper, February 2019, https://sistemas.colmex.mx/Reportes/LACEALAMES/LACEA-LAMES2019_paper_321.pdf

11 Hossain, *The Aid Lab*.

12 Prajal Pradhan, Luís Costa, Diego Rybski, Wolfgang Lucht, and Jürgen P. Kropp, 'A systematic study of sustainable development goal (SDG) interactions,' *Earth's Future* 5, no. 11 (2017): 1169–1179, https://doi.org/10.1002/2017EF000632.

13 In a similar vein, one of my PhD students, Tessa Ubels, identified that effects of Mental Health and Psychosocial Support Programmes can spill over to other thematic areas, such as conflict resolution. So while the aim is reduced individual trauma, there are secondary social outcomes: Tessa Ubels, Sara Kinsbergen, Jochem Tolsma, and Dirk-Jan Koch, 'The social outcomes of psychosocial support: A grey literature scoping review,' *SSM – Mental Health* 2 (2022): 100074, https://doi.org/10.1016/j.ssmmh.2022.100074

14 Amina Khan, 'Three tips for policy-makers on implementing the SDGs,' *Overseas Development Institute*, n.d., accessed 1 February 2023, https://odi.org/en/insights/three-tips-for-policy-makers-on-implementing-the-sdgs/

15 Nienke Oomes, Thierry Belt, Nicolas Berthiaume, Debbie Keijser, Bert van Manen, and Ward Rougoor, *Evaluation of the FMO-MASSIF Fund (2015–2019)* (Amsterdam: SEO Amsterdam Economics, 2020), www.seo.nl/en/publications/evaluation-of-the-fmo-massif-fund-2015-2019/, iv.

16 Ibid., 27.

17 Ibid., 53.

18 The evaluation was very positive and showed a clear impact as it focused on the poorest segments and increased both their productivity and access to finance: Adriana Garcia, Francesco Cecchi, Steffen Eriksen, and Robert Lensink, 'The plus in credit-plus-technical assistance: Evidence from a rural microcredit programme in Bolivia,' *The Journal of Development Studies* 58, no. 2 (2022): 275–291, https://doi.org/10.1080/00220388.2021.1928639

19 Francesco Cecchi and Robert Lensink, *Executive Report: Sembrar-Sartawi Evaluation 2015–2019* (The Hague: FMO, 2021), https://reporting.fmo.nl/FbContent.ashx/pub_1000/downloads/v210629140512/Sembrar%20-%20Sartawi%20Evaluation%20(2015-2019)%20(Report).pdf, 14.

20 Ibid., 14.

21 Simon Davies and James Davey, 'A regional multiplier approach to estimating the impact of cash transfers on the market: The case of cash transfers in rural Malawi,' *Development Policy Review* 26, no. 1 (2008): 108, https://doi.org/10.1111/j.1467-7679.2008.00400.x

22 Ibid., 109.

23 Regional Hunger and Vulnerability Programme, *Dowa Emergency Cash Transfer, Malawi. REBA case study number 1* (Johannesburg: RHVP, 2007), www.calpnetwork.org/publication/dowa-emergency-cash-transfer-malawi/

24 Do you remember the upward price effects of cash transfers in the Philippines (Section 6.2)? These were luckily not observed in the Malawian and Mexican cases. Probably, productivity went up because of the cash transfers, reducing inflationary pressures.

25 Ruerd Ruben, Ricardo Fort, and Guillermo Zúñiga-Arias, 'Measuring the impact of fair trade on development,' *Development in Practice* 19, no. 6: 786, https://doi.org/10.1080/09614520903027049; Sintayehu Hailu Alemu, Luuk van Kempen, and Ruerd Ruben, 'The long shadow of faith-based social networks on agricultural performance: Evidence from Ethiopian apple growers,' *The European Journal of Development Research* 30, no. 2 (2018): 297–319, https://doi.org/10.1057/s41287-017-0094-3

26 It is a mistake that sexual relationships between aid workers and population are only about male aid workers and female local people, as the book *Emergency Sex* shows: Kenneth Cain, Heidi Postlewait, and Andrew Thomson, *Emergency Sex and Other Desperate Measures* (New York: Hyperion, 2004).

27 Isumbisho Mwapu, Dorothea Hilhorst, Murhega Mashanda, Muhigwa Bahananga, and Ruhamya Mugenzi, 'Women engaging in transactional sex and working in prostitution: Practices and underlying factors of the sex trade in South Kivu, the Democratic Republic of Congo,' *Secure Livelihoods Research Consortium* report 10 (2016), https://library.wur.nl/WebQuery/wurpubs/fulltext/401353

28 Christian Groes-Green, ' "To put men in a bottle": Eroticism, kinship, female power, and transactional sex in Maputo, Mozambique,' *American Ethnologist* 40, no. 1 (2013): 102–117, https://anthrosource.onlinelibrary.wiley.com/doi/10.1111/amet.12008

29 Mwapu et al., 'Women engaging,' 5.

30 Pastors and priests scored a meagre 1 per cent of the votes for the category of preferred clients. The study does not mention any reason for this.

31 By no means do I wish to justify transactional sex. One shocking finding of a similar study to the one above relates to unsafe abortions. Of the five hundred interviewed sex workers in the DRC, two hundred had undergone one or more illegal or unsafe abortions. This goes to show

that the burden of unintended effects is most often shouldered by the most vulnerable. Also of importance to note is that not only an influx of blue helmets or development workers can increase transactional sex, but also a more general uptake in economic activity, with business and construction people arriving in an area.

32 Bernd Beber, Michael J. Gilligan, Jenny Guardado, and Sabrina Karim, 'Peacekeeping, compliance with international norms, and transactional sex in Monrovia, Liberia,' *International Organization* 71, no. 1 (2017): 1–30, https://doi.org/10.1017/S0020818316000242

33 Athena Rebecca Kolbe, ' "It's not a gift when it comes with price": A qualitative study of transactional sex between UN peacekeepers and Haitian citizens,' *Stability: International Journal of Security and Development* 4, no. 1 (2015): 44, http://doi.org/10.5334/sta.gf

34 Sara Kinsbergen, Anne-Fleur Lurvink, and Imke van Mil, 'Understanding sustainable exit strategies of voluntary development organisations: Amical break-up or messy divorce?,' in *The Rise of Small-Scale Development Organisations: The Emergence, Positioning and Role of Citizen Aid Actors*, edited by Hanne Haaland, Sara Kinsbergen, Lau Schulpen, and Hege Wallevik, 154–169 (London: Routledge, 2023).

35 Andrew is not his real name. The case is based on one interview with a founder of a Dutch small-scale development initiative, and complemented with recurrent stories from other interviews that were part of this research.

36 Kinsbergen et al., 'Understanding sustainable exit strategies.'; Emmanuel Kumi and James Copestake, 'Friend or patron? Social Relations across the national NGO – Donor divide in Ghana,' *The European Journal of Development Research* 34, no. 1 (2023): 343–366, https://doi.org/10.1057/s41287-021-00375-3; Melle Leenstra, 'The human factor in development cooperation: An effective way to deal with unintended effects,' *Evaluation and Programme Planning* 68 (2018): 218–224, https://doi.org/10.1016/j.evalprogplan.2017.09.008

Further reading

Alemu, Sintayehu Hailu, Luuk van Kempen, and Ruerd Ruben. 'The long shadow of faith-based social networks on agricultural performance: Evidence from Ethiopian apple growers.' *The European Journal of Development Research* 30, no. 2 (2018): 297–319. https://doi.org/10.1057/s41287-017-0094-3

Argos, Maria, Tara Kalra, Paul J. Rathouz, Yu Chen, Brandon Pierce, Faruque Parvez, Tariqul Islam, Alauddin Ahmed, Muhammad Rakibuz-Zaman, Rabiul Hasan, Golam Sarwar, Vesna Slavkovich, Alexander van Geen, Joseph Graziano, and Habibul Ahsan. 'Arsenic exposure from drinking water, and all-cause and chronic-disease mortalities in Bangladesh (HEALS): A prospective cohort study.' *The Lancet* 376, no. 9737 (2010): 252–258. https://doi.org/10.1016/s0140-6736(10)60481-3

Asadullah, M. Niaz, Antonio Savoia, and Wahiduddin Mahmud. 'Paths to development: Is there a Bangladesh surprise?' *World Development* 62 (2014): 138–154. https://doi.org/10.1016/j.worlddev.2014.05.013

Bandiera, Oriana, Robin Burgress, Selim Gulesci, and Imran Rasul. *Community Networks and Poverty Reduction Programmes: Evidence from Bangladesh. LSE STICERD Research Paper no. EOPP015.* London: LSE, 2010. https://ssrn.com/abstract=1717447

Beber, Bernd, Michael J. Gilligan, Jenny Guardado, and Sabrina Karim. 'Peacekeeping, Compliance with international norms, and transactional sex in Monrovia, Liberia.' *International Organization* 71, no. 1 (2017): 1–30. https://doi.org/10.1017/S0020818316000242.

Cain, Kenneth, Heidi Postlewait, and Andrew Thomson. *Emergency Sex and Other Desperate Measures.* New York: Hyperion, 2004.

Cecchi, Francesco, and Robert Lensink. *Executive Report: Sembrar-Sartawi Evaluation 2015–2019.* The Hague: FMO, 2021. https://reporting.fmo.nl/FbContent.ashx/pub_1000/downloads/v210629140512/Sembrar%20-%20Sartawi%20Evaluation%20(2015-2019)%20(Report).pdf

Davies, Simon, and James Davey. 'A regional multiplier approach to estimating the impact of cash transfers on the market: The case of cash transfers in rural Malawi.' *Development Policy Review* 26, no. 1 (2008): 91–111. https://doi.org/10.1111/j.1467-7679.2008.00400.x

Dercon, Stefan. *Gambling on Development: Why Some Countries Win and Others Lose.* London: Hurst publishers, 2022.

Garcia, Adriana, Francesco Cecchi, Steffen Eriksen, and Robert Lensink. 'The plus in credit-plus-technical assistance: Evidence from a rural microcredit programme in Bolivia.' *The Journal of Development Studies* 58, no. 2 (2022): 275–291. https://doi.org/10.1080/00220 388.2021.1928639

Groes-Green, Christian. ' "To put men in a bottle": Eroticism, kinship, female power, and transactional sex in Maputo, Mozambique.' *American Ethnologist* 40, no. 1 (2013): 102–117. https:// anthrosource.onlinelibrary.wiley.com/doi/10.1111/amet.12008

Hossain, Naomi. *The Aid Lab: Understanding Bangladesh's Unexpected Success.* Oxford: Oxford University Press, 2017.

Khan, Amina. 'Three tips for policy-makers on implementing the SDGs.' *Overseas Development Institute*, n.d., accessed 1 February 2023. https://odi.org/en/insights/three-tips-for-policy-mak ers-on-implementing-the-sdgs/

Kinsbergen, Sara, Anne-Fleur Lurvink, and Imke van Mil. 'Understanding sustainable exit strategies of voluntary development organisations: Amical break-up or messy divorce?' in *The Rise of Small-Scale Development Organisations: The Emergence, Positioning and Role of Citizen Aid Actors*, edited by Hanne Haaland, Sara Kinsbergen, Lau Schulpen, and Hege Wallevik, 154–169. London: Routledge, 2023.

Kolbe, Athena Rebecca. ' "It's not a gift when it comes with price": A qualitative study of transactional sex between UN peacekeepers and Haitian citizens.' *Stability: International Journal of Security and Development* 4, no. 1 (2015): 44, http://doi.org/10.5334/sta.gf

Kumi, Emmanuel, and James Copestake. 'Friend or patron? Social Relations across the national NGO – Donor divide in Ghana.' *The European Journal of Development Research* 34, no. 1 (2023): 343–366. https://doi.org/10.1057/s41287-021-00375-3

Leenstra, Melle. 'The human factor in development cooperation: An effective way to deal with unintended effects.' *Evaluation and Programme Planning* 68 (2018): 218–224. https://doi.org/ 10.1016/j.evalprogplan.2017.09.008

Mobarak, Ahmed Mushfiq, and Alejandra Ramos. 'The Effects of migration on intimate partner violence: Evidence for the exposure reduction theory in Bangladesh.' Working paper, February 2019. https://sistemas.colmex.mx/Reportes/LACEALAMES/LACEA-LAMES2019_paper_321.pdf

Mwapu, Isumbisho, Dorothea Hilhorst, Murhega Mashanda, Muhigwa Bahananga, and Ruhamya Mugenzi. 'Women engaging in transactional sex and working in prostitution: Practices and underlying factors of the sex trade in South Kivu, the Democratic Republic of Congo.' *Secure Livelihoods Research Consortium* report 10 (2016). https://library.wur.nl/WebQuery/wurpubs/ fulltext/401353

Oomes, Nienke, Thierry Belt, Nicolas Berthiaume, Debbie Keijser, Bert van Manen, and Ward Rougoor. *Evaluation of the FMO-MASSIF Fund (2015–2019)*. Amsterdam: SEO Amsterdam Economics, 2020. www.seo.nl/en/publications/evaluation-of-the-fmo-massif-fund-2015-2019/

Pradhan, Prajal, Luís Costa, Diego Rybski, Wolfgang Lucht, and Jürgen P. Kropp. 'A systematic study of sustainable development goal (SDG) interactions.' *Earth's Future* 5, no. 11 (2017): 1169–1179. https://doi.org/10.1002/2017EF000632

Regional Hunger and Vulnerability Programme. *Dowa Emergency Cash Transfer, Malawi. REBA case study number 1*. Johannesburg: RHVP, 2007. www.calpnetwork.org/publication/dowa-emergency-cash-transfer-malawi/

Ruerd Ruben, Ricardo Fort, and Guillermo Zúñiga-Arias. 'Measuring the impact of fair trade on development.' *Development in Practice* 19, no. 6: 777–788. https://doi.org/10.1080/096145 20903027049

Sachs, Jeffrey D. *The End of Poverty: Economic Possibilities for Our Time*. New York: Penguin, 2006.

Ubels, Tessa, Sara Kinsbergen, Jochem Tolsma, and Dirk-Jan Koch. 'The social outcomes of psychosocial support: A grey literature scoping review.' *SSM – Mental Health* 2 (2022): 100074. https://doi.org/10.1016/j.ssmmh.2022.100074

13 Conclusion

'It's the complexity, stupid'

This conclusion provides:

- Three reasons why we need to act on side effects
- A cheat sheet to debunk arguments of those who claim that focus on side effects will lead to negative unintended effects
- Recommendations for the key target audiences of this book: policymakers, practitioners, and evaluators
- A final plea to transform the international development sector

My brother is both a doctor and a philosopher. He taught me to always be wary about what people call 'evidence-based' medicine. In his view, the evidence-gathering in the medical sector is to such a degree pharma-sponsored that double-checking so-called evidence on its independence and reliability is essential. Despite these shortcomings, I was quite envious of the medical sector when I started this research seven years ago: medical interventions are only allowed on the market when approved by official supervisory bodies, and they all need to be accompanied by a leaflet explaining potential side effects. Medical companies are being sued successfully if they underestimate side effects. There is even a hotline for people if they think that a medication has side effects.

While I am a big supporter of international development efforts, I have to be honest: the international development sector does not have the same level of professionalization as the medical sector. In our sector, it is still possible to launch a programme if it seems a good idea to you and you can convince some wealthy friends. Citizens in developing countries who are 'benefiting' from a programme are lucky if their benefactor happens to have a complaints procedure. This book has aimed to change that by putting side effects in the limelight. But the book is doing more than just agenda setting: it also provides the tools to actually understand, measure, and address side effects.

13.1 Three reasons to become more serious about unintended effects

13.1.1 Reason 1: it stops preventable damage to human lives

Try to imagine you were living in one of the refugee camps of Guinea about twenty years ago as an adolescent girl. The humanitarian aid worker tells you that he can arrange a spot for you in school, but in exchange, he wants have sex with you. You feel little

DOI: 10.4324/9781003356851-13

This Chapter has been made available under a CC-BY-NC-ND license.

choice. When you grow up, you realize that what happened to you is wrong. You see that the same aid workers and his friends, who were supposed to help you, have actually exploited you and are now doing the same to younger girls, quite some of them getting pregnant. You try to file a complaint, but there is nowhere to go. Unfortunately, this was a very real scenario just two decades ago, as becomes clear from the assessment report by UNHCR and Save the Children UK from 2002.[1]

Agency workers from local and international NGOs and UN agencies were amongst the prime sexual exploiters of refugee children. They often use the very humanitarian assistance and services intended to benefit refugees as a tool of exploitation. The number of aid workers and agencies that were involved shocks me. We are not talking about a couple of bad apples: 42 agencies and 67 individuals were implicated in this behaviour.[2] The example of the girl receiving access to education is actually an example with a good 'exchange rate' (as the report calls it) for the girl. The report explains:

> The girls usually get very little money, if any at all, e.g. in Liberia, the girls were reported to receive the equivalent of USD 10 cents with which they could buy a couple of pieces of fruit or a handful of peanuts i.e. not a full meal … Payment is more often in kind than in cash, e.g. a few biscuits, bar of soap, plastic sheet, clothes, shoes, books, pencils, etc.[3]

This is the marginalization effect (Chapter 7) or even exploitation effect.

I am not saying that sexual exploitation and abuse are not happening anymore, but ever since this report there has been a flurry of action by humanitarian aid agencies to improve standards and accountability, such as the 'Core Humanitarian Standards.' The 2018 Core Humanitarian Standard (CHS) focuses amongst others on unintended effects. Clause 3.6 of the Standard states that agencies should:[4]

Identify and act upon potential or actual unintended negative effects in a timely and systematic manner, including in the areas of:

a people's safety, security, dignity, and rights;
b sexual exploitation and abuse by staff;
c culture, gender, and social and political relationships;
d livelihoods;
e the local economy; and
f the environment.

It looks as if those folks read my book before it even was published! All agencies that sign up to the CHS need to have a solid complaints procedure, something that could have prevented much sexual abuse in Guinea and across the globe. Unfortunately, only twenty of the one hundred signatories are actually certified against these standards, so an extra push by and towards humanitarian agencies is needed.

But it is not just in the humanitarian system that more checks and balances on side effects have emerged. For instance, also in international development finance, stakeholders that experience adverse effects of foreign finance can seek recourse.

Try to imagine you were one of the over 100,000 tribal persons living in the forests of the Indian state of Gujarat in the 1980s next to the (to be constructed) Sardar Sarovar Dam. The World Bank loaned over USD 200 million to this mega-dam. An evaluation report (that was only commissioned after mass protests) found that in an effort to have the project approved quickly, the World Bank had not ensured that displaced people would be properly compensated or that the environmental consequences of the dam would be properly managed.[5] In other words, there was a big chance that your house and land would be inundated with support from the international community and that you would have to wait years for some compensation, often under abysmal conditions. At that time there was no 'inspection panel' to which you could turn. At any rate, the safeguards were not standardized yet.[6] This would all change in the 1990s.

The World Bank adopted eleven safeguards, providing protections against particular risks (e.g., resettlement) and for particular groups (e.g., indigenous people) and resources (e.g., forests, natural habitats). Besides, an independent review mechanism, the Inspection Panel, was established to hear non-compliance claims by project-affected individuals.[7] The World Bank's standards became the leading standard and the safeguards diffused horizontally into policies and practices of other multilateral development banks (such as the Inter-American Development Bank) and private banks. Interestingly, the safeguards were also diffused 'vertically' into domestic laws. For instance, in 2013, India enacted the Right to Fair Compensation and Transparency in Land Acquisition, Rehabilitation, and Resettlement Act (LAA). Its provisions on social impact assessments were inspired by the Bank's safeguard on involuntary resettlement.[8]

So if a new dam were to be constructed in India today with World Bank support, and you would be a tribal person living in the area that would be inundated, the chance that you would have to wait for a compensation in dire straits for years is much lower. First, the national laws would protect you better. And if you would fall through the cracks of the national law, the safeguards from the World Bank could provide solace. And, if those safeguards would fail on you, there would be more possibilities to file a complaint with the independent inspection panel, which shows that progress in dealing with side effects of international development effects is real.

This does not mean that the job is finished. Far from it: there are many further improvements needed. For instance, let us look at the idea for an 'International Ombudsperson for Humanitarian and Development Aid.' The primary role of an Ombudsperson is dealing with complaints. It should act, as Ombudspersons typically do, as a second-tier appeal function after internal organizational channels have been pursued.[9] While the idea has been floating around (especially after the Oxfam sex scandal in Haiti) and scoping studies have been financed, getting such sector-wide improvements off the ground appears difficult, even impossible. But also the application of the safeguards of the international development finance institutions needs to be strengthened, as the chapters on the dams in Cameroon (Section 11.2) made clear.

13.1.2 *Reason 2: it helps disentangle dilemmas and pull the emergency brake when needed*

In medical science, we can see in hindsight that certain treatments with pernicious side effects had been ignored for too long. For instance, doctors in the United States (US) continued to prescribe heavy opioids (painkillers) even after it became clear that these pain killers led to addiction, abuse, and overdoses. The incentives in the system were stacked in such a way that many doctors neglected the side effects, contributing to the opioid crisis in the US, where 38 per cent of Americans adults (92 million people) used prescription opioids in 2015. The medicines that doctors prescribed led to 18,000 patients dying in the US in 2015 alone, showing how deadly ignoring side effects can be.[10]

Some people claim, such as the Nobel Laureate Sir Angus Deaton, that international development's pernicious side effects mean we should stop it altogether. I reach a more nuanced conclusion. Throughout this book, we have seen that different interventions have different side effects in different contexts. They can also be positive and negative side effects can be exaggerated. Just like it would be nonsensical to stop all painkiller prescriptions across the globe because of the opioid crisis in the US, it would be foolish to stop all international development efforts because of particular side effects in particular cases.

Yet, the opioid crisis shows that something that might seem benevolent (painkillers) can create havoc. Luckily the US government curbed its prescription and death rates are now decreasing. The question is, are there also specific development efforts that create so much havoc that we need to stop it? In this book we have seen some examples where the costs clearly outweighed the benefits, such as the orphanage tourism by Western youngsters during a gap year (Section 7.3). However, I found that the benefits versus side effects estimations often pose real conundrums. The taxonomy provided in this book at least gives us some common vocabulary for disentangling development dilemmas, which we have done for the case of South Sudan (see textbox).

A study that was commissioned by the United States Institute of Peace, executed by the Overseas Development Institute (ODI), found that current humanitarian aid efforts disproportionately benefited the South Sudanese government. This resulted in a dynamic whereby the government now derives its income and international legitimacy in significant part from the international presence associated with the humanitarian operation, thus undermining the social contract between the population and the government. The researchers state that the lesson the elites have learnt from the last thirty years is that the 'humanitarian imperative' will always take precedence, with suspensions of activity never being more than temporary, and that international attempts to demand accountability tend to peter out. The researchers found an institutional unwillingness by the (Western) international community to consider the side effects. They encountered a 'widespread culture of silence around the degree to which the humanitarian operation is under stress.' The researchers didn't propose that humanitarian aid to South Sudan should stop, but that more should be provided directly from neighbouring countries, instead of from Juba. If we compare it to the opioids example: they did not propose a ban on opioids, but a smarter way of prescribing them.

Local and international aid agencies were furious when they saw the report by ODI, and provided so many comments that the report (which I have) was never published. This actually proves the point of the researchers that there is indeed a culture of silence that prevents a proper analysis and weighing of side effects. This is such a pity, as it could have stimulated a more fundamental rethinking of humanitarian aid to South Sudan and other countries such as Haiti.[11] But there are solutions: instead of undermining the social contract, humanitarian and development agencies can strengthen it, as they did in Bangladesh (Section 12.1).

13.1.3 Reason 3: it finally makes the discussion about aid effectiveness and efficiency an honest one

Over the last decade or so, there has been a strong focus on the 'effectiveness' of aid. There has been a 'Value for Money' push by many parliaments and donors and a push for 'Effective Altruism' in the non-profit sector. Supported by evidence from Randomized Controlled Trials (like those in the medical sector) and spearheaded by Nobel Laureates Bannerjee and Duflo,[12] there has been a welcome professionalization of the international development sector. There is now a clearer insight on how effective the 'treatment' is for

Table 13.1 Should I stay or go? Benefits versus side effects of humanitarian aid in South Sudan in 2017

Benefits	Negative side effects
In 2016, 5.1 million people were reached with assistance under the Humanitarian Response Plan: more than 4 million people provided with food assistance, 2.5 million people provided with access to clean water, and around 700,000 children and pregnant or lactating women treated for acute malnutrition (both in rebel-held and other territories). A regular injection into the South Sudanese economy is a significant reason why the Juba-based economy has not entirely collapsed in the last two years. For example, it is estimated that for each food aid shipment, an associated USD 10,000–20,000 in cash arrives in the local area to pay the people hired to clear and guard the site (ripple effects).	*Type of unintended effects: conflict effects* **Subtype: direct conflict effects – security threats faced by staff of aid agencies** (in 2017, 27 aid workers had been killed, and detentions happened on a weekly basis). **Subtype: direct conflict effects – funds for the rebels.** At one point in 2017, getting a convoy of trucks from Juba to Bentiu cost USD 2,000 in checkpoint fees alone. **Subtype: direct conflict effects – looting.** In 2016, there were 97 reported incidents of looting (amongst which 20,000 gallons of diesel worth almost USD 30 million) from a WFP warehouse in Juba. Supplies from this warehouse likely contributed to the government's ability to mount offensives in the autumn of 2016. *Type of unintended effects: marginalization effects* **Subtype: elite capture – diversion of food aid.** 73 per cent of respondents to the Bureaucratic Access Impediments survey indicated that they experienced interference during the selection of beneficiaries. *Type of unintended effect: governance effects* **Subtype: democracy effects – aid provides legitimacy to government.** Ministers and local leaders claim the development results as their own achievements. **Subtype: tax effects – aid provides funds to the government through taxation.** The employee taxes, work permits (USD 3,500 per year), and exchange rate taxation provide substantial funds for the government, without increasing productivity. **Subtype: corruption effects – aid fuels corruption.** The government of South Sudan created extra layers of governance (28 districts), leading to many more 'requests' for (personal) financial support from those providing aid.

Sources: InterAction, *A Response to 'The Unintended Consequences of Humanitarian Action in South Sudan: Headline Findings' by the United States Institute of Peace and the Overseas Development Institute* (Washington, DC: InterAction, 2018), accessed on request.; South Sudan NGO Forum, *South Sudan NGO Forum Response to the USIP/ODI Paper: Unintended Consequences of Humanitarian Action in South Sudan* (Juba: South Sudan NGO Forum, 2018), accessed on request; United States Institute for Peace and ODI, 'The unintended consequences of humanitarian action in South Sudan: Headline findings,' 4 January 2018, accessed on request.

intended objectives, which is great. However, by focusing on intended effects only ('measuring impact against design'), we obtain an incomplete and often incorrect view of the effectiveness of an intervention.

While medical trials are only approved if side effects are taken into consideration integrally, in the development sector you can still declare victory even though you ignore side effects. Whereas medical researchers understand that the body is a complex system where unforeseen reactions occur, development effectiveness research can still cling to linear models creating false certainties.

These false certainties lead to unrealistic management systems in international development. Far-away donors steer with fixed overhead percentages and expected rates of return to increase the efficiency of operations. They hope that with this push of 'Value for Money' more results can be obtained with less funding. Unfortunately, the reality is more complex than current management practices allow.

Let me start with the fixed overhead percentages of aid agencies. For instance, the European Union (EU) still has a blanked overhead percentage of 7 per cent, meaning agencies can spend 7 euros out of every 100 euros on costs to maintain their operation. While this might be realistic for some long-term capital-intensive countries and sectors (e.g., roadbuilding in Ghana), this is nonsensical in fragile environments with labour-intensive programmes (e.g., peacebuilding in Chad). With aid agencies always looking for funding to advance their mission, it can sometimes take work to say no to a donor. An organization where I am on the Board of Directors finally did this, when the EU wanted a peacebuilding programme in Somalia with this percentage. My organization said they couldn't perform all the required 'do no harm' checks for this amount and declined the contract. In the end, a rooky NGO that took the unintended side effects less seriously grabbed the contract with the EU that we had declined. This isn't 'Value for Money,' but 'Money for Recklessness'! This shows that current development management practices contribute to rogue behaviour in the development sector.

Let's turn to the expected rates of return. Development finance institutions (DFIs) such as bilateral development banks are also often required to achieve a blanket economic rate of return from their bilateral donors, across geographies and sectors. Development finance institutions can achieve the expected economic rate of return more easily in stable countries such as Ghana than in poorer but more 'difficult' countries such as Chad. Risks of default are lower in these stable markets, and risks of side effects are higher in volatile countries. Conversely, the development rate of return is higher in Chad, because less private capital is available. Unfortunately, because donors punish development finance institutions for costs related to dealing with side effects, donors risk pushing DFIs out of these markets where they have the most added value.

By openly integrating the price of dealing with side effects in the costing equation, we get a more honest dialogue on aid effectiveness and risk-taking. This means that we need to stop managing by fixed overhead percentages and rates of return. It shouldn't matter if your NGO has an overhead ratio of 20 per cent, as long as you achieve development results and deal with side effects: it all depends on the country, the sector, and the activity. It doesn't matter if your economic rate of return as a DFI is just per cent 0.5 per annum for certain sectors and regions, if your financing is additional and you have adequately dealt with side effects in thorny environments.

Just like in medicine, the willingness to accept side effects ought to depend on the severity of the situation. If a patient is on the verge of collapsing, interventions with more chances of side effects are warranted. If there are costs associated with dealing with these side effects, they are accepted lock, stock, and barrel. In short, despite the push for 'Value for Money,' the development sector is still pennywise and pound-foolish. For true value for money, we need to incorporate side effects.

13.2 The unintended effects of focusing on unintended effects: cheat sheet

Writing this book, I did not leave my friends and family off the hook: whether they wanted to or not, I virtually forced them to read draft chapters. At one point, I would only go for drinks with them if they agreed to provide feedback and later people were only invited for my birthday if they had read a draft version of the book. Their feedback was quite harsh, and I doubt whether it was because I was force-feeding the material to them. From their experience, my main takeaways could be counterproductive: this focus on complexity would drive up overhead costs, leaving less money for the target group.

They compiled a list of all the checks and systems an agency needs to have in place before it intervenes in a new context if they follow my recommendations:

- Contribute to the development of local independent research hubs (to track potential backlash effects of Chapter 3)
- Measure the impact of aid workers and on aid workers themselves (to gauge the conflict effects of Chapter 4)
- Include those who have left the intervention area as well as new arrivals in impact measurement (to detect the migration effects of Chapter 5)
- Compensate local structures that are weakened because of international activities (to deal with brain drain effects of Chapter 9)
- Perform a political-economy pre-intervention analysis (to address amongst others the governance side effects of Chapter 10)
- Measure impact beyond the direct target group (to measure the ripple effects of Chapter 13)

This could ultimately mean that fewer actors become active in the places that are most in need (see the Chapter 11 testimony on potentially crippling safeguards), smaller actors go out of business, or that parties with less safeguards take over. How to respond to these concerns? I collected the outcomes of many discussions with friends, family, and peers into one cheat sheet so that you'll be better prepared for concerns than I initially was!

Once you have addressed those concerns with this cheat sheet, it is time to move to the practical takeaways. When putting together all the suggestions I gave throughout the book (over a hundred!), clear red threads emerge.

13.3 What to do: integrate complexity into the programme cycle and overcome boundaries to learning

Of course, first, don't do international development if your objective is not actually international development. If you want to reward geopolitical allies, boost your exports, reduce migration, or just feel good, side effects will abound and working through side effects checklists will not do the trick. Under certain stringent conditions, a mutual benefit approach might be acceptable, but international development always ought to be about 'the promotion of the economic development and welfare of developing countries.'[13] Taking interests and values in the regions where you would like to contribute as the starting point (instead of your interests) reduces the chances of unwanted side effects. Of course, it is not always easy to prevent double agendas, but at least be cognizant of them. These hidden objectives are often key drivers of side effects (e.g., tolerance of corruption in aid programmes).

While some actions need to be taken at the system level (e.g., compensating local structures whose capacities are weakened by international actors), others need to be taken at the organizational level (e.g., creating a culture that rewards out-of-the-box thinking). Yet, other lessons need to be learned at the specific intervention-level (e.g., ensuring that the biodiversity offsetting mitigation hierarchy is respected). While these

Table 13.2 Cheat sheet on the concerns about more focus on unintended effects

Concerns about more focus on unintended effects	*Response and approaches to mitigate the concerns*
You drive investment out of the places most in need because of higher costs.	• The problem is not costs associated with an increased focus on unintended effects, but that donors are accounting for them in the wrong way. They are not overhead but programme costs. • Anyway, donors need to abolish fixed overhead fees and fixed expected rate of returns, and adapt those based on the true costs. • A higher focus on unintended effects can partially be achieved without extra costs.[14]
You drive up costs of the intervention, leaving less funding for target groups. Next to gender, and conflict advisors, soon you will have to cover salaries of (expat) unintended effects advisors.	• Costs should be seen in relation to results: operating costs will decrease compared to results as more adaptive programming will prevent failures from materializing. • Most unintended effects can be detected by creating a safe working space and listening better, which is free.
You drive smaller actors out of the market because of higher costs.	• A valid concern. Hopefully, it stimulates agencies to collaborate better. • Mitigating measures should be proportionate to the size of the organization.
You promote a zero-tolerance approach to risk, leading to the exclusion of the places most in need.	• Nowhere do I argue that there shouldn't be a zero-tolerance approach to risk: I only argue that risk analysis should be comprehensive and that appropriate risk management strategies should be adopted.
You push Global South countries into the hands of less scrupulous donors (e.g., Chinese development banks).	• Instead of lowering our standards to Chinese standards, we should push Chinese actors to increase them. This can be done by working with host governments to have strong safeguards for international investments and development efforts. • If countries and companies prefer support from other non-Western countries such as China, it would be neo-colonial to prevent that from happening.
You disillusion the next generation and feed the critics of international solidarity by being so open about everything that can go wrong.	• It is better that the next generation has a realistic understanding of what can go wrong to ensure that less will go wrong. • Fewer side effects will lead to fewer scandals.

recommendations address different levels, they all start and end with individuals (meaning you!) taking action.

13.3.1 *For everybody in the international development sector: learn*

In Chapter 2, I explained the bounded policy learning model: how ideological, institutional, and technical boundaries shrink the possibilities for learning in the development sector. Here are some tips and tricks to overcome these limits to learning.

Free your mind and overcome ideological boundaries to learning. We all have deeply held beliefs, leading to certain blind spots. Unintended effects mushroom and can fester in these blind spots, so please try to put a spotlight on them. Your attitude matters most: do you look away if you happen to see something strange, or does it attract your interest? To be able to see side effects, it is key to be honest with yourself and others.

Challenge short-term organizational interests and overcome institutional boundaries to learning. Strong organizational (and sometimes even sector-level) incentives exist to ignore side effects. Therefore, building in extra feedback loops such as independent complaints mechanisms is important. Next to building systems, it is also about your attitude: continuing to be critical-constructive about your organization's practices despite short-term pressure to not do that.

Be creative to overcome the technical boundaries to learning. Reality is out there for us to capture, but many pre-existing evaluation models don't allow that. Capture the messy reality of international development by working with models based on complexity thinking rather than linear models. Work together with people on the ground and innovate to capture side effects better.

In addition to what all of us can do, there are specific takeaways for the key target audiences of this book.

13.3.2 Policymakers: stimulate adaptation and collective action

Promote collective action to address sectoral negative side effects

- Forge and stimulate strong partnerships with local actors to provide you with a better contextual understanding of regional and ethnic inequality, potential elite capture and conflict effects, etc., and share this knowledge.
- Stop promoting competition. Stimulate cooperation in the sector (and reduce fragmentation) with strong minimum enforceable standards on 'doing no harm' and taking side effects more seriously.
- Collaborate with other actors to avoid too much aid dependency. Plan together so that local resources are mobilized right from the start. Avoid that countries and organizations become too dependent on foreign aid inflows and ensure that the domestic social contract is strengthened.
- Promote and fund independent research into unintended effects. Donor-driven research hardly finds unintended effects, unless researchers are granted full freedom and are appropriately funded.

Stimulate adaptive programming and locally led development

- Promote innovative communities of practice and intervention methods. Examples are the Thinking and Working Politically Community of Practice, which promotes a focus on power relations and other contextual factors, and the Problem-Driven Iterative Approach, which allows for much more adaptive programming and complexity than regular programmes.
- Abandon top-down linear programming and support development actors in the Global South in charting their trajectory. See how you can contribute to decolonizing international development by developing empowering projects rather than creating dependency.

Stimulate open and empowering communication

- Don't reward inflated success stories. In the digital age people will find out, and it will backfire. Instead, communicate openly about trade-offs and dilemmas so that a nuanced, realistic picture of impact emerges.
- Avoid white saviour narratives. This disempowers and further marginalizes the already marginalized. Strengthen (enforceability of) communication codes of conducts of aid industry associations to ensure empowering communication.
- Avoid flag planting. Highlighting the role of foreign donors in development efforts undermines the social contract. Emphasize instead domestic contributions that strengthen the relationship between the government and the recipient population.
- Don't always communicate. To prevent a backlash donors must work more under the radar. Especially if they work on sensitive issues or if there is a risk that local authorities will cast the intervention in an 'us versus them' frame, it is better to work with local partners, not to engage in 'megaphone diplomacy.'

13.3.3 Practitioners: embrace complexity, don't shun it

Design your organization for complexity

- Design your organization so that there are no thematic silos (e.g., create cross-thematic teams).
- Organize your evaluation and monitoring system to capture mobilization and demonstration effects, interconnections between the target area and the non-target area, and long-term effects.
- Create an incentive structure that stimulates employees to adapt to unforeseen feedback loops, moves by adaptive agents, interconnectivities, alternative impact pathways, and non-linearities.

Design your intervention with an unintended effects-lens

- Improve substantially the quality of entry-tests of proposals by juxtaposing the proposed intervention against the evidence body with respect to unintended behavioural, 'do no harm,' and 'leave no-one behind' effects.
- Plan in an integrated and holistic way. Plan in a way that integrates both environmental and economic objectives.
- When supporting and strengthening vulnerable or marginalized groups, prevent a backlash, e.g., by taking more powerful groups along in the process.

Design an open communication practice

- Communicate your outreach products so that (local) stakeholders can access them and verify whether they are correct.
- Communicate openly about uneasy facts from the intervention area so they can be acted upon.

13.3.4 Evaluators: find what you are not looking for

Look broader

- Measure impact beyond the direct target group. And don't only look for negative effects, but also positive ones such as demonstration and mobilization effects.
- Look beyond the thematic silo of the intervention as the unintended effects often occur in a different thematic area.
- Include those who have left the intervention area and new arrivals. Substantial attrition rates between pre-test and post-test cannot be accepted without understanding what has happened to those who moved (and why they moved).

Look back

- Measure the impact several years after the end of a programme. Because behavioural effects are often the result of a feedback loop, it might take some time for these side effects to materialize.
- Test the assumptions flowing from contextual and evidence analysis and the efficacy of the mitigation measures.

Look differently

- Look with a local lens: have long-term contracts with local research hubs and employ local researchers as a standard practice.
- Use a broad concept of well-being. When analysing the well-being of affected populations, do not only look at quantitative socio-economic indicators, but also qualitative perceptions of well-being.

Let others look

- Understand that your presence affects the system. Measure the impact of aid workers and their cash by letting others look at how your presence influences behaviour.
- Develop local and independent research hubs. Don't rely on remote monitoring uniquely, but always try to have people on the ground without a stake in the development intervention to understand what is happening.
- Ensure the most vulnerable are included in the research design or even perform part of the research.

13.4 Transforming international development to better address global challenges

The global challenges that we are up against as humanity, such as climate change, skyrocketing inequality, and rising autocracy, are convoluted and interdependent. While our old linear way of working has had its successes in the past, it will not be able to deal with current urgent intricacies. To deal with these issues, a forward-looking and comprehensive and above all professional international development sector is needed. However, the international development sector is in crisis and defence mode. The political left criticizes the environmental and social side effects of the development bank loans. The political right points its finger at the 'fat cats of aid' and the scandals in the sector. Those in power often cut aid budgets or divert them from those who need it most. Despite the increasing number of people who are hungry and displaced, the end of international development and solidarity may be near, unless we learn from the criticism and radically transform it.

It often seems that there are only two options for the international development sector. One option is to give up on international development because it is getting too complicated. But giving up on international solidarity altogether, as the opponents like to see it, is not on the table for me. Another option is to board up all international development efforts: make safeguards more comprehensive and stricter to reduce risks to zero. But this is neither possible nor desirable. Just like in medical sciences, risk needs to correspond to return. Potential returns of international development are enormous: remember the internationally supported health insurance in Rwanda that Placide explained in the introduction of this book? Without some risk-taking, Rwanda would not have been as healthy as it is now.

The global challenges we are facing will eventually come to everybody's doorstep. They won't go away by looking away. Sustainable progress can only be achieved with international solidarity. So we need to develop a third option, a nuanced and humble one, in which calculated risk-taking in international development efforts is encouraged and defended. Humility needs to replace the arrogance of Western-based (white) aid policymakers and professionals (like me), who think that with the development of grand designs they can steer 'development' in far-flung places. As we have seen repeatedly in this book, international development efforts set processes in motion with many unknown effects. We know what we put into the system, but we are often surprised by what emerges from it because of feedback loops, interconnectivities, alternative impact pathways, non-linearities, and adaptive agents. So let's be modest about our expectations while remaining confident about the need for international solidarity.

'It is the complexity, stupid,' is what I often think when I see the lack of nuance in discussions about international development. Those within the sector promote it, often against better judgement, as the panacea, while those opposing international development efforts deliberately exploit the smallest mistakes. This book is a call to take a headlong rush into a third way, with a confident nuance and humility.

We need a transformed international development sector to make headway in dealing with global challenges. One that isn't based on 20th-century top-down linear thinking, smelling of colonialist practices, but one that is ready for the 21st century: based on complexity thinking, evidence-based decision-making, and equal partnership. Luckily, plenty of initiatives in the sector are already taking up this challenge. Please join these efforts and strengthen them: up to us to transform the sector and make it more effective in addressing global challenges.

Notes

1 UNHCR and Save the Children UK, *Sexual Violence and Exploitation: The Experience of Refugee Children in Liberia, Guinea and Sierra Leone* (Geneva: UNCHR, 2002), www.parliam ent.uk/globalassets/documents/commons-committees/international-development/2002-Report-of-sexual-exploitation-and-abuse-Save-the-Children.pdf
2 Ibid., 9.

3 Ibid., 10.
4 CHS Alliance, Groupe URD, and Sphere Association, *Core Humanitarian Standard on Quality and Accountability* (Geneva: CHS Alliance, 2018), https://spherestandards.org/wp-content/uploads/CHS-in-2018-Sphere-Handbook.pdf
5 Mark T. Buntaine, *Giving Aid Effectively: The Politics of Environmental Performance and Selectivity at Multilateral Development Banks* (Oxford: Oxford University Press, 2016).
6 Philipp Dann and Michael Riegner, 'The World Bank's Environmental and Social Safeguards and the evolution of global order,' *Leiden Journal of International Law* 32, no. 3 (2019): 537–559, https://doi.org/10.1017/S0922156519000293
7 Ibid.
8 Ibid., 546.
9 Humanitarian Knowledge Exchange, *International Ombuds for Humanitarian and Development Aid Scoping Study* (The Hague: KUNO, 2018), www.kuno-platform.nl/wp-content/uploads/2019/02/Final-report-International-Ombuds.pdf
10 National Institute on Drug Abuse, 'Drug overdose death rates,' 9 February 2023, https://nida.nih.gov/research-topics/trends-statistics/overdose-death-rates
11 Rodrigo Mena and Dorothea Hilhorst, 'Path dependency when prioritising disaster and humanitarian response under high levels of conflict: A qualitative case study in South Sudan,' *Journal of International Humanitarian Action* 7 (2022): 5, https://doi.org/10.1186/s41018-021-00111-w
12 Abhijit Banerjee and Esther Duflo, *Poor Economics: A Radical Rethinking of the Way to Fight Global Poverty* (New York: Public Affairs, 2011).
13 OECD, 'Official development assistance,' n.d., accessed on 1 February 2023, www.oecd.org/dac/financing-sustainable-development/development-finance-standards/official-development-assistance.htm
14 Focusing more on unintended effects in existing evaluations doesn't necessarily drive costs upwards. Let me take the example of Search for Common Ground. In a well-researched article, Lemon and Pinet demonstrate that this organization was successful in getting a much better grip on its side effects within just a couple of years. Once the monitoring and evaluation team started to employ more open evaluation methods and focus on side effects, the percentage of evaluations that focused on it rose from 18 per cent in 2013 and 2014 to 46 per cent in 2016: Adrienne Lemon and Mélanie Pinet, 'Measuring unintended effects in peacebuilding: What the field of international cooperation can learn from innovative approaches shaped by complex contexts,' *Evaluation and Programme Planning* 68 (2018): 253–261, https://doi.org/10.1016/j.evalprogplan.2017.09.007

Further reading

Banerjee, Abhijit, and Esther Duflo. *Poor Economics: A Radical Rethinking of the Way to Fight Global Poverty.* New York: Public Affairs, 2011.
Buntaine, Mark T. *Giving Aid Effectively: The Politics of Environmental Performance and Selectivity at Multilateral Development Banks.* Oxford: Oxford University Press, 2016.
CHS Alliance, Groupe URD, and Sphere Association. *Core Humanitarian Standard on Quality and Accountability.* Geneva: CHS Alliance, 2018. https://spherestandards.org/wp-content/uploads/CHS-in-2018-Sphere-Handbook.pdf
Dann, Philipp, and Michael Riegner. 'The World Bank's Environmental and Social Safeguards and the evolution of global order.' *Leiden Journal of International Law* 32, no. 3 (2019): 537–559. https://doi.org/10.1017/S0922156519000293
Humanitarian Knowledge Exchange. *International Ombuds for Humanitarian and Development Aid Scoping Study.* The Hague: KUNO, 2018. www.kuno-platform.nl/wp-content/uploads/2019/02/Final-report-International-Ombuds.pdf.

InterAction. *A Response to 'The Unintended Consequences of Humanitarian Action in South Sudan: Headline Findings' by the United States Institute of Peace and the Overseas Development Institute*. Washington, DC: InterAction, 2018. Accessed on request.

Lemon, Adrienne, and Mélanie Pinet. 'Measuring unintended effects in peacebuilding: What the field of international cooperation can learn from innovative approaches shaped by complex contexts.' *Evaluation and Programme Planning* 68 (2018): 253–261. https://doi.org/10.1016/j.evalprogplan.2017.09.007

Mena, Rodrigo, and Dorothea Hilhorst. 'Path dependency when prioritising disaster and humanitarian response under high levels of conflict: A qualitative case study in South Sudan.' *Journal of International Humanitarian Action* 7 (2022): 5. https://doi.org/10.1186/s41018-021-00111-w

National Institute on Drug Abuse. 'Study suggests need for improved access to evidence-based pain management.' 31 July 2017. https://web.archive.org/web/20180924033534/https://www.drugabuse.gov/news-events/news-releases/2017/07/pain-relief-most-reported-reason-misuse-opioid-pain-relievers

National Institute on Drug Abuse. 'Drug overdose death rates.' 9 February 2023. https://nida.nih.gov/research-topics/trends-statistics/overdose-death-rates

OECD. 'Official development assistance.' n.d., accessed on 1 February 2023. www.oecd.org/dac/financing-sustainable-development/development-finance-standards/official-development-assistance.htm

South Sudan NGO Forum. *South Sudan NGO Forum Response to the USIP/ODI Paper: Unintended Consequences of Humanitarian Action in South Sudan*. Juba: South Sudan NGO Forum, 2018. Accessed on request.

UNHCR and Save the Children UK. *Sexual Violence and Exploitation: The Experience of Refugee Children in Liberia, Guinea and Sierra Leone*. Geneva: UNCHR, 2002.

United States Institute for Peace and ODI. 'The unintended consequences of humanitarian action in South Sudan: Headline findings.' 4 January 2018. Accessed on request.

Afterword and acknowledgements

I am a white, forty-plus man with a permanent contract working for a donor government. How have all these privileges affected this book and research on international development? How has my position affected the independence of this research? Because I am acutely aware of the biases that come from my background and position, I have assembled a Feed Forward Group with members who differ from me in many aspects: gender, regional background, academic discipline, and age.

This magnificent Feed Forward Group accompanied me during the writing process of the book. During six intensive feedforward sessions they enriched the chapters with their unique viewpoints. Their inputs led to a – what I hope – more balanced book, in which viewpoints from the Global South and Global North, from various academic backgrounds, age groups, positions in the aid system, and genders come together. Naturally, any remaining biases and mistakes are my own responsibility.

It took me seven years of research to be able to write this book. At no point did the Ministry aim to interfere with the research. At one point a minister scribbled on an update memo on the research whether 'there were not more urgent things to research by Dirk-Jan,' but nowhere did they intervene. So if there was any censorship, it must have been self-censorship. While I read the book back in the editing stage, I felt that there were no taboos, but I stand to be corrected.

Actually, having these two hats (policymaker and an academic) also had many advantages. The contacts and inside information that I have as a policymaker fed straight into this research. After a couple of years, my colleagues at the Ministry of Foreign Affairs knew that I was working on research into side effects, and more than once colleagues would ask to share confidential documents with me:

> *I know you care about the issues in these files and nobody knows about this outside a select group of people. I totally disagree with what we're allowing to happen here, but I can't do anything about it. Just don't tell anybody you got them from me.*

My recommendations focus a lot on 'courage,' and daring to challenge your organization and the system. I fully realize that it is much easier to make these types of recommendations in my secure position: I neither need to fear for contract renewal, nor for funding cuts for my organization. In that sense, it might come across as cheap recommendations, impossible to follow up on for those in more precarious positions. While I have always had a relative privileged position (being white and having had access to a top education system), I have always been vocal if I thought something was going

Gloria Nguya is Lecturer at the University of Mwenu Ditu, DRC. She holds a PhD from the Institute of Social Studies, The Hague (2019).

Mayanka Vij is Policy Analyst at the OECD Development Cooperation Directorate (AMID graduate, Radboud University class of 2018).

Cindy Chungong has been serving as one of the regional directors for International Alert.

Zunera Rana is AMID Lecturer at Radboud University. She finished her PhD at the same university in 2021.

Salomey Afrifa is a lecturer and holds a PhD from the Institute of Social Studies in the Hague (2020).

Jorrit Oppewal is Executive Secretary at the Development Aid Committee of the Advisory Council of International Affairs of the Dutch government.

Figure 14.1 The Feed Forward Group for this book.

wrong, even though when I was still looking for a job. I encourage you to do the same. In my experience, critical – yet constructive – thinking is in the end always appreciated.

It is impossible to thank everybody who was involved in this preparatory phase, but special thanks go to my colleagues at the Radboud University and the Netherlands Ministry of Foreign Affairs. Starting with the university, Lau Schulpen supported the unintended effects research angle right from the start, even though there were many sceptics. Sara Kinsbergen kept on commenting on draft versions of the book proposal until it was finally good enough to be accepted (which took a while!) and also commented on the entire draft book. Also my (former) colleagues at the strategy department of the Netherlands Ministry of Foreign Affairs, Roel van Veen, Marc Gerritsen, and Arjan Uilenreef were very relevant for this book, as they enabled me to combine my work at the Ministry with my professorship and this research with full academic freedom.

This book would be much more boring without the testimonies, which were carefully drawn up by Saskia Hesta, and without the cartoons, made by Maarten Wolterink. The book would be much harder to read without the editing by both Meindert Boersma and Indhumathi Kuppusamy. This book is based on approximately ten published peer-reviewed academic papers, which were co-authored and researched (in alphabetical order) by: Meindert Boersma, Marieke van den Brink, Olga Burlyuk, Dion McDougal, Anna Gunn, Lena Gutheil, Maria van de Harst, Sara Kinsbergen, Annelie Kroese, Louise Kroon, Joost de Laat, Lau Schulpen, Elric Tendron, Jochem Tolsma, Tessa Ubels, Gijs Verhoeff, Marloes Verholt, Jolynde Vis, Yue Wang, and Francis Weyzig.

A random crew of people responded to my LinkedIn post where I asked for input for this book. Thanks to Xavier Bardou, Noor Cornelissen, Irene de Goede, Lena Gutheil, Roelof Haveman, Dik van de Koolwijk, Nelly Moleka, Tessa Terpstra, and Gertud Wagemans for reading the draft chapters – or even the entire book – and commenting on them.

I am blessed with many friends who help me out when I need them. I was glad that Stijn Jansen, Tijmen Rooseboom, Sjoerd Sjoerdsma, and Jorim Schraven were all willing to read the final draft when I was still doubting about the framing of the book. They pointed at useful – albeit often opposing – directions, but it certainly supported me formulating the takeaways.

I am grateful to the Routledge team (Alexandra de Brauw and Helena Hurt) who tested the sales pitch I made to them. I told them that 'this is the book that I should have read when I did my Development Studies Masters at LSE twenty years ago.' They sent the book proposals out to three Development Studies course convenors to ask if it lived up to this claim. Luckily, the reviewers concurred wholeheartedly, and the result you find in front of your eyes, also because of the all-round support of Routledge's Katerina Lade. The University of Amsterdam will offer a course for their development studies research master with this book as required reading, closing the circle for me.

Let me conclude by thanking the strong women who made this book possible. Often it is said that behind every man, there is a woman. In my case, there are four of them: my wife Annelies, my two daughters Olivia and Elodie, and of course my mother Monique. Neither me, nor this book, would exist without their love and care.

Discussion group questions about 'Foreign Aid and its Unintended Consequences'

1 Koch presents five myths about unintended effects in the introduction. What are those five misunderstandings about unintended effects? Did you – before reading this book – also have one of those misunderstandings?
2 After having read the book, can you provide a concrete example of one of the myths that can be dismantled?
3 In the theoretical chapter (Chapter 2), Koch introduces five concepts from complexity thinking that might explain the emergence of side effects in international development. What are those key concepts? Which one do you recognize in your own work?
4 In Chapter 2, Koch also introduces the concept of 'bounded policy learning.' Can you explain what it is, and can you give an example of this in your own environment?
5 From Chapter 3 until Chapter 12, the author introduces ten different categories of side effects. Which three of those are according to you most relevant for you or your agency?
6 Koch highlights also that for some of the side effects relevant steps have been taken to address them. What are examples of good practices of dealing with the side effects?
7 Are there any unintended effects of international development efforts that are lacking from the proposed taxonomy according to you?
8 Chapter 12 proposes three different ripple effects. What are those three ripple effects? Which ripple effect merits more attention according to you?
9 In the conclusion, Koch makes a plea that more attention for the positive and negative side effects is needed. Do you agree? Which of the three arguments he proposes do you find most convincing, and which argument least convincing?
10 In the conclusion, Koch provides various recommendations to take unintended effects more seriously. Which three recommendations do you find useful to explore further? And which recommendation do you find most challenging?

Index

Nepal 1, 99, 108, 110
Netherlands 31, 47, 70, 80, 83, 94, 101, 102, 160, 170–171, 173n5, 178, 186, 209
neutrality, principle of 47–48, 49, 50, 54
New Development Bank (NDB) 65–66
Nigeria 15, 40n24, 51, 52, 53, 110, 111, 130, 131–132, 145, 147, 185
'no one left behind' 104
non-linearities 14, 16, *17*, 17, *19*, 20, 172, 203, 205; and conflict effects 44; and unintended governance effects 142–143
North Kivu 3, 78–79, *78*

ODI (Overseas Development Institute) 197
OECD (Organisation for Economic Cooperation and Development) 7, 22, 23n3, 78
official development assistance 23n3, 31, 150, 162, 171, 174n23, *179*
offsetting carbon footprint 164
open communication 203
Organisation for Economic Cooperation and Development (OECD) 7, 22, 23n3, 78
orphanage tourism 92, 93, 99–100, *100*, 197
Overseas Development Institute (ODI) 197
Oxfam 77, 78, 196

Pakistan 49, 136, 152, 161, 180; 'brain drain' in 127–129, *127*
pandemic: COVID-19 6, 35, 70, 111, 132; HIV-AIDS 124, 130, 131–132, *131*
Paris Declaration on Aid Effectiveness 130
Payment for Environmental Services (PES) 51, 108, 109, 115, 116
PDIs (private development initiatives) 16, 100, 186
peacekeeping: in Congo 28; in DRC 2, 28, 76; in Haiti 1–2, 37; and migratory pull effects 60, 68; in Somalia **144**; in Somaliland **144**; and transactional sex 185
performance-based financing programmes 116
permanence 116, 166, **166**, 172
PES (Payment for Environmental Services) 51, 108, 109, 115, 116
Philippines 74, 82, 190n24
piracy **144**
planning 14, *15*, 21 172, 181, 188
policy learning 14, 22, 77, 111, 134; bounded 21–23, 36, 134, 163, 201, 210
policymakers 9, 11n38, 83, 111, 113, 116, 202–203; backlash effects 38; conflict effects 54; marginalization effects 103–104; migration effects 71; negative spillover effects 136–137; price effects 85; resettlement effects 71; ripple effects 188; unintended behavioural responses 119;

unintended environmental effects 172; unintended governance effects 153
political-economy analyses 153
politicians 11n38, 16, 21, 32, 34, 38, 153
poor countries 28, 151–152
poultry 170–171
poverty 5, 8, 28, 32, 37, 65, 67, 81–82, 94, 114, 146, 159, 160
practitioners 2, 8, 9, 11n38, 29, 114, 203; backlash effects 38; conflict effects 54–55; marginalization effects 104; migration effects 71; negative spillover effects 137; price effects 85; resettlement effects 71; ripple effects 188; unintended behavioural effects 119; unintended environmental effects 172; unintended governance effects 153; price disincentive effect 80
price effects 74–85, *75*, *76*, *78*, *81*, *84*; and alternative impact pathways 75; downward 74, 77–80, *78*, 81; and interconnectivity 75; upward 74, 190n24
primary leakage 134, *135*
private development initiatives (PDIs) 16, 100, 186
professionalization, of international development sector 6, 9, 194, 197–198
programme cycle 200–204, **201**

racism 7, 46, 99, 102, 126
Radi-Aid 102
Rana, Zunera 135–136, *209*
reading guide, to this book 8–9
rebound effects 72n14, 108, 113, 119, 119n1
refugee manipulation 49
refugee warrior effect 44, 48–50
refugees 3, 7, 44, 48–50, 55, 69, 150, 195
regional refugee centres 61
regressive targeting effects 92
relationships 113, 176, 185, 186–188, *187*; gay 32; sexual 185, 190n26; spousal 113
Research and Evidence Facility 112, 113
resettlement: aid-induced 60, 61–67, *61*, *64*; effects of *see* resettlement effects; hidden costs of 61–62, *61*; involuntary 60, 61–66, *61*, *64*, 70, 196; safeguards for 66, 71; voluntary 60, 61–66, *61*, *64*, 70
resettlement effects 60–71, *61*, *64*, *68*; and alternative impact pathways 61; and interconnectivity 60–61
rich countries 7, 151–152
ripple effects 176–189, *177*, *179*, *181*, *183*, *184*, *187*; and adaptive agents 177; and interconnectivity 176
risk appetite 54–55
risk-taking 199, 205
Rwanda 3, 6–7, 44, 48, 51, 79, 80, 142, 148, 151, 155n28, 205

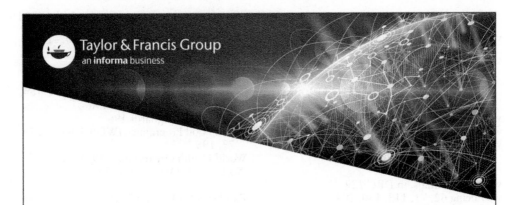

Taylor & Francis eBooks

www.taylorfrancis.com

A single destination for eBooks from Taylor & Francis
with increased functionality and an improved user
experience to meet the needs of our customers.

90,000+ eBooks of award-winning academic content in
Humanities, Social Science, Science, Technology, Engineering,
and Medical written by a global network of editors and authors.

TAYLOR & FRANCIS EBOOKS OFFERS:

A streamlined
experience for
our library
customers

A single point
of discovery
for all of our
eBook content

Improved
search and
discovery of
content at both
book and
chapter level

REQUEST A FREE TRIAL
support@taylorfrancis.com